LATIN AMERICAN MANAGEMENT
Development and Performance

LATIN AMERICAN MANAGEMENT
Development and Performance

Compiled by
ROBERT R. REHDER, University of North Carolina
Graduate School of Business Administration

ADDISON-WESLEY PUBLISHING COMPANY
READING, MASSACHUSETTS · MENLO PARK, CALIFORNIA · LONDON
DON MILLS, ONTARIO

SERIES IN BUSINESS MANAGEMENT

STANFORD UNIVERSITY GRADUATE SCHOOL OF BUSINESS

DAVID E. ALLEN, JR.
Business books translated from English: 1950-1965

HARPER W. BOYD, Jr., et al
Marketing Management: Cases from the Emerging Countries

HARPER W. BOYD., et al
Casos en "Marketing" ↔⟩ *see Harvard stuff - don't qse*

ICAME
Lecturas escogidas en "Marketing"

HARRY R. KNUDSON, JR.
Management of Human Resources: Concepts for Developing Nations

HARRY R. KNUDSON, JR.
Organizational Behavior: Cases for Developing Nations

ROBERT R. REHDER
Latin American Management: Development and Performance

ARNULFO D. TREJO
Bibliografía comentada sobre Administración de Negocios y Disciplinas Conexas

All passages quoted in this text are used with the express oral and/or
written permission, obtained by the author, of the individuals and/or
companies concerned.

REPRODUCED BY ADDISON-WESLEY FROM CAMERA-READY COPY PREPARED BY THE AUTHOR.

FOREWORD

The essential objective of Stanford University's International Center for the Advancement of Management Education is to make a contribution to the practice of business management and to the economies of the developing countries. One of the ways in which ICAME is trying to meet this objective is through the publication of a series of books which focus on the problems and opportunities of business and education for business in these countries. Latin American Management: Development and Performance is one of this series. It is designed to shed light on some of the special issues concerned with the development of management resources in Latin America--issues which must be clearly understood and acted upon if that critical part of the world is to fulfill its potential toward modernization of management and education for management.

Professor Robert R. Rehder is unusually well-qualified to probe the questions raised in this study, with depth and clarity. He has been closely associated with ICAME for a number of years. Both he and his contributing authors have had extensive experience in Latin American business education--as teachers, researchers and consultants. I believe that Dr. Rehder will, through this book, make a significant contribution to understanding and knowledge of a critical problem for the developing countries of Latin America.

Thomas A. Graves, Jr.
Director of ICAME
Stanford, California
1967

PREFACE

This book is concerned with the development of Latin American management resources and the relationship to its modernization process.

Managerial manpower development has gained international recognition during the past decade as a major force in industrialization and economic development. In advanced industrial countries, institutions of higher education purposefully oriented toward the development of high-talent human resources for industrial development are the major source of this vital manpower. All too often, universities in developing countries, including Latin America, have resisted adapting traditional educational programs to meet their national modernization goals. Rising economic and social pressures, however, since World War II have greatly intensified, and major changes in Latin American education are now quite evident. In no area has change been more dramatic than the explosive evolution of management education with hundreds of new programs developing in every conceivable form and institution.

While the supply of managerial manpower is clearly shown to be improving, the quality of education in those countries studied is seen to be largely inadequate to meet the challenges of modernization. These studies both quantify and support the scarcity of financial and qualified faculty resources. In addition they identify other major contributory problems such as the wholesale importation of North American management concepts and curriculum often incongruent with Latin American values and social economic environment.

This book first surveys a broad range of Latin American problems and analyzes their complex interrelationships with management in both the public and private sectors. It seeks to identify how the Latin American cultural value systems, thought processes, and social-economic constraints affect management's personal and organizational goals, strategies and behavior. With this general background, the problems of fitting Latin American managerial education to the needs of four Latin American countries are then analyzed by North and South American social scientists who have been living and working with these problems in these countries. Particular attention is given to the identification of those institutional strategies, curriculum concepts and analytical tools which have proven of significance to Latin American management development and performance. It is the authors' hope that this inquiry will stimulate broad discussion and further study of management education in Latin America.

This volume was made possible by the contributions of many individuals and organizations throughout North and Latin America. While I cannot recognize each one individually, I would like to take this opportunity to express sincere appreciation to all of them. This book would not have been possible without the financial support of the Ford Foundation and the close cooperation of its Latin American offices. I am equally indebted to Stanford University and the University of North Carolina for both the financial support and the close cooperation provided by their Schools of Business Administration.

Robert R. Rehder

Chapel Hill, North Carolina
January, 1968

CONTRIBUTORS

DOLE A. ANDERSON

Professor of Business Administration, Michigan State University, and
Chief of Party of the Midwest Universities Consortium/Ford Foundation
Project at the National Institute of Development Administration, Bangkok,
Thailand. He has spent nearly twelve years in three institution-building
projects in Brazilian higher education. From 1952-1957, he was Chairman
of the Economics Department of the Instituto Tecnológico de Aeronáutica,
São Paulo, Brazil. In 1959, he joined the Brazil Project of Michigan
State University as advisor at the University of Bahía. From 1961-1966
he was advisor at the São Paulo School of Business and served, during
the last two years, as chief of the Michigan State University Party in
Brazil.

STANLEY M. DAVIS

Sociologist and Assistant Professor at Harvard University Graduate
School of Business Administration. At present, he is Visiting Research
Professor at both the Business School of the University of Chile (INSORA),
and the Latin American Faculty of the Social Sciences (FLACSO), in
Santiago, Chile, where he is conducting research on the social context
of the modernization of enterprise. He is a consultant to foreign and
multi-national businesses on cross-cultural problems and organizational
behavior. He has taught in executive training programs in Europe and
Latin America, and teaches a course on Comparative Business and Culture
at Harvard. He received his Bachelor degree from Brandeis University
and his M.A. and Ph.D. in sociology from Washington University, St. Louis.

GUILLERMO S. EDELBERG

Director of Research, Institute for the Development of Executives in
Argentina, I.D.E.A. (Buenos Aires), and Professor at the School of Economic and Social Sciences, Argentine Catholic University. He has broad
experience in both North and South American Universities, research
institutes and international corporations. He was the first Latin
American to earn his Doctor of Business Administration at Harvard University and served as a research assistant there and at the University
of California, Berkeley. From 1961 to 1964, he was Director and Senior
Researcher, Center for Economic Research, Torcuato Di Tella Institute
(Buenos Aires). He is currently coordinating a feasibility study concerning the creation of a Graduate School of Management in Argentina.

JORGE RIQUELME PEREZ

Sub-Director, Center for the Economic and Social Development of Latin
America, D.E.S.A.L. (Santiago, Chile) and advisor to the Ministry of
Education for Human Resources and Economic Affairs Educational Planning.
He has completed post-graduate studies in management and human resource
planning at the University of Chile (Escolatina), University of Paris
(IEDES), and the Massachusetts Institute of Technology where he received
his Master of Industrial Management. He has served as Professor of
several faculties at the University of Chile and was Chilean delegate
to International Human Resource Development and Planning conferences.

TABLE OF CONTENTS

CHAPTER I

MANAGERIAL RESOURCES AND ECONOMIC GROWTH IN

LATIN AMERICA

The relationship of high-level human resources to economic growth has received the attention of internationally recognized social scientists during the last decade.[1] In more recent years their work has helped achieve an established position for manpower planning in national development policy. Particular attention has been focused by these scholars on the high-talent manpower necessary to create and administer the public institutions and private organizations through which they are able to accomplish the functions essential for national development. These critical functions, which include the efficient coordination of financial, human, and physical resources toward the production and distribution of goods and services, are frequently identified as managerial functions. On a comparative basis, however, the development and professional identification of those who carry out these functions, and more important, the manner and effectiveness of their performance, are strongly influenced by their national social-economic environment, including its total educational process.

While formal education, at most, is but a portion of the total intellectual growth process, it does represent in advanced nations a key determinant of the directions and levels of development of its human resources. A country's educational system, in addition, reflects and affects virtually every aspect of its social, legal, political, and economic systems.

Higher education in particular plays a major role in the development of the high-talent manpower needed for the continued economic growth and modernization of today advanced industrial nations. An extensive international analysis of human resource development in both quantitative and qualitative dimensions by Frederick Harbison and Charles Myers concluded:

> "There is a high correlation and presumably some causal
> relation between enrollments in education (and hence
> investment in education) and a country's level of eco-
> nomic development as expressed by GNP per capita. It
> is also clear that this correlation is higher in the
> case of second and third level enrollments than in first
> level enrollments. It is possible, however, for a
> country to invest inefficiently in human resource
> development to emphasize the wrong kinds of formal
> education and to fail effectively to integrate formal
> education with in-service training."[2]

In newly industrializing countries the quantitative and qualitative interrelationships of manpower development problems are particularly difficult because the future results of alternative educational

1

investments of limited human and financial resources are most important
and yet uncertain. Universities in Latin America increasingly are
undergoing vast expansions and are reorganizing their traditional systems,designed for a small professional elite,to develop the large numbers of scientific, technological, and administrative high-talent manpower needed for continued growth and modernization.

The explosive evolution of management education with hundreds of
new programs developing in every conceivable form and institution is
most dramatic evidence of this reorientation. Latin America has widely
adopted the North American concept of specialized higher education for
public and business administration, as well as its theory and curriculum, often with little purposeful adaptation to meet the special needs
of Latin American management. In addition, this imported curriculum
material is greatly influenced by the methods of instruction and the total
system of Latin American formal education.

With the explosive growth rate of programs and enrollment in
administration continuing, there is reason for pause: first, to analyze the demand for specific levels and types of managerial skills and
problem-solving capabilities required within the particular social-
economic frameworks of representative Latin American countries, and
second, to evaluate existing national efforts to meet these managerial
manpower requirements through educational development and the utilization of human resources.

Managerial Resources and National Development.

Advanced industrialized countries have modern institutions of
higher education oriented to provide the large numbers of high-talent
manpower necessary to sustain continued growth. The United States
trained 1,672,800 college graduates in the applied and theoretical
science fields between 1926-58.[3] The Soviet Union during the same
period trained forty percent more graduates in the same fields and is
currently maintaining an annual flow of scientific, technical, professional manpower from its higher educational system two times larger
than the United States.[4] A comparative analysis of high-level manpower resources for Japan, Great Britain, Germany, Sweden and other
advanced industrial countries reveals the accelerating reliance placed
on their universities to develop the high-talent personnel necessary
for their continued development.[5] Although the source of managerial
manpower in the advanced industrial countries is increasingly centered
in their higher educational systems, the areas of specialization from
which they are drawn are as yet diverse. In the Soviet Union a high
premium is placed on highly specialized scientific and technical education with these specialists in all segments of their economy employed to a degree unknown in the United States.[6]

In North America, management education is highly integrated within
the university with increasing emphasis placed on scientific analysis
using mathematical and behavioral tools. Since World War II, Europe
has also begun to develop specialized courses and university programs
in management education. The recently published British report on
higher education prepared under the chairmanship of Lord Robbins

2

recommended establishment of at least two major Graduate Schools of Business, as well as an expansion of business studies in other universities and scientific and technological institutes. The Committee recognized the warnings of its many witnesses that Britain could not retain its position in the modern age without better business management education.[7]

The less developed industrial countries reflect an even greater diversity of needs for managerial manpower development. India, for example, undertaking planned accelerated industrialization, soon discovered the inadequacy of her existing managerial resources and her system of education through which they might be generated. Indian universities, developed largely by the British over 200 years, were traditionally concentrated in Law and Letters. Engineering and/or technological schools were few and their graduates did not enjoy high social-economic status. Also highly emphasized within the Indian universities were the traditional faculties of commerce, which were of low quality and overcrowded. They largely concentrated on the functional aspects of commerce and administration and developed a predominance of administrative clerks and bookkeepers for both the private and public sectors. Charat Ram, Chairman of the Jay Engineering Works, India, speaking at the 1963 CIOS Conference summarized the current situation:[8]

> ". . . business education in India suffers from two
> drawbacks: firstly, there is an acute scarcity of
> faculty who are themselves familiar with the concepts
> of scientific management and are also able to communi-
> cate them to a student body so that they become a part
> of their knowledge and managerial behavior--the faculty
> also usually suffer from a lack of good industrial
> experience; secondly, the students who have gone through
> these courses do not always find occasion to utilize
> their training. Often they come back to organizations
> that are not ready to assimilate their new knowledge."

At its present stage of development, the educational system is developing human resources ill-equipped to initiate, build, or adminis-ter new organizations, or afforded the opportunity to develop and rise within existing organizations. Despite considerable emphasis on man-power planning resulting in increased enrollments in basic scientific and engineering faculties, India has 64% of its university enrollments in faculties of humanities, fine arts, law, and social sciences, in-cluding commerce. Due to their present level of development, the demand for these graduates is not sufficient to permit their productive employment.[9]

There is every evidence that communist China fully appreciates the vital role of human resource development in its industrialization goals. During the ten-year period 1950-1959, China increased its higher education enrollment six times, and this does not include con-tinuing education programs which have been made a required part of all factories, public offices, and scientific research organs.[10] Higher education has been almost totally redirected toward industrialization with strange emphasis given to the development of scientific knowledge and technological skills. China, since 1949, has become the third

largest producer of engineers in the world following the U.S.S.R. and
the U.S.A.[11]

High-Level Manpower Resources in Latin America: The Need

According to United Nations calculations, the population of the
twenty Latin American republics is expected to increase from 199 to 293
million between 1960 and 1975. This average rate of 2.6% yearly is
higher than the rate for any other continent. The population of Latin
America could overtake that of North America as well as the Soviet Union
by approximately 1975.[12]

A very great disproportion between population figures for school
age children and adolescents in Latin America and school system capacities continues to exist. This situation is likely to worsen in line
with the exceptional rate of population growth in this continent.
Following a lengthy statistical analysis of the educational situation
in Latin America in 1960, UNESCO and ECLA came to the following conclusions:[13]

1. At the present time there are approximately fifteen million
   children of school age who are not attending primary schools.

2. Of the adult population, approximately 40% is illiterate.

3. Opportunities for secondary and higher education are in
   practice denied to large sectors of the population who
   cannot afford the expense involved.

4. The number and variety of professional workers trained by
   the Latin American schools and universities are not commensurate with the countries' development requirements.

5. A vigorous impetus should be given to the teaching of
   science and to associated research in fields relating
   to the development of Latin America.

6. Adult education systematically organized on a permanent
   basis as a complement for or an extension of primary
   schooling is almost non-existent.

In summary:

> The Latin American educational structure is based on a vast
> number of barely literate or illiterate persons, a very
> small intermediate sector comprising those who have received
> secondary schooling, and a higher sector, much smaller still,
> consisting of those who have followed university or equiva-
> lent courses. This structure does not correspond to the
> needs and aims of the Latin American countries with respect
> to their social and economic development.[14]

These general conclusions based on aggregate Latin American statistics do not, however, reveal the significant divergencies, particularly
among the South American countries, qualitatively as well as quantitatively, nor the plans and programs under way to meet their particular needs.

The worldwide analysis of levels of human resource development compiled by Professors Harbison and Myers substantiates the wide disparity between Latin American countries.[15] According to their composite index[16] the levels of human resource development ranged from Guatemala (10.7) to Argentina (82.0) as ranked on the following page.

Seven of the twelve Latin American republics included fall into Level II category, "Partially Developed," which are characterized in this study as having started the uphill climb to economic and political maturity but faced with both critical shortages of high level strategic manpower (particularly scientific and technical personnel) and surpluses of university graduates in Law and Humanities.[17] Again there are wide differences within this category as evidenced by contrasting Guatemala's low university enrollment ratios with Peru, which already has several characteristics of Level III.

Brazil might be selected as a representative country of the Partially Developed Level II countries on the basis of its Composite Index. However, again its diverse levels of economic and social development, great size and population do not lend themselves to generalizations at any level. Certainly the northern part of Brazil would be included in Category I; however, the highly developed state of São Paulo would fall in a semi-advanced category. As the country is large, it faces great problems at every level of its educational system. Over 50 per cent of the nation's population is illiterate and the shortage of adequately trained elementary teachers was judged so great by a U.S.A.I.D. survey team early in 1964 that any immediate massive attempt to educate the growing millions of children would be frustrated.[18]

The striking contrast in levels of elementary and secondary educational attainment between the United States and Brazil in 1960 is illustrated in Chart II. Of particular significance to this study, as an indication of the inadequate supply of high-level manpower, is the number of Brazilians currently receiving higher education. This is currently estimated to be about 108,000, or less than the total number of university students in New York City.[19] Of this number, approximately 13,000 students are enrolled in Engineering and 60,000 in the Schools of Law, Philosophy and Arts, which is entirely inadequate in view of the manpower needs of Brazil's developing society of over 75 million inhabitants. While since 1950 the total university enrollment has doubled, the population has grown from 50 to 75 million as the country rapidly industrialized.[20]

The Federal Government of Brazil has at present a legal mandate to spend 12 per cent of its tax revenue on education. In addition, the Government has taken promising steps in the recent formation of new plans and organizations which clearly indicate a recognition of the vital role of high-level human resources in the future development of Brazil, and the need for change and development of the educational institutions which will produce them.

Semi-Advanced Countries

The four Latin American republics included which fall into the Semi-advanced countries, Level III, are Mexico, Venezuela, Chile, and Uruguay.

CHART I

SELECTED LATIN AMERICAN COUNTRIES RANKED BY COMPOSITE INDEX

	Composite Index	Stock of High-Level Manpower			Measures of Educational Development: Enrollment Ratios				Orientation of Higher Education: Percent Enrolled	
		Teachers 1st & 2nd Levels	Engineers Scientists/ 10,000 pop.	Physicians & Dentists/ 10,000 pop.	1st Level Unadj.	1st & 2nd Adj.	2nd Level Adj.	3rd Level Unadj.	In Science & Technology	In Humanities, Law, Arts
Level II										
GUATEMALA	10.7	34.9	NA#	1.2	28	29	6.7	0.8	23.7	33.6
BOLIVIA	14.8	28.3	NA	3.5	19	21	8.3	1.3	NA	NA
BRAZIL	20.9	48.9	NA	5.0	46	48	12.9	1.6	18.6	39.1
COLOMBIA	22.6	41.1	NA	5.0	41	46	13.6	1.8	32.7	39.8
PARAGUAY	22.7	78.3	NA	6.0	64	63	11.2	2.3	8.8	37.2
ECUADOR	24.4	40.8	NA	3.0	49	49	11.9	2.5	28.3	24.2
PERU	30.2	44.4	NA	3.0	48	59	16.2	2.8	31.3	41.6
Level III										
MEXICO	33.0	36.0	NA	4.5	52	55	10.5	4.5	18.3	8.1
VENEZUELA	47.7	59.4	NA	6.5	62	70	26.2	4.3	21.9	28.9
CHILE	51.2	NA	NA	7.5	69	71	28.7	4.5	17.2	26.7
URUGUAY	69.8	NA	NA	13.0	65	71	31.8	7.6	5.4	51.5
Level IV										
SWEDEN*	79.2	79.5	63.5	13.1	74	89	38.7	8.1	30.4	48.8
ARGENTINA	82.0	88.1	12.5	17.5	68	70	32.0	10.0	14.9	36.1
U.S.S.R.*	92.2	65.2	48.1	16.7	67	79	33.9	11.8	45.3	7.6
U.S.*	261.3	135.1	61.7	18.0	88	104	95.3	33.2	22.7	NA

#NA = Not Available

*Non-Latin American countries included in Level IV for comparison purposes.

Source: Data taken from Tables 5, 6, 7 & 8 in EDUCATION, MANPOWER AND ECONOMIC GROWTH, by Harbison & Myers. 1964. McGraw-Hill Book Company. Used by permission.

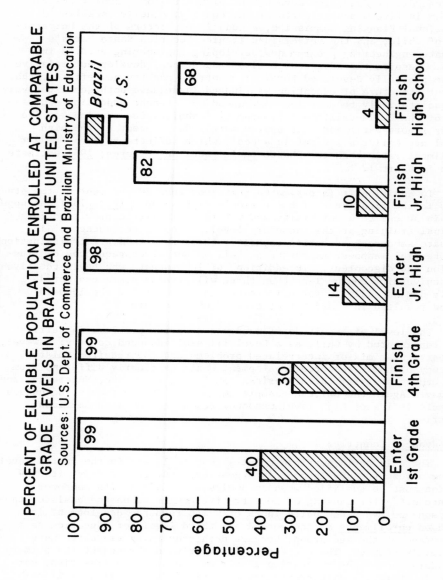

CHART II

PERCENT OF ELIGIBLE POPULATION ENROLLED AT COMPARABLE
GRADE LEVELS IN BRAZIL AND THE UNITED STATES

Sources: U.S. Dept. of Commerce and Brazilian Ministry of Education

Brazil
U. S.

Chile is representative of the average semi-advanced countries in the worldwide sample included in the Harbison and Myers study with a composite index $2\frac{1}{2}$ times that of average Level II countries such as Brazil and Colombia. It is currently recognized as a leader in Latin American Higher Education development with a regional Junior College program in five separate parts of the country, a newly established Educational Planning Commission, a Council of Rectors of the Universities of Chile, and the Universidad Técnica Federico Santa María's graduate engineering program now developing Engineering Ph.D.'s in Chile. Despite the advanced level of educational development relative to the partially developed Level II countries and its new efforts, the present structure of education was judged inadequate both quantitatively and qualitatively to meet the task ahead by a recent education study team of the Chile-California Program of Technical Cooperation.[21] The latter report estimated that approximately 90 per cent of the high school age children are not in school, which reflects an even smaller enrollment ratio than the UNESCO Basic Facts and Figures; 1961 estimate given in Chart I.

In addition it is estimated that less than 20 per cent of the students in the final year of the nation's high schools (colegios) can hope to gain access to a university, and yet there is little provision for terminal training at the secondary level.[22] As a consequence of inadequate secondary education capacity, there results a great dissipation of potential manpower resources as well as social consequences of frustration and discontent. In addition, of 10 students who begin the five-year university course less than three will graduate. A projected supply-demand analysis for university and manpower for the 1960-1970 period resulted in a deficit of over 18,000 graduates.[23]

The level of magnitude of manpower resource problems is fairly well represented by Chile as a Level III semi-advanced country; however, its particular mix of interrelated problems and the required related strategy of human resource development would be clearly different from such other Level III Latin American countries, as Mexico, Venezuela, and Uruguay. Again the Chilean example emphasizes the contrasts and unique characteristics of high level manpower resources in Latin American countries.

The Advanced Countries

The only Latin American country that falls within the fourth level of human resource development is Argentina, and, fortunately, its inclusion must be qualified when an analysis is made of its manpower resources.[24] The ranking of seventy-five countries on the basis of the Harbison and Myers composite index of human resource development is based on enrollments at the second and third levels of education as a percentage of the age group, because data concerning graduates were relatively scarce. The extremely high attrition throughout the primary, secondary, and higher education levels of education in Argentina, compared in Chart III with France and the United States, clearly illustrates the distortion produced in the case of Argentina by the use of enrollment figures as an index of its human resource development.[25] Large numbers of students enroll in Argentine universities, as they have

CHART III

SCHOOLING PYRAMIDS FOR 1000 STUDENTS
WHO BEGIN THE FIRST GRADE

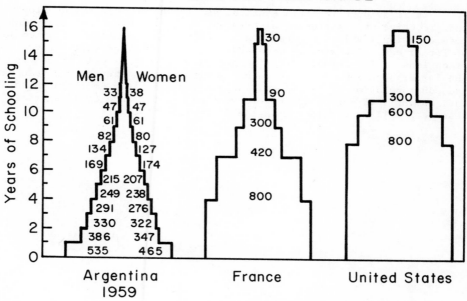

Argentina
1959

France

United States

Centro de Investigaciones
Económicas
Instituto Torcuato di Tella
Buenos Aires, Argentina

relatively open admission requirements and low tuition. Once the students
are enrolled they may attend classes on a part-time or intermittent basis
over seemingly endless years without having to complete established requirements, or simply withdraw.

The orientation of higher education in Argentina again is not
characteristic of the more typical advanced (Level IV) country, with
heavy enrollments in the traditional Humanities, Arts and Law, and a
very low percentage enrolled in Science and Technology. Although
Argentina ranks above Sweden in group IV, it has less than half the percentage of students enrolled in Science and Technology. However, institutions such as the José Antonio Balseiro Institute of Physics and the
Bariloche Atomic Center have made substantial progress in both teaching
and research in the Physical Sciences in Argentina, and the extension of
these new standards of organization, teaching, and research to other
disciplines and institutions of higher education is in evidence.

It is evident in Latin America, as elsewhere, that the development
and effective utilization of high-talent human resources necessary for
modernization involves a great deal more than the quantitative dimensions
of formal education systems. In addition, the study of qualitative
dimensions of its formal education process will not reveal influences of
the larger social-political-economic environment on the early development
and adult behavior of high-level manpower. This Latin American cultural
environment's effect on the development and performance of managerial
resources will be considered in the following chapter.

NOTES AND REFERENCES

1. Examples are as follows:

    M. F. Millikan and W. W. Rostow, A Proposal: Key to an Effective
    Foreign Policy (New York: Harper & Brothers, 1957), p. 61.

    Everett E. Hagen, On the Theory of Social Change - How Economic
    Growth Begins (Homewood, Illinois: Dorsey Press, 1962).

    H. Correa and Jan Tinbergen, "Quantitative Adaptation of Education
    to Accelerated Growth," Kyklos, XV, (No. 4, 1962).

    Albert H. Hirschman, The Strategy of Economic Development (New
    Haven, Connecticut: Yale University Press, 1958).

    Theodore W. Schultz, "Investment in Human Capital in Poor Coun-
    tries," Foreign Trade and Human Capital, edited by Paul D. Zook
    (Dallas, Texas: Southern Methodist Univ. Press, 1962).

    John Kenneth Galbraith, Economic Development in Perspective
    (Cambridge, Massachusetts: Harvard University Press, 1962).

    Theodore Schultz, "Investment in Human Capital," American Economic
    Review, LI (March, 1961).

    John Vaizey and Michael Debeauvais, "Economic Aspects of Educa-
    tional Development," in A. H. Halsey, ed., Education, Economy and
    Society (Glencoe, Illinois: Free Press of Glencoe, 1961).

2. For a detailed expansion of the broad "managerial resource" defi-
    nition see Frederick Harbison and Charles Myers, Management in the
    Industrial World (New York: McGraw-Hill Book Company, 1959), Ch. 1.

3. Nicholas DeWitt, "Education and Professional Employment in the
    U.S.S.R.", Office of Scientific Personnel, National Academy of
    Sciences, 1963.

4. Ibid.

5. Frederick Harbison and Charles Myers, Education Manpower and
    Economic Growth. (New York: McGraw-Hill Book Company, 1964).

6. Nicholas DeWitt, op. cit.

7. Higher Education Report of the Committee appointed by the Prime
    Minister under the Chairmanship of Lord Robbins, 1961-63, pre-
    sented to Parliament by the Prime Minister, October 1963. London:
    Her Majesty's Stationery Office, Cmnd. 2154.

8. Charat Ram, "Management Development in the Developing Economy," CIOS. Council for International Progress in Management, Paper No A12C (New York: 1963).

9. Frederick Harbison and Charles Myers, Education, Manpower, and Economic Growth, p. 106.

10. Professional Manpower and Education in Communist China, by Leo A. Orleans, National Science Foundation, U. S. Government Printing Office (Washington: 1960).

11. Frederick Harbison and Charles A. Myers, Education, Manpower, and Economic Growth, p. 88.

12. Provisional Report of the Conference on Education and Economic and Social Development in Latin America, Economic Commission for Latin America, Tenth Session, May 1963 (Mar del Plata, Argentina: 1963), p. 223.

13. Ibid., p. 334.

14. Ibid., pp. 334-336.

15. Frederick Harbison and Charles Myers, Education, Manpower, and Economic Growth, p. 33.

16. "The composite index which is the basis for slotting 75 countries into these four levels (Level I, underdeveloped; Level II, partially developed; Level III, semi-advanced; and Level IV, advanced) is simply the arithmetic total of (1) enrollment at second level of education as a percentage of the age group 15 to 19 adjusted for length of schooling, and (2) enrollment at the third level of education as a percentage of the age groups multiplied by a weight of 5."

    Ibid., pp. 31-32.

17. Ibid., pp. 74-75.

18. Direction for Education in Brazil, 1964, Survey team internal U.S.A.I.D. report made available to the author by U.S.A.I.D. Education Division.

19. Enrollment in Universities 1962, Servicio de Estadísticas de Educación y Cultura.

20. R. L. Cardwell, R. D. Larson, W. N. Peach and Charles Wagley, An internal study team report on Higher Education in Brazil for A.I.D., April 1964, p. 2. This report was made available to the author by the A.I.D. Mission to Brazil, Rio de Janeiro.

21. Report of Third California Task Force Participants by J. Graham Sullivan, Chile-California Program of Technical Cooperation, November 1963, pp. 82.

22. <u>Report on Chilean Education</u>, Messrs. Edwards and McIlroy,
    U.S.A.I.D. Mission, Santiago, Chile, February 1963. An unpub-
    lished report made available to the author by the U.S.A.I.D.
    Mission, Santiago, Chile.

23. Manpower and Educational Planning in Chile by William J. Platt,
    Al M. Loeb, R. G. Davis for the Chile-California Program of
    Technical Cooperation, Santiago, Chile, June 1964.

24. Harbison and Myers are the first to qualify its inclusion on
    qualitative educational basis. See <u>Education, Manpower, and Eco-
    nomic Growth</u>, p. 131, Footnote 1.

25. <u>Los Recursos Humanos de Nivel Universitario y Técnico en la
    República Argentina</u>, Parte I, Centro de Investigaciones Económicas,
    Instituto Torcuato di Tella, Buenos Aires, Argentina, p. 58.

CHAPTER II

MANAGERIAL DEVELOPMENT AND PERFORMANCE:

ENVIRONMENTAL FACTORS

We will, in Chapter II, center our analysis on fundamental Latin American cultural characteristics, their complex interrelations with other social-economic factors, and their potential effect on the development and performance of its managerial resources. The major Latin American studies of such authors as Alexander, Brandenburg, Fayerweather, Fillol, Hagen, Lauterbach, Whyte, and Williams have established the significance of the social variables with the economic in industrial development.[1]

> ". . . to understand why some traditional societies enter
> upon economic growth sooner than others we must understand
> the internal structure and functioning of these societies,
> for both the barriers to growth and the causes of growth
> seem to be largely internal rather than external."[2]

Social Stratification and the Emerging Middle Classes

Every known culture of any size has a ranking of its people into class strata based on various values considered important by the society. The Hispanic influence in the cultural development of Latin American countries is predominant; however, there are major differences in its manifestations from country to country as well as regions within countries. This is due in part to the great variations in size and cultural characteristics of the indigenous Indian population from region to region and its interaction with the Spanish and Portuguese as well as other European and African immigrants at later periods.

A contrast of cultures between the Andean Indian and the Aborigine of the Selva or Jungle will reveal striking contrasts. The resultant Spanish cultural impact on these different cultures is, in addition, very great. The large concentration of Indian population within Peru and Mexico (estimated to be as large as 9,000,000 in Peru at the time of Pizarro's conquest) could not be driven off the land, but was integrated as a subordinate, subjugated class.

This was not the case in Chile and Argentina, for example, where Indian populations were quite small and the resultant social structure was less rigidly established. For the most part, however, the Latin American social structure was strongly polarized until the early 1900's, with a thin layer of professionals squeezed between a small oligarchical elite and the masses belonging to the lower classes. The latter were identified primarily on the basis of manual labor, occupation, dress, and degree of Spanish literacy. The upper class were distinguished by family membership ties to the landed and mercantile aristocracy including the leadership of Church, State, and the Military.

14

Since World War I a combination of factors including immigration, industrialization, education, and state function development have contributed to the rapid development of the middle classes. Estimates of the size of the middle groups vary with their definitions; however, there is agreement that they currently range from a third to a half of the total population in Argentina, Chile, and Uruguay to less than a tenth in the predominantly Indian populated Andean countries.[3,4] The depth and understanding of social structure study in Latin America is greatly increasing as research moves from macro statistics of occupation and education to intensive field research. A series of sub-classes have now been identified and inter-class relationships and social change have increasingly drawn on interdisciplinary resources involving years of research. The Vicos studies in Peru are exemplary and well illustrate the complexity and scope of problems involved in guiding social change.[5]

Particular attention and study has been directed in recent years to the strategic role of the mobile middle classes in social economic change. In 1950 the Pan American Union published in six volumes Data for the Study of the Middle Class in Latin America which clearly recognized the importance of what was then identified as the emerging middle sectors.[6] The fifteen years following this study have resulted in accelerated growth, heterogeneity, and mobility in the middle sectors. The term middle class has been used to indicate the diversity of backgrounds and lack of class consciousness -- a Peruvian Indian's son raised and educated on a coastal hacienda and offered a white-collar job on that hacienda is a member of this middle mass, as is the Lima entrepreneur and part-time professor at the national University. The former may through University education and industrial job opportunities rise well into the upper middle class professional group and the latter may join the lower levels of the upper class if his managerial talent and economic rewards are commensurate.

The entrepreneur has been the focus of interdisciplinary study concerning his social and psychological characteristics and role in economic development. Cultural variables are found to be particularly significant in four recent studies by the United Nations of Argentine, Brazilian, Chilean, and Colombian entrepreneurs. In surveys of entrepreneurs in these countries, 29% of the sample were found to be foreigners in Argentina and 48% in Chile.[7]

The growth in numbers of the middle classes has only been exceeded by their rising expectations and aspirations for the material and educational benefits now present in the modern world. Historically, the growth of large middle sectors has not guaranteed sustained economic growth nor the public consensus needed for a stable government in the more highly developed Latin American countries; however, it has largely favored the development of public education and industrialization.[8] The influence and pressures created by the middle classes are dramatically seen in the elections of Frei in Chile and the overthrow of Goulart in Brazil. The stresses they are experiencing as their high social and economic expectations conflict with the prevailing characteristics of the traditional outline and economic problems are equally strong and dramatic.

Prevailing Cultural Characteristics

The aristocratic Hispanic hierarchical order transplanted into
Latin America with landed titles of nobility, and its born ruling and
subject class with its supporting values, is yet very much in evidence
in Latin America. The traditional social institutions and their cultural and religious values support and perpetuate this ruler-subject
ideology.[9] Fayerweather, writing of contemporary Mexican culture,
states: "The Spanish tradition of 'imposition, dogma and faith' has
deeply influenced the lives of educated Mexicans."[10] Fillol, in
describing the Argentine basic personality structure, states: "In summary, then, great success is obtained by waiting, by hoping, by the
favor of the saints, or by luck -- not primarily by thrift, work and
enterprise."[11]

Work was regarded as a necessary burden for those unfortunate
enough not to be born to leisure and not a measure of success or form
of personal fulfillment. If a member of the upper classes worked at
all, it was only with his mind. The Protestant ethic regarding work as
a means of salvation with its related great value on time, productivity,
and economic goals was not a cultural characteristic of colonial Latin
America.

The impact of the Protestant Reformation and the Intellectual
Renaissance was little experienced in Portugal and Spain, and the
children of their Latin American colonies are still influenced to accept and adapt to the dictates of supernatural power and superior
authority over which they have no control in the three major social
institutions of Family, Church, and School.

Family Structure, Values, Orientation, and Continuity

The "elite" born into the patrilineal, extended family, introduced
from Spain during the colonial period, have little cause to question
their inherited authority over the masses, and the latter, for the same
reason, are more apt to accept this authority. The Latin American
family extended beyond blood and marriage relationships through such
institutions as "compadrazgo" or godfatherhood including commitments
which first involve loyalty to its members. The Latin American uses
both the mother and father's names. This is a great source of pride
and plays a very important role in structuring the society at all levels. The family name identifies lineage, economic, social, and
political position and religion. Great emphasis is placed on family
relationships and connections in developing the structure of both public and private enterprise.

Within the extended family the eldest male typically dominates the
age-sex hierarchy as in the commercial and political spheres of the
Latin American culture. There has been far less tendency for the fe-
male to encroach on the male-dominated society in Latin American than
there is evidenced in the United States. The father establishes rules
for the household and administers punishment for the children in a
dominant superior-obedient subordinate relationship sanctioned by traditional Latin cultural values such as the model of the macho, the
whole man, proud, fearless, strong, and romantic. The childhood

environment tends toward early emphasis on protective restraint with later development highly directed and controlled. Hagen sets forth the effect of authoritarian parenthood in traditional societies as follows:

> "In the name of training, the parents unwittingly give him the perception that except in a few activities the interaction between his initiative and the world around him is necessarily an anxious process, and that the anxiety is to be avoided by submitting to authority. No doubt he has repressed his rage at his parents and simply feels obligation toward them."[12]

In support of Hagen's analysis, Mr. Ramirez, a Mexican executive described the traditional Mexican family:

> "The state of dependency of the child is extremely strong. It is difficult for him to break his links with home. It's a very painful process. When he wants to get married he usually needs the approval of the parents, and this may well not be an economic matter. He may be earning more than his father, but emotionally he needs his approval."[13]

The literature concerned with the complex interrelationships between personality and social structure is growing rapidly and incorporates a variety of research tools including clinical observations and various tests of personality traits applied over wide geographical distribution. The findings therefore are often inconclusive and there is not as yet an established advanced body of verified and interrelated principles. There is, however, some consensus on the following general principles.

The more restrictive and authoritarian the parents during infancy and childhood, the less likely are the independent achievements of children and open, responsive relations with their peers. In addition, the events of advanced childhood and subsequent years have the potential to perpetuate or remake the developing personality.

Throughout the literature dealing with Latin American early personality formation and resultant distinguishing mature orientations, the following basic[14] characteristics emerge and are generally consistent with the above empirical research findings concerning highly structured, traditional societies:[15]

1. Fatalism or resignation to fate and destiny in an arbitrary and threatening world which is not amenable to analysis nor responsive to initiative.

2. Reliance on authority and structured rules in response to uncertainty, including interpersonal relations whose nature is not clear.

The literature concerning personality development further supports the importance of later years in reinforcing or changing the personality patterns tentatively developed during infancy and childhood within the home environment.[16]

In Latin America, as previously discussed, the highly structured, extended family relationship typically continues into adulthood and tends to perpetuate the rigidity of character structuring of the child. In addition, educational institutions of church and state continue to reinforce the early patterns.

Education and Continued Personality Development

C. H. Haring in his thorough work of the Spanish Empire in America summarizes its early influence on the development of education in Spanish America as follows: "Spain gave to the colonies what it had. [17] Whatever shortcomings there were existed also in the mother country."

The system of education which Spain and Portugal gave to its colonies was developed to provide a professional education strongly influenced by the church for the privileged aristocracy. The colonial school systems and programs instituted by and for the upper classes were of little practical value to the masses even where schooling was available as it was intended "to prepare the flower of colonial youth towards the Church and towards Letters."[18]

Primary and secondary educational programs were oriented to prepare the select for higher education, and further shared two distinguishing characteristics: (1) severely limited access to primary and secondary education, as indicated by the relation between the number of children of school age and the actual enrollment;[19] (2) authoritarian instruction emphasizing the verbal commitment to memory of the wisdom of high authorities.[20]

Latin America received the medieval University structure through Spain and Portugal, as well as content and form from the Napoleonic Code. University education in Latin America antedates that of North America by a hundred years with both the University of San Marcos, in Lima, Peru, and University of Mexico, established by royal charter in 1551. Its traditions are well established.

The university professional curriculum was in part an extension of the early titles of nobility and land grants from the Iberian Kings. The university professional title was largely regarded as an end in itself, providing social identification and prestige whether or not the profession was practiced. The university academic programs were correspondingly theoretical in orientation and directed toward letter, law or medicine in isolated, independent schools of professional training incorporated nominally under university heading. Traditional professional or letter degrees were an important measure of social distinction, and only when a profession was not obtainable was another occupation such as commerce considered. Financial achievement in business could not compensate for the lack of professional status.

Within the traditional university system in Latin America there was little correspondence between the degree received, the effective knowledge acquired, and the subsequent activities of the degree recipient, again in keeping with values centered on "being" as opposed to "achievement".

The university organization, which had its origin in the Middle Ages, was comprised of an exclusive and limited number of separate and semi-autonomous professional schools. Each school was organized around a powerful and autonomous faculty and headed by a Dean elected from and responsible to his faculty peers. The deans in turn were members of the University Council presided over by the Rector who was elected or appointed by the faculties, the state, the church, or with various methods of combined procedure. Rudolph P. Atcon reflects the basic political nature of the traditional Latin American University in his description of the Latin American University Council.

> "The University Council has nothing in common with the U.S. managerial system, where powers are delegated and only decisions on general orientation are taken jointly or laid down by superior authority. A system of private loyalties and obligations, of person-to-person dealings, preempts the possibility of arriving at decisions of general interest or at objective considerations of long-range needs. After the horse trading of private interests has ended, grounds for agreement are of a nature so non-descript as to affect no vested interests. This "least denominator" is usually so low as to be ineffectual."[21]

Each school's pre-established curriculum was taught exclusively to those students enrolled in its five-year professional career program. The Institutions of Cátedra (Chair) and its legally prescribed holder, the Catedrático (Professor) were again adopted from European Institutions and provided the professor with absolute rule over his subject area for life. However, social, political, and economic considerations played major parts in the nomination of Latin American professors for chair positions designed to be conferred on a basis of individual capacity, knowledge, and experience. Consistent with the Latin American concept of the University as a social-political institution, the professor received little or token direct financial remuneration from the university. Rather, this status position formed a base from which to launch and maintain a successful professional and/or political career.

The rigidity of the university organization structure with its classic, fixed curriculum and protective chairs predictably oriented the professors' time and efforts away from the academic and toward the social-political system and values which the university shared, pre-served, and transmitted. The professors elected or appointed to political office retained their university position, title, and foremost loyalty to this system of higher education through which they advanced.

The university's organizational rigidity, combined with its traditional verbal, theoretical, and authoritarian teaching orientation, did not readily lend itself to the adoption and adaptation of the scientific curricula and research methodology so rapidly developing in Europe and North America by the turn of the century. The human resources, libraries, and laboratories necessary for scientific and technological growth were consequently little developed within the university during the first half of the 20th century.

The stability and nature of this traditional social political university system and the role of the Latin American student are both exemplified by the university student reform movement originating in Cordoba, Argentina, June, 1918 which subsequently spread throughout Latin America.

The reform's basic objective was to free the university from domination by disinterested and unqualified professors holding life-time appointments and teaching a limited number of rigid, professional curricula for a privileged elite. The reform intended to reorient the university from its traditional objectives, organization, and curriculum toward an active contribution to the country's social and economic development, including scientific and technological curriculum.

The reform's general aspirations were unified in a World Congress in Mexico in 1921 and, following many extended and often violent student strikes, representation within Latin American University Government was generally won by the students. "Cogobierno" (cogovernment), as it is identified commonly, took the form of student and alumni representation on the university councils, and legally institutionalized direct student and alumni involvement in its highest administrative and academic policy decisions.

The Student University Reform furthermore strongly identified with national social reform movements. Among those students' names who promoted the university reform are many of the subsequent major political leaders of popular reform in Latin America. In Peru, for example, a major leader of the student university reform of 1919 was Víctor Raúl Haya de la Torre, who in 1931 established the powerful, popular Aprista Party.

In the years following the reformist movement of the early 1900's, the students and alumni university government involvement has further developed and extended as an integral part of the university's social-political role.[22]

What began as a student reform of the traditional Latin American University problems further developed as a student problem. The students were fully institutionalized as active members of the social-political system and thereby further developed the university's vital part in that system.

The extent and reverberations of the students' and the university's involvement in internal and national politics are interpreted as follows by Rudolph Atcon:

> "Whenever secular excesses become too numerous or too unbearable for society at large, the University, led by its student body, would protest. Emotional reactions to emotional situations resulted in strikes, demonstration, manifestos, and open violence... When the students suffered, the country had martyrs. If the government fell, the nation had heroes. Either way students were bound to acquire ever-increasing status, prestige, and

political power. They also acquired a divine right to inter-
fere. But martyrs or heroes do not make good students... In
consequence students develop a tendency to shout down their
adversaries, to use slogans and stir emotions rather than reason on facts."[23]

The direction and extent of educational reform which has been
accomplished since the statements of intent summarized above, at the
World Congress in Mexico in 1921, has been highly diversified within the
20 Latin American republics and their 233 institutions of higher education, including 88 universities. The causes for the varied patterns
and degrees of university reform are many. The common historical elements in the university's founding and early growth resulted in a
prominent pattern of general characteristics which allow the abstraction and useful analysis of a "Latin American University." However,
the social-economic environments in which the universities develop,
including the total educational system on which they build, are significantly heterogenous as evidenced quantitatively by the diversity of
levels of human resource development discussed in Chapter I.

The qualitative variances in contemporary institutions of higher
education in Latin America are equally great and represent a critical
variable in the high-level manpower problems of Latin America.

Representative contemporary universities and other non-university
formal institutions of higher education will be analyzed in the following country study chapters with emphasis given to their strategies to
orient about the diverse needs of their respective national and local
problems.

It should be emphasized that the cultural elements of any one social
class or subgroup describe characteristics which are commonly found and
shared by its members and provide both group stability and continuity.
These frequently found cultural characteristics do not indicate, however, that each member of the group shares all of these characteristics.
Individual members of a culture, or group subculture, may deviate considerably from its integrated pattern of values, attitudes, and practices. This distinction is particularly important when considering the
attitudes and administrative practices of Latin American Management in
the following section as they include many individuals with diverse
ethnic and educational backgrounds. The important entrepreneurial role
of the large numbers of immigrants to Latin America since the latter
half of the 19th century has been frequently cited.[24]

Certainly many cultural characteristics are shared by the large
numbers of Mediterranean immigrants and the native Latin American society; however, a considerable degree of individual social deviation is
evidenced by such active value orientations as drive for achievement.
The Northern European immigrant's value orientations assimilated into
Latin American organization and administration are readily apparent,
although their relatively small numbers, social isolation, and accomo-
dation have reduced their impact as agents of social change. Albert
Lauterbach furthermore does not expect that either the British or North

American pattern of entrepreneurship will be repeated on a comparable scale in Latin America due to its historical and cultural character-istics:[25]

> "It is far more likely that the pattern there will continue to be a combination of private and public development initiative, bolstered by increasingly objective standards of executive selection and promotion, expanding facilities and requirements for executive training, periodic inter-change of trained executive talent between the private and public sectors, growing awareness of productivity factors on the part both of the enterprise managers and their workers, etc."

Contemporary Organization Structure and Administrative Behavior

The first portion of this chapter discussed individual behavior, growth and development related to Latin American cultural character-istics, including the major social institutions of Family, Church, and School. Recent cross-cultural empirical studies of similarities and differences in managerial attitudes and practices suggest that administra-tive behavior appears as strongly influenced by such cultural elements as by degree or kind of industrialization.[26] Unfortunately, there is yet little empirical research dealing with managerial attitudes, be-liefs, and practices in Latin America. However, it is increasing, and there are now several Latin American country studies written by highly qualified social scientists, describing in depth the organization and administration characteristics of individual Latin American countries. Although their backgrounds, education, and research methodology are highly diversified, their basic findings are in surprising accord.

Two separate research studies, involving the contemporary adminis-trative behavior and organization structure in each of the following countries, were selected for comparative analysis: Argentina, Brazil, Chile, Colombia, Mexico, Peru. In addition, two comparative studies of Management by Albert Lauterbach and Frank Brandenburg were included, involving each of these countries between 1959-63.

Argentina — Fillol, Social Factors in Economic Development — The Argentine Case (Cambridge, Massachusetts: MIT Press, 1961).
      — Alexander, Labor Relations in Argentina, Brazil, and Chile (New York: McGraw-Hill, 1962).

Brazil   — Alexander, Labor Relations in Argentina, Brazil, and Chile.
      — Siegel, Gilbert B., Adm. Values and the Merit System in Brazil; Perspectives of Brazilian Public Administration, Robert Daland, Editor, (Los Angeles: University of Southern California, The School of Public Administration, 1963).

Chile
- Alexander, Labor Relations in Argentina, Brazil, and Chile.
- Myers, Charles A., "Management in Chile," in Harbison and Myers, Management in the Industrial World (New York: McGraw-Hill, 1959), Chapter 9.

Colombia
- Hagen, On the Theory of Social Change (Homewood, Illinois: The Dorsey Press, Inc,, 1962), Chapter 15.
- Lipman, El Empresario Industrial en América Latina Naciones Unidas, Comisión Económica para América Latina

Mexico
- Fayerweather, The Executive Overseas (Syracuse: University Press, 1959).
- Vernon, The Dilemma of Mexico's Development (Cambridge, Mass.: Harvard University Press, 1963).

Peru
- Whyte and Williams, "Supervisory Leadership: An International Comparison," CIOS XIII (1963) Symposium B3 Paper No B3c.
- Holmberg and Whyte, "Human Problems of U.S. Enterprise in Latin America," Human Organization, XV (Fall, 1956), 10-11.

Lauterbach, "Executive Training and Productivity: Managerial Views in Latin America," Industrial and Labor Relations Review,XVII (April, 1964), 377.

Brandenburg, Frank, 'The Development of Latin American Private Enterprise', National Planning Association, May 1964. Washington, D. C.

These interdisciplinary studies indicate that the contemporary Latin American private and public sector organization and operating characteristics are generally consistent with the attitudes and cognitive patterns developed within the social institutions previously described.[27] The Latin American cultural attitudes and cognitive functions are instilled by the parental, church and school social institutions long before the individual joins or develops an organization which itself is a part of the wider culture.[28] If the surrounding work group behavior and organization characteristics are consistent, his opinions and beliefs will have little opportunity for change. Fayerweather's conclusion from his study of the Mexican executive is exemplary and further indicates the process of cultural accommodation necessitated by foreign firms organizing in Latin America.

"Most of the Mexican executives observed in this study showed relatively individualistic tendencies. This is a reality around which the organizations had to be built. Specifically it meant that the capacities for cooperation of many men at lower levels was limited, so that, if decisions were to be reached on interdepartmental matters they often had to be made by superiors.... All of these actions create to a degree an authoritarian atmosphere. They are necessary as adjustments to the cultures of many foreign countries. If the business of a company is to move

> ahead, the organization must function. And it can function
> only if the systems are accommodated to the personalities
> of the personnel."

Recognizing the traditional elements of the Latin American culture and the rising impact of industrialization and modernization, what are the major, prevailing characteristics of the contemporary organization structure and administrative behavior?

Administrative Authority and Organization Characteristics

The central findings of the authors previously cited concerning the most common administrative authority and organization characteristics in the six Latin American countries studied were generally consistent. Management leadership behavior was most often characterized as authoritarian and/or paternalistic. Fillol,[29] Whyte,[30] and Fayerweather,[31] in their respective country studies emphasized the prevalence of highly individualistic, personalistic management characteristics, emphasis being on an innate individual worth as a basis for authority. Management was correspondingly described as reluctant to delegate authority due to a general lack of trust in subordinates and sensitivity to errors which may reflect on it personally.[32]

Decision Making Systems

Decision making systems were characterized as predominantly highly centralized in each of the countries studied. The concentration of ownership within the family, its extended relationships, and the relatively small size of most Latin American firms were frequently identified with the highly centralized and paternalistic management characteristics.[33]

Mason Haire, Ghiselli, and Porter, in their comparative study of managerial attitudes, found management leadership attitudes in fourteen countries tended to follow common cultural tradition rather than level of industrialization.

Four European countries with predominant Latin backgrounds -- Spain, France, Italy, and Belgium -- tended to cluster on the scales distinguishing such managerial leadership attitudes as participative decision making and nature of controls.[34]

There was further general consensus among the authors involved that the decision processes of the Latin American manager deviate in several dimensions from the currently held characteristics of optimal scientific methods of problem solving. For the purposes of this study it is not necessary or practical to enter into a discussion of current economic or behavioral models of decision making[35]; rather, we will draw upon the consolidation of research on various phases of the decision process as described by Brim, Glass, Lavin, and Goodman in their study of Decision Processes to provide a basis for comparative analysis of Latin American decision process characteristics.[36] (1) Identification of the problem; (2) obtaining necessary information; (3) production of possible solutions; (4) evaluation of such solutions; (5) selection of a strategy for performance; and (6) actual performance of an action or actions; and subsequent learning and revision.

Fayerweather, in his study of Mexican management characteristics, includes steps 1-5 in the above decision process classification under analysis.[37] He defines the analytical approach to management as both the process in which the problems and ideas are organized, examined, and developed in the search for effective patterns of action and an orderly logic in thinking. He concludes that while the analytical approach to management decision processes appears to be gaining ground in Mexico, it faces strong opposition from two traditional approaches: established rules and impulses. The utilitarian concern for results is competing with the value of the action as a release and means of expressing inner urges.

Attempts to equate culturally biased definitions of optimal decision processes with degree of rationality have little value without first identifying the rules and the success of the solutions satisfying the needs and purposes of the decision maker. Fayerweather, for example, identifies Proyectismo as an additional element in the Mexican culture which affects both management's analytical effectiveness and the 6th decision process characteristic, actual performance of an action. He describes Proyectismo as the tendency to construct plans with little or no analysis and then assume, wish, and believe the plans are an accomplished fact.[38-39] Again satisfaction appears to be gained from the planning process as an end in itself regardless of the likelihood of its success.

Whyte, Holmberg,[40] and Lauterbach[41] further note that the non-financial considerations appear to have a more important role in Latin American management evaluation of a possible solution. The prevalent family ownership basis of Latin American firms, with its extended relationships, position, varied interest, and individualistic and non-material personality characteristics previously discussed, provides a complex set of values by which to judge the rationality of Latin American Management.[42] Whyte and Holmberg[43] suggest: "the profit motive, far from being the sole determining factor, is often only a limiting factor in executive decisions. The executive decides what ought to be done and then plans as best he can to make his actions pay." The time element enters into the decision-making discussions within the country studies under the analysis in several ways. Whyte and Holmberg state that the Latin American manager does not share the North American's high value of time.[44] He does not equate time with money and therefore does not value the measurement and control of time as highly, nor tend to associate punctuality with responsibility in the evaluation of men to the extent of his North American counterpart. There is considerable emphasis by several of the authors involved that Latin American managers tend to be oriented toward the short run in the generation, evaluation, and selection of a strategy for performance.[45,46,47]

Fayerweather distinguishes between future-time orientation in the generation of the analysis and actual performance of an action or actions. He cites the abundant and elaborate plans in Mexican history and the contemporary development programs as evidence that the middle and upper class Mexicans are quite aware of the future. However, he concludes they exhibit a tendency to avoid analytical thoroughness in their evaluation, selection, and performance of actions, as evidenced historically by the frequency of program failures in Mexico. Fayer-weather relates the above to proyectismo already noted and the past social, political, economic environment which combined to make the future very uncertain in Mexico. The final characteristic in the decision is described by Brim et al, following the actual performance of action, as subsequent learning and revision or control. And as one might expect, there appears to be a logical relationship between managerial authority characteristics, the decision-making system, and the control processes predominating.

Management control procedures in Latin American are most frequently identified with highly centralized and involved financial procedures and closeness of personal supervision at all levels. Fillol notes that in Argentina it is not unusual for a board to supervise in detail all operations of the firm, and that this characteristic is conspicuous through all levels of management.[48,49] Peruvian workers correspondingly were found by Whyte to be more accustomed and acceptable to close supervision and pressures for production than the North American workers.[50] It is noteworthy that the Brim et al. empirical research study of personality and decision processes indicated: "general values and orientation toward life together with the cultural background of the respondent seem to account for more variability in decision-making than the more traditional personality traits", such as verbal intelligence, which was found to have a negligible relation to the decision process characteristics. Individual personality dimensions, such as belief in fate and supernatural causes and dominance in child-rearing attitudes, were found to be closely related to such decision processes as consideration of smaller numbers of possible outcomes of actions and optimistic evaluation of outcomes.[51]

Recruitment, Placement, and Development Characteristics

The recruitment, placement, and development of personnel in Latin America remains strongly influenced by family, personal acquaintances, and political connection, according to the authors included in the analysis.[52,53,54,55,56,57] Again the predominance of family and closely held firms promotes nepotism and emphasis on experience as criteria for selection and succession. Japan has incorporated technical and professional management education criteria in its patrimonial system, and has extended its family to adopted professionals selected on education and performance criteria.[58] Latin America, however, little evidences this emphasis on functional education within or outside of the firm in its manpower staffing and development. Alexander, in his Argentine, Brazil, and Chile studies, concludes that most skilled workers learn their skills from practice, as there are few in-plant training programs in these three countries.[59] Lauterbach's study of managerial views of executive training in eleven Latin American countries, including the above, concludes that the training of Latin American executives at this point is rather haphazard, both in facilities available and actual instruction.[60] Top managements' rare appreciation of employee development needs and their association with productivity, combined with highly centralized family organization characteristics, do not develop social mobility, but tend to center efforts on securing present positions. Here again both cultural and level of industrialization factors are involved. Latin America's continued modernization may result in recruitment, succession, and development characteristics more closely aligned to Japan than to North America. Whyte and Holmberg note, however, that rapidly growing industrial opportunities in Latin America are creating a void of people with technical and managerial skills which is increasingly being filled by people of the lower classes and contributing to the development of the middle class.[61]

The lack of technically trained workers and capable middle management is widely believed to be one of the greatest obstacles in the course of Latin American industrialization.

External and Internal Interrelationships: Complex Systems

Social scientists have long recognized the existence of environmental factors and their systemic interrelationships with the internal organization and administrative behavior of productive enterprises.[62] The complexity and extent of these interrelationships are now more fully revealed and understood, as a result of increasing interdisciplinary research of the modernization process utilizing systems concepts.[63,64,65,66] One excellent example of such interdisciplinary experimentation in modernization process research was that carried out at the center for International Studies at Massachusetts Institute of Technology by a group of social scientists in 1960. The results were later edited and published by two of the authors, Max F. Millikan and Donald L. M. Blackmer, under the title, The Emerging Nations Their Growths and United States Policy.[67] The following summary statement from this study is exemplary of the true complexities involved:

> "We have emphasized the great complexity of the process of social, political, and economic change through which all the societies we refer to as underdeveloped are passing. The complexity results partly from the fact that modernization involves interaction among psychological, political, social, economic, and cultural factors and partly from the fact that the histories, traditions, resources, and values of the process of continuous interaction among so many variables in so many different circumstances would be impossible to trace and to describe with precision even if all the variables could be described in mathematical terms and each assigned a firm statistical weight. Obviously, in dealing with men and societies, neither the qualitative relations nor the quantities can be firmly and unambiguously established."[68]

The authors in the country studies under consideration in this chapter devote unusual efforts to illustrate and analyze the comprehensive interrelationships existing between the organization and its environment, all changing rapidly under national modernization pressures, as illustrated by this excerpt from Fillol's Argentine study:

The "high profits per unit" philosophy has been unquestionably nourished by the protectionist policies followed by the Argentine government since the mid 1930's. Protectionism breeds and will continue to breed inefficiency. Barred from the influence of foreign competition, Argentine industry has been able to pass to the consumer the increased costs of governmental labor policies and has adapted itself comfortably to producing large profits on the smallest possible volume... We must also keep in mind, however, that such an approach to profits is partly the consequence of a "trader" business mentality not unrelated to cultural characteristics which induce the Argentine to maximize his immediate advantage (in this case the business's short run profit), while neglecting adequate consideration of future goals and long-run profitability. Furthermore, the "mass markets at low unit profits" philosophy is only possible where a mass market exists at all.[69]

Comparative management studies concerning a country's administrative needs and practices isolated from its complex environmental interrelationships are quite popular today. However, the receptivity of the enlightened nationals offered such advice is understandably diminishing.

If the development and performance of Latin American managerial resources and organizations are to be better understood and improved, it will necessarily involve their study as an integrated part of each country's unique social-economic system. While this is the ambitious intent of the following authors in the five countries selected for study, the focus will remain on managerial resource development in formal educational institutions.

NOTES AND REFERENCES

1. A complete citation of the studies under consideration in this work, by the authors mentioned, is quoted on page 22 of this chapter.

2. Everett E. Hagen, On the Theory of Social Change (Homewood, Illinois: The Dorsey Press, Inc., 1962) p.55.

3. Report on the World Social Situation Social Development in Latin America, U. N. Economic and Social Council, E/CN.5/375Add.2, 4 March 1963, pp. 16-18.

4. John Johnson, Political Change in Latin America: The Emergence of the Middle Sectors (California: Stanford University Press, 1958), p. 2.

5. Richard Adams and others, <u>Social Change in Latin America Today</u>,
    Chapter II, "Changing Attitudes and Values in Peru: A case study
    of Guided Change," by Allan R. Holmberg, (New York: Random House,
    1960).
    See also: Whyte and Andrew, <u>Two Cities of Latin America: A
    Comparative description of Social Classes</u> (Garden City, New York:
    Doubleday and Company, 1964) and
    Oscar Lewis, <u>Life in a Mexican Village: Tepoztlan Restudied</u>
    (Urbana: University of Illinois Press, 1963).

6. T. R. Crevena, ed., <u>Data for the Study of the Middle Class in
    Latin America</u> (Washington, D. C.: Pan American Union, 1950-51).

7. <u>The Industrial Entrepreneurs in Latin America</u>, U. N. Economic
    Commission for Latin America, E/CN.12/644/Add.4, March 18, 1963.

8. Johnson, <u>op.cit.</u>, pp. 181-187.

9. William S. Stokes, <u>Latin American Politics</u> (New York: Thomas
    Crowell Co., 1959). See Chapters 1 and 2 for an analysis of forces
    which inhibit social mobility in Latin America.

10. John Fayerweather, <u>The Executive Overseas</u> (Syracuse: University
    Press, 1959), p. 64.

11. Tomás Roberto Fillol, <u>Social Factors in Economic Development-The
    Argentine Case</u> (Cambridge, Massachusetts: M.I.T. Press, 1961),
    p. 12.

12. Hagen, <u>op.cit.</u>, p. 25.

13. Fayerweather, <u>op.cit.</u>, p. 25.

14. Abram Kardiner, <u>The Psychological Frontiers of Society</u> (New York:
    Columbia University Press, 1945), pp. 7-8. Dr. Kardiner proposes
    that the basic personality elements for a society is that personal-
    ity configuration which is shared in common by the society's mem-
    bers as a result of common culturally patterned experience within
    the family and its other social institutions.

15. William F. Whyte and Allan R. Holmberg, "Human Problems of U.S.
    Enterprise in Latin America," <u>Human Organization</u>, XV (Fall,1956), pp.
    10-11.

    - Fillol, <u>op.cit.</u>, pp. 10-19.

    - Hagen, <u>op.cit.</u>, p. 369.

    - Fayerweather, <u>op.cit.</u>, pp. 21-30.

    - Ozzie G. Simmons, "Drinking Patterns and Interpersonal Performance
      in a Peruvian Mestizo Community," <u>Quarterly Journal of Studies in
      Alcohol</u>, XX (1959), pp. 104-105.

- William F. Whyte, "Culture, Industrial Relations, and Economic Development: The Case of Peru," Industrial and Labor Relations Review, XVI (July, 1963), pp. 587-592.

- Lewis, op.cit., pp. 317-318.

- Samuel Ramos, Profile of Man and Culture in Mexico (Texas: University of Texas Press, 1962), pp. 126-132.

- Albert Lauterbach, Industrial and Labor Relations Review, XVII (April, 1964), p. 374.

- Harold Orlansky, "Infant Care and Personality," Psychological Bulletin, XLVI (1949), pp. 35-38.

16. Hagen, op.cit., pp. 128-129.

17. C. H. Haring, The Spanish Empire of America (New York: Oxford University Press, 1947), p. 213.

18. Fernando de Azevedo, Brazilian Culture (New York: MacMillan Co., 1950), p. 336.

19. The severity and continuity of the quantitative educational access problem is reflected in the following 1950 statistical abstract from Reports of the Conference on Education and Economic and Social Development in Latin America, U.N. Economic Commission for Latin America, March 1962, Santiago, Chile:

    In the year 1950 in Latin America of the population over 15 years of age:
    - 49% had not attended school at all or had dropped out before completing one year.
    - 7% had completed primary education.
    - 6% received secondary level education with 2% completing the course.
    - 1% entered a university.

20. "The clinging to dogma and authority, scholastic and literary tradition, the almost total lack of interest in science, the repugnance to technical and artistic activities, were necessarily to characterize in the colony all the education which was modelled on that of the home country which had remained closed and bitterly opposed to the critical analytical spirit, to research and experimentation." Azevedo, op.cit., p. 335.

21. Rudolph Atcon, "The Latin American University," Universidad Nacional Autónoma de Honduras, Tegucigalpa, D. C. (March 31, 1961), p. 20.

22. The following sources present an excellent review and analysis of
    the historical development and contemporary orientation of Latin
    American University Higher Education:

    - Harold Benjamin, Higher Education in the American Republics
      (New York: McGraw-Hill, Inc., 1965).

    - Gabriel C. Del Mazo, Estudiantes y Gobierno Universitario (Buenos
      Aires, Argentina: Imprenta Universitaria, 1949).

    - Abraham Flexner, Universities: American, English, German (New
      York: Oxford University Press, 1930).

    - John Tate Lanning, The University in the Kingdom of Guatemala
      (Binghamton, New York: Vail-Ballao Press, Inc., 1955).

    - Ismael Rodríguez Bou, La Educación Superior en América Latina,
      Preparado por la Comisión Especial para Promover la Programación
      y el Desarrollo de la Educación, la Ciencia y la Cultura en
      América Latina de la Organización de los Estados Americanos,
      Enero, 1963.

    - Luis Alberto Sánchez, La Universidad Latinoamericana, 1a. ed.
      (Guatemala: Imprenta Universitaria, 1949).

23. Atcon, op.cit., p. 30.

24. El Empresario Industrial en América Latina, Naciones Unidas,
    Comisión Económica para América Latina, E/CN.12/642/Add.1, 10 de
    febrero de 1963.
    The high proportion of people of foreign extraction in the group
    of entrepreneurs that was surveyed in the four countries (Argentina,
    Brazil, Chile, and Colombia) was striking. For example, in Chile
    48% of the entrepreneurs surveyed were of foreign extraction.

25. Albert Lauterbach, "Executive Training and Productivity: Managerial
    Views in Latin America," Industrial and Labor Relations Review,
    XVII (April, 1964), 377.

26. Mason Haire, Edwin Ghiselli, Lyman Porter, "Cultural Patterns in
    the role of the Manager," Industrial Relations, II (February,
    1963), 102.

27. Raymond Vernon, The Dilemma of Mexico's Development (Cambridge,
    Massachusetts: Harvard University Press, 1963), pp. 158-159.
    "Indeed, as one tries to describe the principal characteristics
    and values of Mexico's business leaders, he finds that the same
    characteristics and values seem to apply to Mexican leadership in
    general, whether that leadership appears in business, in politics,
    or in other areas. And it is the history and culture of Mexico
    itself that provides the richest clues to an understanding of
    these leadership characteristics and values."

28. Branislaw Malinowsky, Magic, Science, and Religion and Other Essays (New York: Doubleday Company, 1955).

29. Fillol, op.cit., p. 14.

30. Whyte, op.cit., pp. 6,7.

31. Fayerweather, op.cit., p. 137.

32. Vernon, op.cit., p. 159; Fillol, op.cit., pp. 19,57,59; Whyte, op. cit., p. 27; Holmberg, op.cit., p. 36; Fayerweather, op.cit., pp. 34,136; Myers, op.cit., pp. 173,178; Alexander, op.cit., pp. 48, 173; Lauterbach, op.cit., p. 369.

33. Lauterbach, op.cit., p. 376; Alexander, op.cit., pp. 48,133; Myers, op.cit., p. 173; Whyte, Holmberg, op.cit., p. 7; Fayerweather, op. cit., p. 28.

34. Haire, Ghiselli, Porter, op.cit., pp. 102-103.

35. For an excellent discussion and bibliography of the limits of rationality see Herbert A. Simon, Administrative Behavior 2nd Ed. (New York: The MacMillan Company, 1961), pp. 22-39.

36. Brim, Orville and others, Personality and Decision Processes: Studies in the Social Psychology of Thinking (Stanford, California: Stanford University Press, 1962), p. 9.

37. Fayerweather, op.cit., p. 62.

38. Ibid., pp. 65-66.

39. The author's several years of experience in executive and graduate level management education and study in Peru would strongly support the prevalence and impact of proyectismo in administration in that country.

40. Whyte, Holmberg, op.cit., pp. 9-10.

41. Lauterbach, op.cit., pp. 376-377.

42. Simon, op.cit., pp. 75-77.

43. Whyte and Holmberg, op.cit., p. 10.

44. Ibid., p. 9.

45. Lauterbach, op.cit., pp. 376-377.

46. Fillol, op.cit., pp. 13, 14, 95-96.

47. Fayerweather, op.cit., pp. 77-79.

48. Fillol, op.cit., p. 60.

49. Orville G. Brim, Jr., David C. Glass, David E. Lavin, Norman Goodman, Personality and Decision Processes (Stanford, California: Stanford University Press, 1962).

50. Whyte, op.cit., pp. 6-7.

51. Brim, Glass, Lavin, Goodman, op.cit., p. 234.
    Discussion with directors of executive development programs in Chile, Brazil, Argentina, and Colombia combined with the author's experience in Peruvian and Chilean management programs would indicate that in these countries it is very difficult for top management to be absent from their organization for periods of time longer than one week. The very rapid growth of management continuing education in these countries is therefore almost totally scheduled after normal working hours although considerable effort has been spent to promote full-time concentrated courses.

52. Fillol, op.cit., pp. 22, 57, 61.

53. Whyte, Holmberg, op.cit., p. 4.

54. Fayerweather, op.cit., p. 106.

55. Myers, op.cit., p. 178.

56. Alexander, op.cit., p. 49.

57. Lauterbach, op.cit., p. 360.

58. Harbison and Myers, op.cit., pp. 260-262.

59. Alexander, op.cit., pp. 116-117, 223-228, 339-340.

60. Lauterbach, op.cit., p. 366.

61. Whyte, Holmberg, op.cit., p. 35.

62. The introduction of the systems approach to anthropological research emphasizing the functional interrelationships between cultural elements including institutions and organizations is generally credited to the British Scholar, Bronislaw Malinowsky, who, in 1944, wrote A Scientific Theory of Culture and Other Essays (Chapel Hill, N. C.,: University of North Carolina Press).

63. Early biological theories of the firm's behavior, such as that proposed by Kenneth Boulding, emphasized the integration of the organization within the environment and its stable unity ("homeostatic equilibrium") resulting in a process of gradual change often involving generations. There was, however, little recognition given to the deliberate ability of the firm's

management to effect changes in its environment. Kenneth Boulding, _A Reconstruction of Economics_ (New York: John Wiley & Sons Ind., 1950).

64. Jean Boddewyn, "The Cultural Approach to Business Behavior," in Joseph W. McGuire, ed., _Interdisciplinary Studies in Business Behavior_ (Cincinnati: Southern Publishing Company, 1962).

65. John T. Dunlop, _Industrial Relations Systems_ (New York: Henry Holt and Company, 1958), p. 383. "An industrial-relations system is comprised of three groups of actors -- workers and their organizations, managers and their organizations, and governmental agencies concerned with the work place and work community. These groups interact within a specified environment comprised of three inter-related contexts: the technology, the market or budgetary constraints and the power relations in the larger community and the derived status of the actors. An industrial-relations system creates an ideology or a commonly shared body of ideas and beliefs regarding the interaction and roles of the actors which helps to bind the system together."

66. A more recent comparative study of Richard Farmer and Barry Richman, using a comprehensive systems approach, considers the effect of economic, political-legal, educational and sociological environmental constraints on managerial behavior and effectiveness. Richard N. Farmer and Barry M. Richman, _Comparative Management and Economic Progress_ (Homewood, Illinois: Richard D. Irwin, Inc., 1965).

67. Francis M. Bator, Donald L. M. Blackmer and others, _The Emerging Nations - Their Growth and United States Policy_, ed. by Max F. Millikan and Donald L. M. Blackmer (Boston: Little, Brown and Company, 1961), p. 93.

68. _Ibid._, p. 93.

69. Fillol, _op.cit._, p. 58.

CHAPTER III

MANAGERIAL RESOURCE DEVELOPMENT IN ARGENTINA

by

Guillermo S. Edelberg

Social - Economic Environment for Managerial Resource Development.

Historical Development. Many students of Argentina's socio-economic
history concur in pointing to the 1880's as the period during which the
country started its road towards modernization. Until then, and almost
since becoming independent from Spain in 1816, Argentina had suffered
from a series of internal political and economic struggles which hindered her institutional organization as a modern nation. However,
political stability was achieved by the 1880's, and shortly thereafter
a period of rapid expansion and striking changes took place.

Since it is not the objective of this section to discuss in detail
Argentina's socio-economic history after that date but rather to isolate factors that influenced managerial resource development, we have
chosen to deal here with two interrelated aspects bearing heavily on
this whole area; namely, immigration and the change in the economic
structure, from an almost purely agricultural economy to one which
includes a very important industrial sector.

During the 100-year period that runs from 1857 to 1954, over
4,000,000 immigrants chose Argentina as the country of their permanent
residence. The peak of the wave was reached in the first decade of
this century with over 1,100,000 immigrants.[1] The Census figures are
quite clear in this respect: while the 1869 Census indicated that the
Argentine population numbered then 1,900,000 inhabitants, the one taken
in 1895 showed 4,050,000. Furthermore, the 1914 Census counted
7,900,000 inhabitants. This meant in fact that between 1869 and 1914
the Argentine population doubled every fifteen years.

Such heavy inflow of immigration changed the social composition of
the country's population. By 1914 one third of Argentina's inhabitants
were people born elsewhere; the proportion changing to 15% by 1954. If
only the Buenos Aires metropolitan area is considered, the figures show
that by 1914 some 50% of its inhabitants were foreigners.[2]

The vast majority of the immigrants came from Southern Europe --
Italy and Spain, mainly. The influence of the Italian immigrants, for
example, may be noted in many aspects of Argentina and contributed to
differentiate her from most other Latin American countries. Although

35

Italy and Spain were not then leaders in the development of industrial activities, only a small proportion of the newly arrived settled in rural areas in occupations related to agriculture. A very important reason was that the relatively small number of native families which concentrated the ownership of land succeeded throughout the years, with minor exceptions, in maintaining the control over their large estates. These families constituted the aristocracy of the country, and until 1916 were almost exclusively the sole providers of Argentina's political leaders.[3] Thus, the immigrants, despite their number, were not able to change the "status quo."[4]

The newly arrived established themselves in urban areas, especially in Buenos Aires, and became the providers of labor for petty trades, all sorts of services, small workshops, and home construction activities. By the turn of the century, however, relatively few industrial establishments existed in Argentina, mainly producing export goods derived from agriculture and cattle exploitations. No large consumer goods industries, i.e., textile plants such as those that existed in other countries then, could be encountered in Argentina. With the exception of those goods produced by craftsmen or "family shops", a large proportion of consumer goods were imported from abroad.

As the concentration in urban areas increased, so did a market for consumer goods. In addition, the rapid development of the country's railroad system enlarged the growing markets even more. As a result of this briefly described process, a number of small entrepreneurs originating from among the immigrants organized industrial establishments, as indicated in Table 1, the quantity and importance of which increased, though slowly, throughout the years. World War I favored the growth of the industrial sector, although the same did not happen in the immediate post-war period. The process accelerated somewhat during the Great Depression, but it was World War II and its aftermath that strongly reinforced the tendency to industrialize. The inability of the traditional foreign suppliers to provide goods that had been imported for many years, the government's policies for the promotion of industrialization, the industrial activities directly undertaken by government agencies, and the new wave of immigrants and foreign investments that arrived when the war was over put Argentina, as a number of economists assert, in the "take-off" stage of her economic development. Table 2, for example, illustrates this fact: approximately 62% of the industrial establishments that existed in 1946 started operating after 1930. By 1966, the industrial sector employed a proportion of the work force larger than that engaged by the primary sector, and its share of the Argentine gross national product was as large as that corresponding to agriculture (21 percent, approximately).

By 1966, the sons of the immigrants born in Argentina and identified with local habits and traditions, and the people that attended colleges, especially in the technical branches of education, and participated in civic activities provided an important proportion of the technical abilities and leadership that made many establishments achieve a modern stature.[5] Thus, the dramatic changes in the ethnic

characteristics of the country's population reinforced by the consequences of World War II influenced the entire development of the managerial resources throughout more than 80 years, up to present times.

Attitudes regarding business. It is not surprising that the landed
aristocracy, which for a long time succeeded in monopolizing all roads
of access to the different manifestations of power -- political, economic, and social -- was the elite that determined for many years the
attitudes towards business and administration.

By 1880, the upper class viewed the extensive exploitation of land
and the opening to agriculture of virgin soil as the most highly regarded economic activities. Consequently, other economic activities
that gave support to such point of view were well accepted. Thus, the
laying of thousands of miles of new railroad tracks, the establishment
of banking services, the modernization of ports to facilitate the
export-import trade, and the establishment of meat-packing plants by
foreign firms were all encouraged.

During a period of about 50 years, the "estancieros" made
phenomenal profits. In that long interval, and with the exception of
the short periods during which a number of local or foreign crises
affected the country, the foreign exchange provided by the export of
commodities such as wheat and beef was more than enough, as compared
to the quantity needed for the importation of all consumer goods,
including those for conspicuous consumption. In general, then, industry was not regarded as a desirable activity for members of the upper
class. Thus, it found little encouragement for its development.

The immigrants who early in the century started to engage in
small-scale industrial activities could not easily compete with prices
and quality of foreign producers, and the conflict between protection
and free trade started to grow and to become a permanent issue in the
country's economic policies. World War I provided an opportunity for
local industry to grow, but when peace returned the policy of free
trade was again followed. It was not until the Great Depression and
World War II that Argentina's industrialists gained stature and power.
Thus, although the landed elite viewed the accumulation of wealth as
an acceptable social value, the road to industrialization was mostly
led by immigrants, i.e., "self-made men".

Other sectors relevant to business and administration had also
grown in the meantime; namely, Federal agencies and foreign firms.
The attitude toward these, from the point of view of the ruling class,
differed from that held towards local industry. Members of the upper
class occupied executive posts in Federal agencies, while the other
jobs were performed by members of the growing middle class. Not
unfrequently, the patronage of the aristocracy greatly helped one to
become a civil servant. Whichever the case, activities in government
agencies carried some degree of prestige and status. As far as the
foreign firms are concerned, individuals from the upper class became
members of their local boards of directors or were their local lawyers.

These, undoubtedly, were positions of prestige.[6] However, more important perhaps is to note that those members of the middle class that performed technical and professional activities in these foreign firms received a certain amount of management training.

Taking a historic view of the attitude towards business and administration, we may conclude that Argentina as a whole -- and not only a small group of visionaries -- caught up with modern and "international"approaches to industry and management by the mid 1940's. Perhaps the economic policies followed then were not the most appropriate ones for the promotion of investments in the industrial sector. However, it may be said that the development of a local industry was then fully accepted as a national goal, and the human resources available, perhaps underutilized, were ready to perform the task, if not at an optimum level, at least at an acceptable one. It might be added that the sector which lagged behind in its approach to management was agriculture -- precisely the sector which half a century before had been at the forefront of the country's progress. It seemed as if its main concern was the improvement of techniques rather than the improvement of management practices.

By the mid-1960's, the starting of a career with the hope of becoming a top executive in any sector of industry was a most desirable goal for young men of ambition. The position carried social status, power, and prestige.

Class structure.[7] Following Harbison and Myers'[8] approach to the study of management in the industrial world, it may be observed that by the mid-60's the three types of patrimonial, professional and political management coexisted extensively in Argentina.

In making a broad generalization, it may be said that in most Argentine private firms, regardless of size, the top executives belong to the family that owns or controls the firm, while the second layer of executives and the technical staff belong to the professional management type. Private firms run by professional managers in the United States style would be hard to find in Argentina although slow changes in this direction may be noticed as the industrial tradition of Argentina grows older.

The top executives of the Government's enterprises, i.e., the members of their boards of directors, are appointed on the basis of political decisions, while the second and following layers of managers in general, belong to the professional type. Political appointees in this second layer, however, are not uncommon, as is probably the case in many other countries. It is worth noting that, in the case of Argentina, the image of the political appointees deteriorated in the last 30 years or so, due to their frequent lack of technical competence.

Finally, in the case of the foreign firms, all layers of management are professional although it would be difficult to ascertain the following: a) what proportion of the management of the head office in the country of origin of the foreign firms belong to the patrimonial type; b) what proportion of the foreign firms have definite policies for or against having local executives reach the number one position in the local affiliate (although a number of foreign firms having Argentine nationals in that high position may be identified).

The preceding description should be qualified by the fact that Argentina may be classified as an open society where social mobility is pretty high. Thus, members of the managerial classes have changed from one category to the other with relative ease. Also, the move to a higher social status has been achieved with relative frequency in one or two generations. Finally, the existence of numerous professional associations facilitates the communication among members of the different managerial groups.

But whichever the path of progress in the social ladder may have been, the fashion for social behavior is still set by the landed aristocracy. This is evidenced by club membership, schooling for the children, summer resort attendance, "manners"...[9]

Attitudes of managerial elite.

> Argentine entrepreneurs have been widely critized for their tendencies toward cartelization, monopolies, nepotism, and, in general, concentration of ownership. They have also been critically judged for their unwilling- ness to take risks and reinvest earnings "productively," and for their prevailing philosophy of high profits per unit of sale rather than mass markets at low unit profits. These criticisms are all valid, well-founded, and obviously constructive from an economic-development point of view.[10]

The preceding observations made by Fillol in his book about the influence of social factors in the economic development of Argentina require some comments.[11]

The statement on the concentration of ownership was confirmed by the Argentine Industrial Census of 1954, which reported that 1% of the establishments employed 47% of the labor force,[12] and by information contained in a book on the country's leading groups.[13] The other criticisms in the quotation, however, rather seem to be a kind of statement of the obvious, i.e., "Argentine entrepreneurs are not like their United States counterparts". The question is not whether the described behavior is "incorrect" as measured by standards of advanced industrial countries, but rather whether such behavior is really a deterrent to Argentina's industrial development. And, if so, whether changes are possible or are taking place in the right direction.

Assuming the observations correctly describe businessmen's behavior, it is difficult to say whether a different behavior is possi- ble within the country's political, social, and economic setting. Is

it reasonable to expect an economic behavior that fits a country like
the United States to fit a country whose industrial history is only 40
or 50 years old (or less, perhaps)? Furthermore, each country has a
series of problems which are outside businessmen's control. In the
case of Argentina, factors in this category are, among others, government decisions affecting business, political instability, a chronic
inflation, scarcity of capital and foreign exchange, and small markets.
Thus, the problems for businessmen as such are not how to stop inflation
and political instability, but rather, how to live with them. In this
sense, it seems that the behavior of "modern" managers is of little
help.[14] Perhaps under such conditions the behavior described by Fillol
is the only one possible in Argentina or elsewhere under similar conditions. It is not easy to answer these questions -- especially when
the quantity and quality of statistics available do not permit a good
appraisal of the country's industrial development.[15] Therefore, due to
lack of strong evidence and in view of the frequently adverse circumstances, perhaps an opposite conclusion is true: businessmen ought to
be congratulated for their ability to survive and grow. Thus, the
question on the "goodness" or "badness" of businessmen's behavior in
Argentina, from the point of view of her economic development, remains
unanswered.

Leaving then that question aside, it may be said that some of the
traits, though not all of them, observed by Fillol, are correct. During
the course of a survey conducted in 1962 under the auspices of the
United Nations' Economic Commission for Latin America,[16] twenty-seven
industrialists were interviewed. In spite of this being a rather small
number, as recognized by the author of the study,[17] a profile of
Argentine top managers, based on information furnished by them, is
attempted:

> The Argentine industrial entrepreneur considers
> himself a "doer" rather than an innovator or organizer.
> Thus, he is concerned when he meets obstacles that
> hinder the achievement of his goals.

> ...he is a middle-aged person (45-50 years old), born
> in an Argentine town of European immigrant parents also
> coming from urban areas. He has more schooling than
> his parents: i.e., fourteen years of schooling, which
> is a little bit more than high-school level.

> He has been some fifteen years in his firm, having
> performed very different tasks during this period.
> He works over eight hours per day, and most of his
> time is devoted to general management and financial
> problems.

> He does not have a very clear idea about his role
> in society. He believes that the basis for success in
> Argentina is hard work, education, and honesty. He
> strives for his economic security but looks for oppor-
> tunities to help people. As an entrepreneur, he does
> not seek for risks, command, or power. He does not have

a very clear idea about the main satisfactions or
dissatisfactions in his job.

Many of his activities in the firm are performed
through committees... He selects his employees and
top executives mainly based on personality traits,
and secondly on the basis of formal education. He
believes that the authoritarian treatment of subordinates is disadvantageous and prefers to obtain
their consent.

In matters of economic policy, he is a firm believer
of the necessity to protect Argentine industry.
Regarding the concept of "free enterprise", he has
confusing opinions about its ideological content. When
he tries to define it, he brings forward personal
opinions, which sometimes contradict those of manufacturers' associations.

... He favors to sell more at lower prices, even in
the case that total profits remain the same. He
understands his market is nation-wide and that he
might win acceptance for his products if providing
quality.

... He is willing to live through some degree of
inflation if banks would give more credits.[18]

The preceding "profile", as was said, derived from interviewing
twenty-seven top executives in leading industrial firms. For this
reason, it is difficult to say whether it is representative of those
engaged in mining, agriculture, government enterprises, and small
firms.

Despite the shortcomings of trying to encompass managerial
attitudes in a few paragraphs, as noted above, it may be asserted that
by the mid-1960's a change in attitudes of Argentine businessment, at
least those of men in leading sectors, was evident.[19] It may even be
asserted that they were following the path described by Kerr and others
in a recently published study.[20] They were becoming more sophisticated in the management techniques they utilized; they were becoming
better organized as a profession, and their awareness of their role as
one of the leading groups in the community was increasing.

That they were becoming more sophisticated in the management
techniques they utilized is demonstrated by the following factors:
1) the several thousand men that attended the large number of seminars,
courses, lectures, and round table discussions organized by the
different institutions listed in Tables 15 and 16. For example: one
of these, the Institute for the Development of Executives in Argentina,
IDEA, reported that approximately 3100 individuals participated in the
123 seminars and 25 meetings it organized during 1965;[21] 2) the
increasing demand for improving more and more the quality of the
different seminars offered in Buenos Aires;[22] 3) the increasing use

of services provided by management consultants; 4) the skills required from those applying for managerial positions, as it could be checked almost everyday in the newspapers; 5) the increasing demand for last-year students and young graduates of the new schools of business administration; 6) the increasing use of electronic data processing equipment, both in the private and public sectors; 7) the increasing number of Argentine executives with some sort of training abroad, beyond their local training, which meant in fact they were familiar with the management techniques applied in the industrially advanced countries; and 8) the impact of the 1962 recession with its pressure for the "survival of the fittest".

As far as the professional organization of businessmen was concerned, it may be said that beyond the traditional associations which grouped managers according to their fields of specialization in college or to the economic sector to which they belonged (such as chambers of commerce or manufacturers' associations), new associations of executives as such have emerged. (For example: the Argentine Marketing Association, the Argentine Association of Purchasing Agents, and the Business Leaders Christian Association.)

Finally, the founding of the previously mentioned Institute for the Development of Executives in Argentina, (IDEA), the Foundation for Latin American Economic Research (FIEL), the Di Tella Institute, and the Businessmen Council of the School of Economics of the University of Buenos Aires, for example, and the rapidly increasing support given to a vast number of educational, cultural, and welfare activities indicate that businessmen were well aware of their responsibilities in the Argentine society.

Most of these changes have taken place in less than ten years. Thus, it is not an exaggeration to express that the changes are rather amazing. Unfortunately, the same cannot be said with respect to the public sector. Some effort, such as the founding of the Institute of Public Administration (ISAP), took place in the decade that runs between 1955 and 1965; but factors such as political instability, insufficient budgets, and low salaries relative to other occupations precluded, with some exceptions, significant changes like the ones described for the private sector.

Political power and economic influence. The determination of the political power and the economic influence of managerial groups is a fuzzy question since the group as such is a complex mix of managers of large, medium-size, and small enterprises; of owner, political, and professional managers; of Argentine and foreign-born managers; and of managers frequently working in economic sectors of conflicting interests. Imaz clearly points out that managers have not been articulate in obtaining political power for them as a group, but rather, whenever obtained, the power and influence belonged to the individual who was able to achieve it.[23] He indicates several reasons why the group as such failed in obtaining political power; namely: 1) it is a new group; 2) it is a social sector composed of great diversity from an economic, ethnic, and personal point of view; 3) the lack of vocation for the conquering of political power; 4) the lack of cohesion of the group, which leads to the absorption of individuals into the traditional aristocratic groups whenever they rise very high in the social ladder; and 5) the lack of a strong leadership.

Available indicators of current managerial resources. The question of the supply and demand of managerial resources is one which cannot be readily answered. It involves matters such as the underemployment of potential managers, the plans for economic growth, the ability to up-grade people to managerial positions, and so forth. A thorough study of the problem is beyond the scope of this section.

There exists data, however, which casts some information on this matter. The 1954 Industrial Census, for example, reported that a total of 1,498,115 people were engaged in industry.[24] This total was broken down as follows:

Owners or Managing Directors	224,956
Employees	166,980
Workers	1,055,496
Members of owners' families	50,683
TOTAL	1,498,115

The first category, unfortunately, does not discriminate the owners of small shops, which cannot be properly classified as "managerial resource," while the second category does not help to establish how many of the "employees" are actually "managers."

Another source of information derives from a survey conducted by the end of 1961, during which 2,003 industrial firms, identified as each employing that year more than 100 persons, were investigated one by one.[25] As a result of this study, it was determined that total employment by these firms added up to 764,000 (roughly, 41% of total employment in industry in that year). In addition, using sampling methods and available information regarding firms employing less than 100 people, the occupational structure of industry was tentatively determined, as indicated in Table 3.

The relevant columns in Table 3 from the viewpoint of this section are those referring to firms employing over 100 persons and 11-100 persons (obviously, the 120,000 persons listed in the last column cannot be properly referred to as "executives"). Thus, the leading 2,003 Argentine industrial firms employing over 100 persons had 35,720 people working in managerial, professional, and technical capacities.[26] Other findings of the study were the following:

1) Over 60% of the 35,720 people engaged in management, professional and technical activities, performed duties connected with production, plant and equipment maintenance, and auxiliary technical services;

43

2) Less than 4% of the people included in those three occupational categories performed research activities;

3) Average years of education were as follows: 13 for the whole group; 13.1 for management people; 17.5 for people in professional jobs; and 11.2 for those in technical jobs;

4) Schooling of those in the "management" category was as follows: 15% had only attended primary school; 50%, only secondary school; and about 35% had university training (both complete and incomplete studies are included in these percentages). In connection with these figures, it may be mentioned that another study, which covered "middle managers", showed that those with a college education (both graduates and those who did not finish college) represented approximately 50% of the interviewers.[27] The discrepancy is probably due to the fact that this last percentage refers only to "middle managers";[28]

5) Some 5% of the people performing professional jobs did not have a college degree;

6) Somewhat less than 70% of those engaged in technical activities had formal technical training;

7) There were sixteen professional people with college degrees per 1,000 workers in the whole group of firms. The "chemical production" group showed the highest ratio: 43 professionals per 1,000 workers. It is perhaps worth noting that the General Motors' study earlier mentioned in the chapter showed that college graduates added up to 2% of total employment in the firms studied. In addition, another 5% had reached college level, but left before obtaining a degree.[29]

The study, therefore, indicated that while most people performing professional and technical jobs held the corresponding degrees, those at the management level had attended school for only a few years (as was quoted, 15% had only primary school, 50% had only secondary education, and about 35% had university training). Two conclusions thus seem pertinent: 1) further training for non-college managers is possibly needed in order to raise the productivity and efficiency of their firms; and 2) college graduates do not tend to become "entrepreneurs". Very possibly these two conclusions do not differ much from those applicable to other countries; but there might be a difference in "degree" rather than in "kind".

Finally, other conclusions of the study indicate that 45% and 15% of those holding college degrees in the managerial, professional, and technical   levels are engineers and accountants, respectively.[30] Although this fact is not surprising because these two careers have been taught in Argentina for many years, it illustrates the importance of teaching management courses to college students in those fields.

Other indicators of current managerial resources are obtained by studying the Argentine Government enterprises and the foreign enterprises. Their importance is by no means negligible.

Excluding companies carrying out development and exploration contracts in the petroleum industry of Argentina.., state ownership is already more extensive in Argentina than in Brazil, Chile, or Colombia. The proportion of capital and reserves of large enterprises in Argentina attributable to the public and private sectors, including the long-resident Shell and Esso but excluding recent development and exploration firms in the oil industry (for which reliable statistics are unavailable), are summarized in the following table:[31]

	Largest Enterprise		
	Top 10	Top 20	Top 30
Argentine government	84.5%	67.9%	61.3
Argentine private	10.7	20.4	20.5
Foreign private	4.8	11.7	18.2

Total employment of the Argentine Federal Government adds up to approximately 700,000. Half of these work for seventeen "state enterprises", listed in Table 4, organized under the provisions of Law 13.653. Depending on the individual enterprise, those in managerial functions range from five to ten percent of a firm's employment. This gives a rough idea of the managerial force in the Federal Government as far as their number is concerned.

Turning now to foreign firms in Argentina, it may be said that they are numerous, and their countries of origin vary a great deal. British, German, Italian, United States, French, Japanese, Swedish, and Dutch firms may be encountered. Until the mid-40's the largest foreign investments were of British origin, the peak being reached by "the end of 1934, when the nominal total stood at more than $453 million."[32] Twenty years later, the main foreign investments came from United States sources and added up to much more than $500 million.[33]

Unfortunately, there is no detailed information on foreign firms as a whole, listing their contribution to locally available managerial resources, i.e., people brought into the country for different periods of time. However, partial data is available from information gathered by the Chamber of Commerce of the United States of America in Argentina. The results of a survey conducted by that Chamber may be summarized as follows:[34]

Number of firms that sent in information: 212 (75% of the active members of the Chamber)

Total employment: 76.675 (174 firms)

United States citizens employed: 331 (130 firms)

Another source of information regarding perhaps both quality and quantity of managerial resources is given by the number of Argentine nationals that have been trained abroad. Again, no comprehensive data is available. However, a report prepared by the Institute of International Education indicates that 858 Argentine nationals attended United States academic institutions during the years 1950-1961 (Table 5).

With all the previous information now on hand, the logical question to make is the following: how well-equipped is Argentina with managerial resources? The answer to it, as was said at the beginning of this section, is not easy. However, the information obtained from those who provide selection services enables one to state, tentatively, that from a general point of view, the supply of managerial resources in Argentina has been able to meet the existing demand.[35] Naturally, there are cases in which it is difficult to fill out certain positions. For example: the fact was mentioned that sometimes it is not easy to find a finance manager with knowledge of the English language; also, sometimes maintenance and quality control engineers are difficult to hire, because the existing ones are well paid and tend to remain in their jobs. However, these are isolated cases which do not contradict the general statement given a few lines above. Furthermore, the Buenos Aires newspapers frequently illustrate firms from different Latin American countries which advertise positions available. This fact seems to confirm the adequacy of the Argentine managerial resources.

As far as the demand in the different functional fields is concerned, Table 6 indicates that it is more or less equivalent for the three traditional areas of marketing, production, and finance (in Argentina, accounting and finance are activities frequently performed by the same individual). From the supply point of view, it may be argued from the same table that demand is somewhat greater than supply in the case of positions related to production. This fact was confirmed by executive selection experts.

Table 7 gives information about the educational background of those placed in vacant managerial positions. It may be noticed that the main percentages confirm those quoted from the Almada et al. study earlier referred to in the chapter.

It might be added that economists assert that the industrial growth of Argentina has closely followed the government measures for or against industrialization.[36] Thus, there has always been, at least in the private sector, a latent "spirit of entrepreneurship" ready to take advantage of government incentives.

In spite of this general conclusion, there are several indicators that show maladjustments. In the first place, there exists a low ratio of engineers -- scientists per 10,000 population as compared to other countries.[37] The second indicator is, despite such low ratio, the "exodus" of professional and technical people. For example: the number of engineers that emigrated to the United States during the period 1951-1961 is equivalent to 8% of all engineers that graduated in the

country during the same period[38] (see Table 8). Despite the fact that
figures are not available on how many emigrants returned to Argentina,
this illustrates, perhaps dramatically, how the country may be losing
strategic manpower. This problem has become a national issue, and
different institutions both in the official and private sectors have
taken steps to decrease its importance although the impact of their work
cannot yet be assessed. Consequently, these two indicators show that
either the industrial sector does not know how to maximize the benefits
derived from employing technicians or that there exists an oversupply of
technical people (at least in certain fields), or both.

A third indicator showing that something goes wrong in the supply
and demand of managerial resources is the low percent of national income
spent in education as compared to other countries.[39] This fact may have
hindered in the past, or may hinder in the future, the development of
men with managerial potential, at least from a quality viewpoint. In
addition, it may have influenced, or will influence, the ability to
utilize available managerial skills.

In concluding this section, the following observations may be made:
1) the universities will continue training a large proportion of those
who will occupy managerial positions, both in business and in public
administration; 2) a large proportion of future managers will still have
no college education, for which reason their training in executive
programs, seminars, round-table discussions, and so forth will be
increasingly important.

MANAGERIAL RESOURCE DEVELOPMENT: CONCEPTS,
COMMITMENTS AND STRATEGIES OF HIGHER EDUCATION

Historical role of major institutions of higher education. The
traditional college system of Argentina is composed of the following
eight official universities supported by the Federal Government (thus
the word "national" sometimes attached to their name):

Name	City where located[40]
Universidad de Buenos Aires	Buenos Aires
Universidad de Córdoba	Córdoba
Universidad de Cuyo	Mendoza, San Juan
Universidad de La Plata	La Plata
Universidad del Litoral	Santa Fé, Rosario
Universidad del Nordeste	Resistencia, Corrientes
Universidad del Sur	Bahía Blanca
Universidad de Tucumán	Tucumán

The oldest one is the University of Córdoba, founded in the XVII
century, followed by the University of Buenos Aires and the University
of La Plata, which were founded at the beginning and at the end of the
XIX century, respectively. The other five universities reached the

category during this century -- the youngest two in the 1950's. There exists, in addition, the young National Technological University, which represents a departure from the traditional pattern, since, as indicated by its name, it only trains professionals in technical fields.

Contrary to the United States practice, where undergraduate and graduate education coexist extensively, Argentina's universities teach regular graduate curricula only as an exception. Consequently, engineers, physicians, or accountants, for example, obtain their degrees as a result of undergraduate training -- 5 or 6 years in general, depending on the field of study. These are frequently terminal degrees qualifying their holders for professional practice. Although this is a useful generalization, it should be noticed though that some colleges grant doctor's degrees as a result of further course study and thesis werk. However, those working for a doctor's degree do not commonly plan to follow a teaching and research career. Such a degree holds a measure of prestige; but, broadly speaking, its possession does not make much of a difference in actual professional life.

A study earlier quoted in the chapter analyzed the approximately 150,000 degrees granted by the national university from 1900 through 1960 in careers involving four or more years of study. Its main conclusions are the following:[41]

1) Comparing degrees granted during the period 1951-55 with those granted during 1955-60, architecture, engineering, and medicine, in that order, showed the largest relative increase.

2) Over 60 percent of the graduates completed their studies between 1940 and 1960.

3) The University of Buenos Aires issued over 50 percent of the total degrees granted in Argentina since 1901.

4) From 1901 to 1960 the Argentine universities have granted 32,500 degrees in medicine, 21,000 in law, and 9,700 in accounting. The engineering group is relatively new: almost 11,000 engineers, out of a total number of 16,700, obtained their degrees on or after 1946.

5) Since 1952 the number of degrees awarded in specialized engineering fields has exceeded those awarded in civil engineering.

The preceding data, therefore, constitute a historic review of the result of the work of Argentine universities during the first sixty years of this century, which may cast some idea as to how they met, or will meet, the demands of a process of economic growth. But in order to draw some conclusions, it is also useful to see what trends existed by the mid 1960's.

Table 9 illustrates total college enrollment for 1962 and 1963 in careers considered strategic for Argentina's economic development by the 1965-69 National Development Plan. According to it, those careers (agronomy and veterinary, economics and business administration,

engineering in all its specialized fields with the exception of civil
engineering, and basic sciences) represented a small proportion of total
enrollment and degrees awarded; i.e., only 20% of total enrollment in
1963, and 16% of degrees conferred in 1962. The National Plan notes
that the proportion of those enrolling in the strategic careers is
greater than the related figure for graduates and thus concludes that
the change in emphasis has started. Finally, the Development Plan indicates that enrollment in medicine in 1963 was 30% of total university
enrollment, and the number of physicians graduating in 1962 was 44% of
total degrees awarded. Enrollment in law schools was 18%, and its
graduates, 17.5%.[42]

The preceding figures refer to total university students in
Argentina. It should be noted, however, that total enrollment in the
University of Buenos Aires, by far the largest one in Argentina, adds up
to approximately one-half of the total number of college students in the
country. Therefore, it might be useful, from the point of view of this
section, to review the statistics related to it included in Table 10.
The figures in this table indicate that:

1) total enrollment for 1958 and 1964 was 58,684, and 65,328
respectively, thus showing an 11.3% increase in the six-year
period;

2) the schools which show the largest percentage of increase
in their enrollment, for the 1958-64 period, are the following:
Liberal Arts, Basic Sciences, Agronomy and Veterinary, and
Economics, in that order. The ones that show the largest
decrease are Pharmacy, Medicine, and Dentistry;[43]

3) the School of Medicine had in 1958 the largest enrollment,
while in 1964 the School of Economics ranked first. The School
of Engineering ranked fourth in both years.

It is not possible with the previous information, however, to
reach a definite conclusion as to whether the Argentine universities
have been efficient in providing the quantity and quality of the managerial resources required by the economic growth of the country, both in
the past and in the future.[44] However, the previous figures provide
valuable insights that may move one to believe in an _affirmative_ answer.
The increasing number of college students, the large proportion of
engineers that have graduated in the last 20 years, the increasing number of engineers in areas of specialization other than civil engineering,
and the important proportion of college graduates that earned their degrees since 1940 suggest the following fact: though perhaps in a haphazard way, the universities responded favorably to the need for more
middle-level managerial resources.[45] Obviously, college training does
not make by itself a manager; further on-the-job training and experience
is needed. In addition, precise timing between college training and the
specific needs of a new industry, both in quantity and quality, is not
possible. Men for these jobs have to be brought into the country from
abroad, or men without the appropriate training may have to be upgraded
to perform them. But this is not a problem solely confined to Argentina;

49

it may happen anywhere in the world. It is no secret that "planning of human resources" and "economics of education" are new terms in the experts' vocabulary. Therefore, the previous positive statement seems valid from an overall point of view.

However, the emigration of Argentina's professionals to foreign countries, in spite of the low ratio of engineers and scientists per 10,000 population mentioned by Harbison and Myers, as was earlier quoted, indicates that something has gone wrong. It is not clear, however, whether they leave the country because of the relatively low salaries, the lack of incentives, the country's political problems in the last few years, or little demand for their services. It is not an easy job to determine which factor or factors predominated at a given time; but the large number of executives with no formal college training, as illustrated earlier in the chapter, may explain a tendency to underutilize available professional people. Though perhaps not the only factor, this is possibly a very important one for understanding the exodus of professionals.

Thus, the informal training in the modern approach to management of those Argentine managers who have not had the opportunity to learn about it in the past may be as important for the country as the formal training of professionals at the college level. Such activity, however, has only exceptionally been undertaken by the universities. On those rare occasions when it was done, it was, in general, directed to college graduates. Consequently, the task had to be performed by other institutions as we shall see later in the chapter.

Contemporary concepts and commitments of major institutions of higher education to managerial resource development.

> The economic development plan forsees a moderate increase in university enrollment. The ratio of enrollment relative to the college age bracket (19-24 years old) will increase from 10% to 11%. In this way it is hoped that the college-level human resource requirements of the plan will be met.[46]

Very important changes affecting the concepts and commitments to managerial resource development at the university level have taken place in Argentina since the late 1950's; for example: the change in curricula in the schools of economics and engineering at different universities and the passing of Law No. 14557 allowing the creation of private universities, the privileges of degrees conferred which will be accepted as equivalent to those of official national universities, if certain requisites are complied with.

Up until the late 1950's, the traditional career followed in the country's Schools of Economics led to the degree of "public accountant", which is equivalent to the United States C.P.A.[47] No courses leading to a degree in business administration were offered by the faculties of those schools. Then, the fact that institutions of higher learning could no longer ignore the modern developments in the teaching of business administration and economics started to gain recognition by those faculties. At the same time, the country's stage of economic progress reinforced the feeling that a "catching up" with modern educational concepts was necessary. Consequently, a revision of the programs of study was initiated.

The analysis of the existing curricula by the Schools of Economics with the purpose of giving more emphasis to areas related to business administration and economics, showed in general that a choice, not easy to arrive at, had to be made in order to implement that objective. The alternatives were generally described as follows: either new programs leading to degrees in business administration and economics were to be created, or curricula leading to an accounting degree were to be reorganized and new courses in those areas added. Furthermore, this last alternative had two sub-alternatives: either the undergraduate curricula were to be reorganized, or graduate curricula were to be created for men already having an accounting degree.

There were different factors that weighed in favor of or against the two alternatives. One reason working against the creation of curricula in business administration, fully independent from accounting, was the uncertainty of job opportunities for the prospective graduates, since the traditional demand asked for accountants. This weighed heavily in the case of universities located outside of Buenos Aires where the economic activity is not as heavily concentrated. Another reason working against their creation was that it was felt that since accounting was the traditional career, it might be a better strategy to improve its curriculum rather than create wholly new careers. This seemed to be especially important in view of the usual lack of sufficient resources on the side of the Argentine universities. Finally, if the new careers were to be created, an appropriate teaching staff had to be located, which by itself was not an easy job.

Naturally, different universities followed different paths. The faculty of the School of Economics of the University of Buenos Aires decided to create the new careers, and thus undergraduate degrees in business administration and in economics are now awarded, together with the traditional accounting degree. It should be mentioned that upon creating the new program, the school signed an agreement with Columbia University, later on described in more detail, in order to strengthen the new department of business administration.

Furthermore, a few years after these changes occurred, the authorities of the University of Buenos Aires, concerned with its role in relation with the economic growth of the country, laid a set of priorities for the emphasizing of its activities. At the top of the priorities list were business administration and engineering. Thus, managerial resource creation received clear recognition of its importance.

Although the emphasis of this description is placed on the Schools of Economics, it is worth mentioning that as far as the Schools of

51

Engineering are concerned, courses dealing with Operations Research, Production Management, Statistics, and other functional areas, such as Marketing and Finance, were added to the programs of study. In this way, the young engineering graduates possess a broader understanding of the meaning of management as compared with those of the preceding classes. For the purpose of illustrating trends and figures, Tables 11 and 12 show first-year enrollment and number of degrees awarded from 1959 through 1965 at the Schools of Economics and Engineering of the University of Buenos Aires.

Turning now to the approach followed by other national universities for the establishment of business administration courses or curricula, the following paths may be mentioned:

1) University of Tucumán: early in the 1960's a graduate "program in organization and administration" started operating within the School of Economics for the purpose of providing an opportunity in modern management training to graduates of that School (graduates of other schools could not enroll). Their new program in its initial stages counted upon the assistance of the University of Chile's Instituto de Organización y Administración (INSORA). The program's progress was slow, and by 1966 no one had graduated from it. To give an idea of the order of magnitude, it should be noted that in 1965 total enrollment in the University was 9,899, out of which 808 were enrolled in the School of Economics. At the same time, the program in organization and administration had 26 students. By 1966 this new program was under close scrutiny and the possibility of creating an undergraduate program was starting to be studied.

2) University of Cuyo: during 1966 a new program started operating within the framework of the School of Economics, in the city of Mendoza. Its purposes were twofold: first, to provide training in fields related to business administration to teachers of that school. This, in turn, had the objective of building a team with sufficient potential to provide teachers and researchers if changes leading to the establishment of an undergraduate curriculum were introduced in the current programs of study. The second purpose of this new program was to offer further management training to graduates of the School of Economics. It should be noted that, as in the case of the University of Tucumán, only graduates of the School of Economics could enroll. When the program started, approximately 20 individuals were enrolled in it. Finally, it should be noted that it was not intended to repeat the program, which awarded a certificate (not a degree) of completion after taking eleven courses over a five-semester period, year after year; rather, the idea behind it was that once a core team of teachers and researchers had been built, the program was to be terminated and a regular undergraduate program started.

3) University of Córdoba: as of 1966, new programs of study were enacted at the School of Economics. One of the changes that took place introduced courses related to management training in the curriculum leading to the traditional degree of "public accountant." In addition, a complementary curriculum leading to a graduate degree in business administration was created with the purpose of offering further management training to those holding a degree in accounting.

4) University of La Plata: a new program of studies was enacted in the School of Economics in the early 1960's, as a result of which three undergraduate curricula, leading to degrees in accounting, economics, and administrative sciences, respectively, are offered. The administrative sciences curriculum is an outgrowth of what was formerly the School of Public Administration, which later on became the Institute of Administrative Sciences. It is aimed at providing practitioners of administration both to business and the public sector. It should be noted that those that may obtain a bachelor's degree in this field may pursue further studies leading to a doctor's degree, at which time they have to decide among two possible fields of specialization: business administration or public administration.

As a result of the previous information, it may be concluded that the current tendency in Argentine official universities leads towards the creation of undergraduate curricula. The new programs, furthermore, are the outgrowth of changes introduced in the previously existing curricula at the Schools of Economics, which led to the traditional degree of "public accountant." There exist, however, a few graduate programs in business administration, although admission into them is restricted to public accountants.

As far as programs in the field of public administration are concerned, it is not possible to say that regular curricula have started to appear in most of the Argentine official universities. As a matter of fact, this has happened only exceptionally. It should be noted, however, that Law Schools and Schools of Economics have traditionally included in their curricula a number of courses useful for those that may enter the civil service, such as administrative law and public accounting.[48] Naturally, there are programs such as the one already mentioned in the case of the University of La Plata, or another one in Political and Diplomatic Sciences at the University of the Litoral, but these are the exceptions rather than the rule. An example of a different sort is provided by the graduate curricula offered by the School of Engineering at the University of Buenos Aires, addressed in general to individuals involved in technical functions in different government agencies. Regular curricula concentrating in the discussion of issues affecting public policies, however, are unknown in Argentina.

Major problem areas.[49] The political problems of the 1943-1955 period put the national universities under severe strains. The college atmosphere in those years, to put it mildly, was not the most conducive to the achievement of academic objectives. By the end of the period, the national universities emerged from the crisis with a series of very important problems which persist up to present day. Thus, many educational problems affecting the new programs of business administration, for example, do not differ greatly from the general problems that bear on the universities.

The overall obstacle that encompasses most other problems is the inadequacy of the budget as compared to the requirements of the modernization process of institutions of higher learning. This fact is aggravated by the country's chronic inflation, which forces university presidents to be almost permanently in search of additional funds from government sources. It should be noted that university training is free: no tuition or fees are paid by students attending national universities.

The following fact illustrates the consequences of the unavailability of sufficient funds: 1) Faculty members are paid low salaries; consequently, there is an almost absolute lack of full-time faculty members. As a result of this situation, only small efforts are devoted to research and to the preparation of teaching material. 2) The physical facilities are inadequate, and crowded classrooms are therefore not unusual. The different schools are disseminated in many different buildings apart from each other; 50 buildings, in the case of the University of Buenos Aires.

A second major problem affecting the universities is of a more subtle nature since, it is difficult to measure in quantitative terms how much it damages the progress that is always hoped for in relation with educational establishments. This problem is almost of a political nature and it has become a national issue. According to a special "university law," the national universities are autonomous, and their authorities are selected, through a series of balloting stages, by faculty members, graduates of the university, and the students. Each one of these three groups participates through the representatives they elected in the government of the university.

Student participation in university government is frequently quoted as one of the current "evils" of university life. This has become a "political" issue, and people will or will not agree with the previous statement depending on their personal experience and political views. Whichever the case, the fact is that the national universities are almost permanently under the threat of radical changes in their institutional structure. The experience has shown that whenever this happens, almost automatically, students strike, professors resign, and the universities start a period which is not conducive to the achievement of academic objectives. Thus it may be said that the threat of changes in the legal status of universities, whether it may happen or not, is undoubtedly an important problem in the affairs of university life.[50]

From another point of view, other facts work against the "efficiency" of university life. Among these, the heavy administrative machinery which slows down, sometimes to an unbelievable extent, the process of decision making, stands out prominently. For instance: a) the appointment of regular faculty members[51] requires a contest, all the stages of which may take several years; b) the development of new courses or the dropping of old ones may also demand years until a decision is reached.

Despite the fact that these problems persist, it is very important to note that since 1955 major improvements have been made. It is possible to say that as far as these problems are concerned, change has occurred not in kind but in degree. The University of Buenos Aires, for example, has been very successful in establishing a publishing house, EUDEBA, Editorial Universitaria de Buenos Aires; it has developed a scholarship program, both for undergraduate students to study locally and for graduates to study abroad;[52] it has increased the number of full-time professors and thus improved the amount of research being conducted; it has started to develop, though slowly, what will constitute its future campus; and it has organized a center for applied research. Other national universities have also been making great progress in similar directions. The University of Córdoba, for instance, has a well developed campus and manages one of the best television channels in the country. It would take too long to make a complete enumeration of changes of this sort; but it is possible to say that, compared to the state in which they were in 1955 and in spite of the difficulties previously described, the universities showed a remarkable progress by 1966.

In addition to the solutions to university problems taken by their authorities, it is of prime importance to notice new institutions that have developed in the last few years under government sponsorship. These new institutions have their own objectives, but a very important outcome of their existence is that they complement the universities' activities. For instance: they sponsor faculty members that may want to conduct research; they invite foreign scholars; they offer scholarships to college graduates, and they provide employment opportunities for certain fields of study for which there is, unfortunately, little demand in Argentine industry. Some of these institutions are the following:

a) National Committee for Scientific and Technical Research ("Consejo Nacional de Investigaciones Científicas y Técnicas");

b) National Institute of Industrial Technology ("Instituto Nacional de Tecnología Industrial," INTI);

c) National Institute of Agricultural Technology ("Instituto Nacional de Tecnología Agropecuaria," INTA);

d) National Atomic Energy Commission ("Comisión Nacional de Energía Atómica");

e) Armed Forces Technical Research Commission ("Junta de Investigaciones Técnicas y Experimentales de las Fuerzas Armadas," JITEFA).

The private universities. The second example referred to above as an indication of changes that have recently occurred in the educational structure of the country was the passing of Law No.14.557 permitting the establishment of private universities. So far, the following twelve private universities have been registered as such under the provisions of the law:[53]

Name	Main Location
Universidad Católica de Córdoba	Córdoba
Universidad del Salvador	Buenos Aires
Pontificia Universidad Católica Argentina Santa María de los Buenos Aires	Buenos Aires
Universidad Católica de Santa Fé	Santa Fé
Instituto Tecnológico de Buenos Aires	Buenos Aires
Universidad del Museo Social Argentino	Buenos Aires
Universidad de Mendoza	Mendoza
Universidad Juan Agustín Maza	Mendoza
Universidad de la Patagonia "San Juan Bosco"	Comodora Rivadavia
Universidad Católica de Cuyo	San Juan
Universidad Católica de Mar del Plata "Stella Maris"	Mar del Plata
Universidad del Norte "Santo Tomás de Aquino"	Tucumán

The degrees these universities may confer are equivalent to those of the national universities if certain legal requirements are complied with. Almost all of them teach undergraduate curricula, which in general include fields of specialization related to the development of managerial resources, such as business administration, economics, and engineering.

In order to illustrate the role and order of magnitude of these universities, Table 13 shows some figures for the Argentine Catholic University, probably one of the largest in the "private universities" category. In interpreting these figures, it should be recalled that private universities started operating by the end of the 1950's, only a few years ago.

It is worth noting that, in addition to its regular undergraduate programs, the School of Economics of this university has organized a number of special programs in the field of our interest; namely, a management course for officers of the armed forces which started in 1962 and another one for business executives which started in 1966. Furthermore, the Law School offers, as of 1964, a special course for corporate lawyers in which management tools and techniques are studied.

As it might be expected, the different private universities registered under Law No. 14.557 have followed different paths in their approach to the teaching of programs related to business administration. Thus, while the Argentine Catholic University did not offer a program leading to a degree in accounting, the Catholic University of Córdoba

offered two different programs leading to the degree of "public accountant" and to a bachelor's degree in business administration, respectively. By 1966, 109 students were enrolled in the former program and
158 in the latter.[54]   At the same time, the School of Economics of the
Northern University "Santo Tomás de Aquino," which opened its doors in
1961, offered undergraduate programs leading to the degrees of public
accountant and economist. By early 1966, 86 students were enrolled in
the accounting program, and no one had graduated yet. This School
planned to offer a program in business organization and administration
directed to students it may eventually graduate.[55]

The private universities did not receive funds from government
sources; their income was derived from fees paid by students and grants
received from private sources. As in the case of the national universities, the financial needs seemed to be larger than the available
funds; thus, the practice of part-time teaching, for example, was the
norm.

By 1966, the contribution of the registered private universities,
measured in terms of young graduates entering into professional life,
started to be felt. But it was too soon to be able to make a thorough
appraisal of the problems and contributions of these universities.

The provincial universities. A new development in Argentine higher
education has been the creation of provincial universities. A number
of these, supported by provincial governments, were founded after the
passing in 1958 of Law No. 14.557, which allowed the organization of
private universities. Thus provincial universities were created in the
following provinces: Buenos Aires, La Pampa, San Juan, La Rioja,
Neuquén, Entre Ríos, while other institutions, such as the Universidad
del Centro, located in the City of Río Cuarto, aspired to acquire that
status.

Unfortunately, there was no certainty as to the status attached to
the degrees they could award; i.e., whether they would enable their
holders for professional life, such as the graduates of national and
registered private universities. As a matter of fact, there existed a
legal problem since it was not clear whether or not provincial governments were authorized, according to Argentine law, to register provincial universities within the terms of law 14.557 as was done by the
Federal Government.[56]

Some of these provincial universities offered courses in business
administration, as in the case of the University of La Pampa. In this
specific case, however, the program was given under the general supervision and collaboration of the National University of La Plata.
Furthermore, this last institution would eventually be the one awarding
the degrees. In this way, the graduates of the University of La Pampa
would not meet obstacles for the full recognition and acceptance of
their degrees.

Whichever the case, it is too soon, however, to evaluate the impact and contribution of these new educational institutions.

Non-registered private universities. In addition to the officially registered private universities, there exist a number of institutions which have applied for registration under the terms of Law No. 14.557. Many of them offer courses leading to degrees related to management practice. These degrees, however, will earn no privileges for their holders if the Argentine authorities do not register them as private universities.

There has been feverish activity related to this type of establishment, and "non-registered" private universities have been proliferating in the last few years. This fact provoked the issuance of government regulations against the misuse of the word "university" in the name of an educational establishment.[57]

Although it is not possible to say how many non-registered universities existed in Argentina, it is possible to mention that by mid-1966, 36 of them had their application for registration under study at the Ministry of Education. Out of this total, only three establishments had been admitted into the "observation service," which was the most important step prior to the obtaining of the official registration.

The non-registered universities offered, in general, programs leading to a bachelor's degree ("licenciado") and sometimes, even to a doctor's degree. These programs were frequently of a very specialized nature to an extent which was almost unbelievable. The quality of their teaching and their institutional stability has yet to be proved. For information purposes, Table 14 lists the name of these non-registered private universities.

An order of magnitude is given by the following figures: during 1965, some 1,200 students were enrolled in the various programs offered by the Argentine Business University (Universidad Argentina de la Empresa), while some 650 people participated in the seminars and courses offered by the Sales and Marketing Managers' Association and by the University of Commercial Sciences sponsored by that Association.[58]

Non-university training. Professional associations with membership drawn from those engaged in the different management fields, but not part of manufacturers' association chambers of commerce and associations of college graduates, have been known in Argentina for over thirty years. From a quiet start in 1941, when the Argentine Committee for the Study of Industrial Organization ("Círculo Argentino de Estudios sobre Organización Industrial," CADESOI) was founded,[59] the number of organizations of this type has been steadily increasing, as indicated by Table 15.

Table 16 lists other names which, added to most of those in Table 15, give the spectrum of private (i.e., non-university, whether national, provincial, "registered," or "non-registered" private university)

institutions which offered in Buenos Aires a wide variety of courses
and seminars in the different functional fields of business administration. There is a large variety of institutions among those listed
in Tables 15 and 16. Some were professional associations; some of the
names represented consulting firms; others were affiliated with government agencies. There is little doubt that the list is incomplete as it
is a most difficult job to keep track of new institutions in the field.
Furthermore, large businesses organized, not infrequently, special programs for their managerial personnel.

Beyond the usual role played by government agencies, professional
associations, or consulting firms, it is worth noting, from the point
of view of this study, that if all courses and seminars offered by those
institutions are "pooled" together, almost every area, technique, or
approach to business management may be found among them. Naturally,
participants in these courses varied: they were low, middle, or top-
managers; college or high school graduates, or people with less schooling. On the other hand, the quality of the instructors and of the courses
offered ranged from very good to very poor. In addition, there existed
overlapping, duplication of efforts, competition for a "small market"
of participants, and mechanical repetition of same classes by the same professors in different institutions.

In spite of these shortcomings, the important aspect to emphasize
from this impressive list of institutions and courses is how much they
have contributed to the upgrading of Argentine managerial resources. An
order of magnitude is given by the figure already quoted: during 1965,
over 3,000 people participated in seminars and other activities organized by the Institute for the Development of Executives in Argentina
(IDEA).

Furthermore, it is also illustrative to mention data included in
the General Motors' report quoted earlier in the chapter;[60] namely:
1) the Institute for the Development of Executives in Argentina (IDEA)
and the Productivity Center (CPA) attracted a large proportion of the
individuals that attended management seminars (40% approximately); 2) a
few firms sent members of their staff for further training outside
Argentina; but, considering these firms only, that figure shows that
most of the people traveled to the United States to study some specialized aspect within the engineering field; 3) the number of firms that
offered training opportunities to college students was steadily increasing.

The previous information refers to training in the private sector
of the Argentine economy. In contrast with all the enthusiasm for business management development, nothing similar was encountered for public
administration. Obviously, many civil servants probably participated
in courses or seminars such as those described in this section. But as
far as non-university training was concerned, only one existing institute
solely concerned itself with this area: the Instituto Superior de
Administración Pública, ISAP (Superior Institute of Public Administration), later on described in more detail.

Current strategies, results, and indications of future outcomes of management education. If a foreign expert in management education who visited Argentina in 1955 returned to the country 10 years later, he would hardly recognize the situation existing then from the view point of his field of specialization.

During his first visit, business administration courses as such were not known in local universities. Management training offered by private institutions was almost unknown. Public administration as a field of study was perhaps only approached from a legal or public accounting point of view or with the objective of making administrative procedures more efficient (or "rational," as was frequently expressed). Private foundations for the sponsoring of teaching and research in the social sciences were to a large extent non-existent.

By 1965 the situation was completely different. The leading Argentine universities, both national and private, offered curricula that led to undergraduate degrees in business administration. Courses and seminars offered by private institutions were so numerous -- to a perhaps unbelievable extent -- that it would have been almost impossible to keep track of all of them. Public administration was a major field of study in at least one national university, and a government institution had been created for improving the training of civil servants. In addition, the School of Engineering of the University of Buenos Aires included graduate programs, such as highway or railroad engineering, for young engineers who would eventually join government agencies. Furthermore, the most important Argentine universities had by 1965 a permanent full-time staff of highly-trained economists producing valuable research material, some of it very useful for businessmen.

Government agencies, such as the previously mentioned National Committee for Scientific and Technical Research, the National Institute of Industrial Technology, the National Institute of Agricultural Technology, the Balseiro Physics Institute, and the Atomic Energy Commission, were by 1965 elaborate organizations complementing in some way the work of the universities. The National Development Council ("Consejo Nacional de Desarrollo," CONADE) and the Federal Investments Council ("Consejo Federal de Inversiones," CFI) may also be included in this category.

Private foundations and other non-profit institutions for the encouragement of teaching and research in the social sciences were by no means lacking in 1965. The Di Tella Foundation and the Di Tella Institute had already organized the latter's Center for Economic Research ("Centro de Investigaciones Económicas") which, when founded, distinguished itself from other local institutions in these respects: it offered the possibility of a professional career in a special branch of the Social Sciences at salaries competitive with those paid in private industry; it offered the possibility to Argentine students in the United States working toward their Ph.D.'s to return to Argentina to work on a thesis topic related to this country; and it offered foreign scholars a place to settle and do research on Argentina. In addition, by 1965 the Di Tella Institute had already organized its Center of Comparative Sociology ("Centro de Sociología Comparada") while at the same time the Public Administration Center was in the process of being organized.[61]

The Foundation for Latin American Economic Research ("Fundación de Investigaciones Económicas Latinoamericanas," FIEL) started operating, by mid-1965, under the joint sponsorship of four leading Argentine institutions (the Argentine Chamber of Commerce, the Rural Society of Argentina, the Buenos Aires Stock Exchange, and the Manufacturers' Association). The Institute for the Development of Executives in Argentina, I.D.E.A., already mentioned, was operating at full-scale both in training and research. Last, but not least, The Ford Foundation and the United States Agency for International Development were active in supporting Argentine institutions.

A number of diverse institutions, some of them already mentioned, and others such as the Pan American Union, different Rotary Clubs, and the Argentine-United States Cultural Institute[62] offered different scholarship programs which enabled many aggressive young graduates to study abroad in fields related to management. Finally, a growing number of leading business firms were sending members of their staffs to executive development programs in the United States. Some of these firms even organized local executive training programs as a part of their regular activities for the improvement of management efficiency.

Thus, the 1955-1965 period witnessed in Argentina an accelerated process of "catching-up" with modern concepts of managerial resource development. The reason for the accelerated pace is almost surely explained by its stagnation during the immediately preceding period. In order to understand how this process of innovating in management education and training took place, a close look at a few leading programs before concluding the chapter is useful. To this effect, the Department of Business Administration at the School of Economics of the University of Buenos Aires, the Institute for the Development of Executives in Argentina, I.D.E.A. and the Government's Institute for Public Administration will be now studied in more detail.

The Department of Business Administration, School of Economics, University of Buenos Aires. As was earlier mentioned, leading Faculty members of the School of Economics clearly understood by 1957, shortly after the end of the Peron era when a "revival" of academic life was taking place, that the School could no longer ignore the following fact: a program specializing in business administration had to be offered beyond the traditional accounting curriculum if the School has to fill its role in providing the high-level manpower -- managerial resources -- needed by the growth of the Argentine economy. Consequently, the Faculty voted the establishment of a curriculum leading to an undergraduate degree ("licenciado") in business administration. Although the main program remained at the undergraduate level, provisions were taken for requisites leading to a doctor's degree. Thus, this program became the first one of its sort established by an Argentine university.

In addition to the chronic problems afflicting Argentine institutions of higher learning (earlier listed in the chapter), such as an inadequate budget, inappropriate physical facilities, and a heavy administrative machinery, the new program met other difficulties. These were problems such as the lack of experienced teachers with formal training in the field,[63] as well as the lack of teaching materials and of an updated library.

In view of the situation, a faculty mission traveled to the United States in 1958 to request academic assistance, as a result of which an agreement was reached with Columbia University. The memorandum of understanding between the School of Economics of the University of Buenos Aires and the Graduate School of Business Administration of Columbia University, which was put into effect with the support of the United States Agency for International Development and the Argentine Government, stipulated the following: 1) the provision of technical advice and assistance in the strengthening of subject matter, teaching methods and research, and other help needed to strengthen the program; 2) the provision of a series of seminars to be conducted by United States professors on relatively short assignments with the objective of broadening the training of the faculty and students of the local school of business administration, as well as stimulating the interest in management of businessmen and public administrators; 3) assistance in the development of an effective library in the field of business administration; 4) provision of graduate study at Columbia or other selected universities for present and prospective professors of the new local program in order to equip them to teach in the business admini - tration program; 5) the development of an annual work plan to be revised quarterly; 6) the provision of a full-time United States program coordinator to be located in Buenos Aires and a part-time project director at Columbia.

The agreement with Columbia lasted five years -- until 1965. During its life, all aspects of the program were carried out, but undoubtedly the most successful part of it was the training abroad of some thirty graduates of the School of Economics. Most of these earned a Master of Business Administration degree at Columbia, while very few worked for a Ph.D. degree. Upon their return, these young professors taught not only at the new department of business administration, but also in other institutions devoted to management training. In addition, they got involved in translating books and articles related to their fields of specialization into Spanish and doing a small amount of research. Unfortunately, the program did not meet its expectations as to full-time utilization of these men, both in teaching and research, as well as with regard to the introduction of rapid institutional changes. However, although teaching part-time as is traditional in Argentina, the "Columbia group," was able to raise teaching standards and improve the quality and quantity of teaching materials in the University and in other institutions.

Thus, in making an overall evaluation of the results of the program, there is no doubt that its impact upon management education and training in Argentina will be felt for a good many years.

Another innovation that came into effect at the young Department of Business Administration was the creation of the Businessmen Council ("Consejo Empresario"). The Council was founded in 1961 with the participation of leading members of the local business community. Its main objective was that of collaborating with the School's authorities in the education of the future generations of businessmen. To this purpose, the Council donated books, educational films and simultaneous translation equipment and facilitated educational trips of students and educators.

Institute for the Development of Executives in Argentina (IDEA). This private, non-profit, tax-exempt association was founded in 1960 by a group of businessmen representing some twenty companies. Its objectives were to make the modern concepts of management known and to promote the social responsibilities of business leaders. By the end of 1965 the total number of companies and individual membership was close to 200, including most of the outstanding and largest business firms in Argentina.

In translating its objectives into action, IDEA offered every year a number of evening seminars, usually one-week long, in many different topics related to management. In addition, the Institute also carried out a research program. The unusual growth pattern that has characterized IDEA throughout its short life can be illustrated in terms of the training activity: six seminars were organized during 1960 with a total attendance of 360. The following year the number of seminars doubled. By 1964, seventy-six seminars and thirteen conferences were organized, with a total attendance of 2,097. The figures for 1965 show 123 seminars, 25 conferences, and 3,078 participants in all of IDEA's activities. Through different divisions covering different functional fields, the members of the institution contribute directly to the programming of the training activities. Membership in these divisions is made up of representatives of member companies and individuals. IDEA's facilities comprise a library of technical books, periodicals and films, audio-visual teaching material, and simultaneous translation equipment.

The sources of the Institute's finances are mainly membership dues and fees paid by the seminar attendants, the latter varying according to duration and topic. Donations from local sources have been received, and special programs have been carried out with the financial assistance of the United States Agency for International Development and the Ford Foundation.

It is not an easy job to find a brief explanation to IDEA's phenomenal growth and success in its first five years of life. To this effect, perhaps it may help to note that, when founded, it was the first association in Argentina composed of leading businessmen (many of them the highest ranking officers in their respective firms) solely concerned with management as a profession in its broadest sense.

In addition to the previous fact, a number of innovations IDEA was able to introduce, as compared to other non-profit private institutions, may assist in understanding its constant progress, namely:

1) The selection of seminars and speakers was not limited to the study of specific management techniques, but it included the discussion of national issues. A good example is provided by the "political" seminars in which the country's political issues are discussed with the participation of leading politicians belonging to different political parties;

2) The invitation to conduct seminars and lectures to leading foreign scholars;

3) The selection of candidates for scholarships to attend executive development programs at Columbia University and the International Marketing Institute at the Harvard Business School;

4) The creation of a Division of Research to undertake studies on topics related to business and businessmen in the Argentine environment. By early 1966 the Division included four full-time research members and was engaged in the construction of a cost-of-living index for middle managers. The program also provides for the further training abroad of members of the research staff who, upon their return to Argentina, will resume their research work and teaching activities within IDEA;

5) The emphasis placed in communicating with other social groups in the country which have little opportunity to discuss technical problems or national issues with businessmen. For example: a three-day meeting with Navy officers took place in 1965 at Puerto Belgrano, a large base of the Argentine Navy.

Institute of Public Administration. In 1958, the Provisional Government then in power in Argentina issued Law-decree No. 4027, by means of which the Instituto Superior de Administración Pública, ISAP, was created as a part of the Office of the Present.[64] Its objectives were to provide technical assistance and to conduct or promote courses in different fields for the improvement of the organization and functioning of public agencies as well as for the training of government agents.

In order to fulfill its objectives, the Institute's activities were carried out by three divisions, namely:

1) Public Administration Courses, which took care of courses for top- and middle-level administrators, as well as special seminars;

2) Organization and Methods Service, in charge of work specifically related to problems of structure and procedures;

64

3) Department of Library, Research and Publications, in charge of gathering documentation, preparing teaching materials, and publishing the Public Administration Review ("Revista de Administración Pública")

During 1964 the Government issued Decree No. 5829 which changed the above described structure of ISAP. The Institute was transferred from the Office of the President to the Finance Ministry ("Secretaría de Estado de Hacienda").

In addition, some of the activities it had been performing until then were put under the supervision of other agencies within that Ministry as follows: the Organization and Methods Service was transferred to the Office of the Budget while training activities for middle-level administrators and supervisory personnel were transferred to the Civil Service Bureau. So, ISAP, as such, was left in charge of the training of top-level administrators and of the Department of Library, Research and Publications. It is perhaps worth noting that the 1964 decree emphasized that in its research and publications ISAP should give priority to problems related to the carrying out of programs and projects for the social and economic development of the country.

The following tabulation, which does not discriminate between the old and new structure of the above referred services for ease of interpretation, illustrates the training activities that took place since ISAP was created and until 1965:

Course description	Number of times given	Total Participants
Organization and methods	46	879
Supervision techniques	84	991
Middle-level administration	3	44
Courses for instructors:		
In supervision techniques	5	20
In personnel administration	1	15
In job evaluation	1	4
Top-level administration	4	67
Work-measurement analysis	2	24
Office layout	1	12

In addition, other courses were given in cooperation with other government agencies, and in the interior of the country. A few seminars with the National Development Council and the Federal Investments Council were also offered. In making an overall evaluation, it may be concluded from the preceding figures that most training activities did not concentrate in top- and middle-level administrators.

Almost since the start of its activities, ISAP was able to utilize the help of foreign advisors who come to Argentina under the auspices of the United Nations Technical Assistance Bureau. Also, several members of ISAP and other civil servants related to it obtained scholarships to study abroad, some of them sponsored by The Ford Foundation. By 1966, ISAP had a library which numbered several thousand volumes and had been able to publish its "Public Administration Review" on a continuing basis. But it was too soon, however, to be able to appraise the results of the 1964 reform.

Summary and conclusions. In summarizing the contemporary concepts and commitments of major institutions of higher learning to managerial resource development, it may be said that both in the nationally and privately registered universities the newly developed field of business administration was included in most curricula offered by the mid-1960's.

Public administration curricula, however, were only offered as an exception. A government institute had been created with the objective of training civil servants. In addition, several government agencies offered courses related to public administration. However, none of these programs amounted to a college curriculum.

There were a number of problems that conspired against the efficient operation of the national universities. Among these, the most important were the inadequacy of their respective budgets and the threat of a sudden change in their institutional structure. In spite of these shortcomings, the period from 1955-1965 witnessed a tremendous progress in the quality of college education in Argentina which included the introduction of courses and curricula related to the field of our interest. By the end of the period a number of private institutions existed which greatly contributed to the training of those employed by the important and growing industrial sector of the country.

In view of the described circumstances, it is not difficult to predict at this point that the future will witness the creation of new undergraduate business administration curricula, both in nationally and privately registered universities, and that more private institutions will offer more seminars in many different topics. Also, more foundations and other non-profit institutions will provide increasing financial assistance for management education, training, and research. As far as Public Administration Training is concerned, however, the future is more uncertain. Nevertheless, and in a brief way, these lines express an optimistic outcome of our study.

But there is at the same time, unfortunately, a pessimistic outcome. Argentina lacks a standard-setting institution in the field of our interest in which the search for excellence is a prerequisite to every decision. By this, we mean an institution with a core of highly-trained teachers and researchers devoting full-time to their academic pursuits and teaching to full-time students. It is only in an environment of this sort that activities such as the counseling of students, the production of updated teaching materials, the writing of text books responding to local peculiarities, and the discussion of educational issues can flourish.

It is not easy to say whether an institution such as this should offer undergraduate or graduate curricula, or executive development programs, or perhaps a mixture of these. But the need for standard-setting institutions is there. Until the time when such an educational establishment is created, it will not be possible to say that Argentina has reached maturity in the development of the managerial resources needed for her economic growth.

TABLE 1

CLASSIFICATION OF OWNERS OF INDUSTRIAL ESTABLISHMENTS
ACCORDING TO NATIONALITY IN THE CENSUS OF 1914
(PERCENTAGES OF TOTAL FOR EACH CATEGORY)[1]

	Argentine	Foreign Born	Mixed Ownership
Processing of foodstuffs	38	58	4
Clothing, shoes, and toiletries	15	84	1
Construction and related industries	26	72	2
Furniture and related industries	24	74	2
Artistic and decorative objects	25	73	2
Metallurgical and related industries	20	77	3
Chemical products	24	66	10
Printing, publishing and graphic arts	39	56	5
Textiles	91	8	1
Other	40	52	8
Total	32	65	3

Source: 1914 Census, Volume VII (Industry) p. 246.

[1]It may be also interesting to point out the composition of
the industrial labor force showed by this census: 51% of it was
Argentine, while the remaining 49% was foreign born.

TABLE 2

NUMBER OF INDUSTRIAL ESTABLISHMENTS AND THEIR
LABOR FORCE, ARGENTINA, 1946, BY YEAR
OPERATIONS STARTED

Operations started	ESTABLISHMENTS		PERSONNEL			
			Employees		Workers	
	Number	Percent	Number	Percent	Number	Percent
Before 1851	64	.1	1,110	.8	3,678	.4
1851 – 1870	171	.2	3,026	2.2	10,446	1.1
1871 – 1890	1,171	1.4	8,773	6.5	59,876	6.4
1891 – 1900	1,806	2.1	12,350	9.1	60,921	6.5
1901 – 1910	4,010	4.6	15,769	11.6	97,296	10.4
1911 – 1920	7,708	8.9	20,292	15.0	114,209	12.2
1921 – 1925	6,804	7.9	12,805	9.5	82,087	8.8
1926 – 1930	10,243	11.8	13,905	10.3	92,089	9.8
1931 – 1935	9,856	11.4	13,921	10.3	94,181	10.0
1936 – 1941	18,241	21.1	18,177	13.4	148,665	15.8
1942 – 1946	25,130	29.1	13,031	9.6	150,161	16.0
undetermined	1,236	1.4	2,325	1.7	24,778	2.6
TOTAL	86,440	100.0	135,484	100.0	938,387	100.0

Source: 1946 Industrial Census, p. 9.

TABLE 3

ESTIMATE OF TOTAL EMPLOYMENT IN ARGENTINE
INDUSTRY IN 1961, PER OCCUPATIONAL CATEGORY

Occupational Category	Number Employed						No. Employees
	Over 100 persons Number	Percent	11-100 Persons Number	Percent	1-10 Persons Number	Percent	
Managerial	10,783	1.4	45,791	7.2	70,000	22.2	120,000
Professional	6,818	.9	10,812	1.7			
Technician	18,119	2.4	25,439	4.0	23,000	7.4	
Clerical	117,057	15.3	71,866	11.3			
Skilled worker	292,903	38.3	224,502	35.3	222,000	70.4	
Non-skilled worker	318,338	41.7	257,572	40.5			
TOTAL	764,018	100.0	635,982	100.0	315,000	100.0	120,000

Source: M. A. Almada, M. A. Horowitz, and E. A. Zalduendo, Los Recursos Humanos de Nivel Universitario y Técnico en La República Argentina. 2 vols. Buenos Aires: Editorial del Instituto Torcuato Di Tella, 1963, p. 318.

TABLE 4

ARGENTINE STATE ENTERPRISES ORGANIZED
UNDER THE PROVISIONS OF LAW No. 13.653.
YEAR 1965

Name	Personnel (approx.)
Ferrocarriles del Estado (railroads)	178,000
Flota fluvial (river transportation)	4,500
Subterráneos de Buenos Aires (Subway)	4,200
Administración General de Puertos (port authority)	7,700
Líneas Marítimas Argentinas (ocean transportation)	5,300
Talleres de Reparaciones Navales (shipyard)	1,500
Aerolíneas Argentinas (airline)	6,800
Dirección Nacional de Fabricaciones e Investigaciones Aeronáuticas (Air Force manufacturing plant)	8,700
Seguro Aeronáutico (insurance)	12
Yacimientos Petrolíferos Fiscales (petroleum)	39,000
Yacimientos Carboníferos Fiscales (coal)	4,000
Gas del Estado (gas)	9,200
Agua y Energía Eléctrica (electric power)	14,300
Empresa Nacional de Telecomunicaciones (telephones)	42,000
Astilleros y Fábricas Navales del Estado (Navy shipyard)	6,800
Instituto Nacional de Reaseguros (reinsurance)	400
Dirección Nacional de Industrias del Estado (miscellaneous industries)	1,800
TOTAL (approx.)	334,000

Notes: 1) This tabulation excludes one very small enterprise and three more which are in the process of closing down.

2) This tabulation also excludes those State enterprises not organized under the provisions of Law No. 13.653. Thus, it leaves out important operations such as the Dirección General de Fabricaciones Militares (Army Manufacturing Plant).

TABLE 5

ARGENTINE NATIONALS ATTENDING ACADEMIC INSTITUTIONS
IN THE UNITED STATES, PER FIELD OF STUDY. 1950–1961

Fields of Interest	Total for 1950 – 1961 Period
Accounting	6
Agronomy	26
Anthropology	8
Architecture	25
Atomic Science	2
Biology	24
Business Administration	77
Chemistry	35
Dentistry	22
Economics	61
Aeronautical Engineering	10
Agricultural Engineering	4
Chemical Engineering	23
Civil Engineering	33
Electrical Engineering	36
Electronic Engineering	4
Industrial Engineering	26
Mechanical Engineering	48
Metallurgical Engineering	5
Mining Engineering	4
Petroleum Engineering	12
Sanitary Engineering	2
Textile Engineering	14
Engineering, not specified	31
Geo – Science	11
History	8

TABLE 5 (Continued)

Fields of Interest	Total for 1950 - 1961 Period
Law	79
Library Science	9
Mathematics	28
Medicine	58
Metallurgy	2
Nursing	13
Philosophy	9
Physics	17
Political Science	10
Psychology	18
Public Health	31
Sociology	16
Para-Medical Specialties	11
TOTAL	858

Source: A report prepared from the Roster of Internationally Trained Persons by the Institute of International Education (New York, N. Y. 1963).

TABLE 6

SUPPLY AND DEMAND OF MANAGERIAL PERSONNEL,
AS ILLUSTRATED BY AN ARGENTINE EXECUTIVE
SELECTION AGENCY[1]

Field	Demand %	Supply %	AVERAGE NUMBER OF INDIVIDUALS AVAILABLE PER POSITION[2]
Marketing	26.90	28.65	18.20
Production	32.20	30.40	16.10
Accounting and Finance	31.10	32.70	17.97
Personnel	3.80	3.80	17.17
Administration	5.10	2.65	8.78
Public Relations	.90	1.80	34.75
	100.00	100.00	

NOTES: [1]The percentages indicated in this Table refer to total figures for 1964, 1965 and half of 1966.

[2]These average figures only include suitable candidates, rather than total number of applicants.

Source: Executives S.A.

TABLE 7

EDUCATION OF THOSE PLACED IN VACANT POSITIONS
BY AN ARGENTINE EXECUTIVE SELECTION AGENCY

Field of Study	Production %	Marketing %	Accounting and Finance %	Personnel
Chemical Engineers, Chemists	16.35			7.70
Mechanical Engineers	16.35			
Civil Engineers	7.30			
Mechanical and Electric	12.70			
Industrial Engineers	10.90		1.00	
Construction Engineers	5.45			
Engineers (in general)		2.90		
Engineering students	9.10	8.70		15.40
Psychology majors				7.70
Law students		8.70		30.00
Accounting students		8.70	23.80	15.40
High School graduates (technical and other)	21.85	52.20	41.55	23.00
Business administration majors			0.95	
Philosophy majors		4.30		
Medicine students		7.25		
Architecture students		2.90		
Psychology students		1.45	0.95	
Only grammar school		2.90		
Accountants			17.30	
Doctor in Economics			11.50	
Lawyers			1.00	
Architects			1.00	

SOURCE: Executives S.A.

75

TABLE 8

ARGENTINE PROFESSIONAL AND TECHNICIANS, ADMITTED
AS IMMIGRANTS INTO THE UNITED STATES
JULY 1st., 1950 - JUNE 30, 1964

Profession	Total for Period
Engineers	984
Physicians	925
Teachers	973
Technicians (without specifying)	464
Professionals (without specifying)	249
Chemists	228
Nurses (professionals and students)	248
Accountants	236
Professors	220
Musicians and Music Teachers	189
Draftsmen	129
Lawyers	84
Architects	121
Dentists	87
Pharmacists	58
Geologists	19
Physicists	16
Biologists	9
TOTAL	5,239

Source: United States Justice Department: Immigration and
Naturalization Services

TABLE 9

TOTAL COLLEGE ENROLLMENT IN CAREERS CONSIDERED
STRATEGIC FOR ARGENTINA'S ECONOMIC DEVELOPMENT
1962 AND 1963

Field of study	1963 Enrollment		1962 Graduates	
	Number	Percent	Number	Percent
Total, National Universities	162,355	100	8,153	100
Agronomy and veterinary	4,156	2.55	141	1.73
Science	9,130	5.62	566	6.94
Engineering (other than civil)	15,467	9.52	541	6.63
Economics and business administration	4,041	2.49	69	0.84

Source: Presidencia de la Nación Argentina, Consejo Nacional de
Desarrollo, Plan Nacional de Desarrollo, 1965-69
(Buenos Aires, 1965), p. 339.

TABLE 10

TOTAL ENROLLMENT IN THE UNIVERSITY OF
BUENOS AIRES, BY SCHOOL, 1958 AND 1964

SCHOOL	YEAR 1958		YEAR 1964		CHANGE, 1958-1964	
	Number Enrolled	% of total Enrolled	Number Enrolled	% of total Enrolled	Absolute (number) Change	Relative (%) Change
Law	10,849	18.6	12,260	18.8	+ 1,411	+ 11.6
Medicine	14,986	25.5	10,743	16.5	− 4,243	− 28.3
Engineering	7,186	12.2	7,532	11.5	+ 346	+ 4.8
Liberal Arts	2,264	3.8	5,570	8.6	+ 3,306	+146.0
Agronomy & Veterinary	1,219	2.1	1,834	2.8	+ 615	+ 50.0
Economics	10,329	17.6	15,258	23.4	+ 4,929	+ 48.0
Dentistry	3,485	5.9	2,970	4.6	− 515	− 14.8
Architecture	3,850	6.6	4,297	6.6	+ 447	+ 11.6
Basic Sciences	1,891	3.2	3,035	4.6	+ 1,144	+ 60.5
Pharmacy	2,625	4.6	1,829	2.8	− 796	− 30.4
TOTAL	58,684	100.0	65,328	100.0	+ 6,644	+ 11.3

Source: Universidad de Buenos Aires, Junta de Planeamiento, Comparación entre los Censos Universitarios de 1958 y 1964, Servicio de Documentación, Publicación Interna No. 1, Buenos Aires 1965, p. 31 (mimeographed).

TABLE 11

FIRST-YEAR ENROLLMENT, AND NUMBER OF
DEGREES AWARDED, SCHOOL OF ECONOMICS,
UNIVERSITY OF BUENOS AIRES, 1958 - 1965

Field of study	FIRST - YEAR ENROLLMENT						
	1959	1960	1961	1962	1963	1964	1965
Accounting	2,401	2,216	2,399	2,425	3,304	2,856	n.a.
Business Administration	48	46	114	145	153	337	n.a.

	NUMBER OF DEGREES AWARDED						
	1959	1960	1961	1962	1963	1964	1965
Accounting	282	344	303	259	314	282	489
Business Administration	--	--	--	2	3	9	n.a.

Source: Junta de Planeamiento, Universidad de Buenos Aires.

TABLE 12

FIRST-YEAR ENROLLMENT, AND NUMBER OF
DEGREES AWARDED, SCHOOL OF ENGINEERING,
UNIVERSITY OF BUENOS AIRES, 1958 - 1965

Field of study	FIRST - YEAR ENROLLMENT						
	1959	1960	1961	1962	1963	1964	1965
Civil Engineering	259	168	170	180	180	196	n.a.
Industrial Engineering	229	179	201	200	196	238	n.a.
Naval Engineering	44	28	52	34	21	58	n.a.
Electrical Engineering	490	502	593	614	609	695	n.a.
Chemical Engineering	47	97	113	124	146	164	n.a.

	NUMBER OF DEGREES AWARDED						
	1959	1960	1961	1962	1963	1964	1965
Civil Engineering	173	181	156	98	132	128	100
Industrial Engineering	54	44	21	22	34	56	50
Mechanical Engineering	45	66	66	47	36	24	10
Electrical Engineering	23	33	49	12	13	8	4
Chemical Engineering	18	23	29	18	15	6	10

Source: Junta de Planeamiento, Universidad de Buenos Aires.

TABLE 13

ARGENTINE CATHOLIC UNIVERSITY

ENROLLMENT, 1958-1965

Field of Study	1958	1959	1960	1961	1962	1963	1964	1965
TOTAL ENROLLMENT IN ALL FIELDS	602	624	1.037	1.451	2.090	2.438	2.714	3.411
Economics and Business Administration (undergraduate)	146	156	207	291	395	489	518	535
Science and Engineering (undergraduate)	--	--	50	102	152	212	239	281

Source: Pontificia Universidad Católica Argentina Santa María de los Buenos Aires, Anuario 1965, pp. 24 and 25.

TABLE 14

SOME NON-REGISTERED PRIVATE UNIVERSITIES OFFERING BUSINESS ADMINISTRATION PROGRAMS[1]

Name	English translation of name	Remarks
Universidad Argentina de la Empresa	Argentine Business University	Started operating in 1957 under a different name. Spons. by the Chamber of Corporations of Argentina. Probably the oldest one in category.
Universidad de Ciencias Comerciales	University of Commercial Sciences	Sponsored by the Sales and Marketing Managers' Association (See Table 15).
Universidad Lasalle de Sudamérica	Lasalle University of South America	
Universidad Argentina de Ciencias Sociales	Argentina University of Social Sciences	
Universidad de Belgrano	Belgrano University	
Universidad Bartolomé Mitre de Olivos	Bartolomé Mitre University of Olivos	
Universidad Dante Alighieri	Dante Alighieri University	Located in Rosario, Province of Santa Fe. Affiliated with a traditional high school.
Universidad Argentina John F. Kennedy	John F. Kennedy Argentine University	

[1] The names included in this list are given only for information purposes. No reference as to the quality of their teaching should be made as a result of their inclusion here.

82

TABLE 15

ARGENTINA PROFESSIONAL ASSOCIATIONS RELATED TO MANAGEMENT FIELDS, PER YEAR ACTIVITIES STARTED

Year activities started	Name	Initials commonly used as designation	English translation of names
1941	Círculo Argentino de Estudios sobre Organización Industrial	CADESOI	Argentine Committee for the Study of Industrial Organization
1947	Instituto Argentino de Dirección de Empresas (ex-Instituto Argentino de Dirigentes de Personal)	IADE	Argentine Business Management Institute (formerly, Argentine Institute of Personnel Managers)
1952	Asociación de Dirigentes de Ventas y Comercialización	ADV	Sales and Marketing Managers Association Organized its Sales and Managers School in 1957
1952	Asociación Cristiana de Dirigentes de Empresa	ACDE	Christian Association of Business Managers
1956	Centro Argentino de Técnicos en Estudios del Trabajo	CATET	Argentine Association of Work-Study Technicians
1960	Sociedad Argentina de Investigación Operativa	SADIO	Operations Research Society of Argentina
1960	Instituto para el Desarrollo de Ejecutivos en la Argentina	IDEA	Institute for the Development of Executives in Argentina
1961	Sociedad Argentina de Organización Industrial	SADOI	Argentine Society of Industrial Organization

TABLE 15 (Continued)

1962	Consejo Argentino de Organización Científica[1]	CADOC	Argentine Council for Scientific Management
1965	Asociación Argentina de Marketing	AAM	Argentine Marketing Association
n.a.	Asociación Argentina de Compradores		Argentina Association of Purchasing Agents
n.a.	Asociación de Dirigentes de Empresa	ADE	Manager's Association

[1]Membership in this organization is composed of most of the associations in this table, rather than individuals.

Source: Most of this historic review has been taken from Congreso de Organización Científica de la Empresa, "Antecedentes de Racionalización Administrativa," Revista de la Universidad Argentina de la Empresa (May 1964) pp. 87-90.

TABLE 16

INSTITUTIONS OFFERING MANAGEMENT COURSES IN BUENOS AIRES, ARGENTINA, 1966[1]

Name	Initials used as designation	English translation of name	Remarks
Centro de Productividad de la Argentina	CPA	Argentine Productivity Center	Started operating in 1960. It is one of the centers of the Instituto Nacional de Tecnología Industrial, INTI (National Institute of Industrial Technology). Obtained support from the United Nations Special Fund and from the International Labor Organization.
Bureau des Temps Elémentaires	BTE	Office of Time Elements	Consultants Associated with the Institute of Controle de Gestion, of Paris, France. Founded in 1958.
Centro de Investigación de las Técnicas Matemáticas Aplicadas a la Dirección de Empresas	CITMADE	Center for the Research of Mathematical Techniques Applied to Business Management	Affiliated with the Instituto Nacional de Tecnología Industrial, INTI (National Institute of Industrial Technology).
Centro de Investigación del Metal Estampado	CIME	Research Center Stamped Metal	Specialized in courses for small business management. Received a grant from The Ford Foundation. Affiliated with the Instituto Nacional de Tecnología Industrial, INTI (National Institute of Industrial Technology).

[1]Some of the professional associations listed in Table 15 are very important from the point of view of management training. They are not included in this list to avoid repetition.

TABLE 16 (Continued)

Name	Initials used as designation	English translation of name	Remarks
Fundación Galileo Argentina		Argentine Galileo Foundation	Affiliated with a business firm, Galileo Argentina, S.A.
Instituto Argentino de Control de Calidad		Argentine Institute for Quality Control	
Instituto de Estudios Contemporáneos		Institute of Contemporary Studies	
Escuela Superior Argentina de Relaciones Públicas		Argentine School of Public Relations	
Centro de Investigaciones, Formación y Relaciones Empresarias	CIFRE	Center for Business Research, Training and Relations	
Instituto de Estudios Empresarios	IDEE	Institute of Management Studies	
Instituto Superior Internacional de Relaciones Públicas		International Institute of Public Relations	Affiliated with the International Institute of Public Relations of Rome, Italy.
Instituto Superior de Relaciones Humanas "Marcelino Champagnat"		Institute of Human Relations "Marcelino Champagnat"	Affiliated with a traditional catholic high school.
Asociación del Crédito Industrial Argentino	ACIA	Argentine Association of Industrial Credit	
Asociación Argentina de Propaganda		Argentina Advertising Association	Sponsors the Escuela de Propaganda, (School of Advertising).

TABLE 16 (Continued)

Name	Initials used as designation	English translation of name	Remarks
Instituto de Orientación Económico-Financiero	IDOEF	Institute of Economic and Financial Orientation	Sponsored by the Fundación Argentina para Estudios e Investigaciones Económico-Financieras (Argentine Foundation for Economic and Financial Study and Research).
Instituto Superior de Administración Pública	ISAP	Institute of Public Administration	Founded in 1958. It is a part of the Federal Administration.
Círculo Argentino de Profesionales de Relaciones Públicas		Argentine Association of Public Relations Professionals	Sponsors the Escuela de Relaciones Públicas (School of Public Relations).
Selección Contable	SELCON	Accounting Digest	Affiliated with a publishing house that specializes in topics of business administration.

NOTES AND REFERENCES

1. Gino Gemani, Estructura Social de la Argentina (Buenos Aires: Editorial Raigal, 1955), p. 82.

2. Ibid., p. 81.

3. In this year the ruling class lost a presidential election for the first time.

4. Torcuato S. Di Tella and others, Argentina, Sociedad de Masas (Buenos Aires: Editorial Universitaria de Buenos Aires, EUDEBA, 1965).

5. See Inés Izaguirre de Cairoli, "Estratificación y orientación profesional en la Universidad de Buenos Aires," Revista Latino Americana de Sociología, 65/3. Buenos Aires, 1965.

6. Murmis, Carmes G. Cucullu de, Estudio sobre el prestigio de las ocupaciones, Jornadas Argentinas de Sociología, Departamento de Sociología, Universidad de Buenos Aires, Buenos Aires, 1961, (mimeographed).

7. The observations contained in this section as well as in the rest of the chapter were drawn prior to the revolution that took place on June 28, 1966. They have not been modified due to the fact that it is still too early to see the impact on them of measures taken by the new government.

8. Frederick Harbison and Charles A. Myers, Management in the Industrial World. An International Study (New York: McGraw-Hill Book Company, Inc., 1959), pp. 69–80.

9. José Luis de Imaz, Los que mandan. (Buenos Aires: Editorial Universitaria de Buenos Aires, EUDEBA, 1964).

10. Tomás R. Fillol, Social Factors in Economic Development. The Argentine Case (Cambridge, Mass.: The M.I.T. Press, 1961), pp. 57–58.

11. Fillol recognizes in a footnote: "...the analysis that follows will therefore rely exclusively on personal experiences, observations and opinions. Therefore, the reader should probably allow for some margin of error owing to incomplete information and biased appreciation of the reality." Ibid., p. 57.

12. Dirección Nacional de Estadística y Censos. Censo Industrial de 1954 (Buenos Aires).

13. José Luis de Imaz, op.cit., pp. 162-163.

14. See also Hla Myint "Economic Theory and the Underdeveloped Countries", The Journal of Political Economy, October, 1965.

15. One example often quoted of the lack of reliable statistical figures is the Argentine index of industrial production. The sample from which figures for the updating of the index were obtained did not include, until a few years ago, automobile manufacturers. Thus, the index underestimated for a long time the rate of industrial growth.

16. Eduardo A. Zalduendo, El Empresario Industrial en América Latina. Argentine, Comisión Económica para América Latina, E/CN.12/642/ Add. 1 (Santiago de Chile, 10 de febrero de 1963).

17. Ibid., p. 49. Pages 48 through 69 describe the methodology followed in the survey.

18. Ibid., pp. 45-47. Translated into English by the author of the chapter.

19. Fillol made this point clear in his study (op.cit., pp. 59-61).

20. Clark Kerr et al., Industrialism and Industrial Man. The Problems of Labor and Management in Economic Growth (Cambridge, Massachusetts: Harvard University Press, 1960).

21. IDEArio, Año VI, No. 56, February 1966 (Buenos Aires)

22. General Motors Argentina S.A., Departamento de Personal, 2a. Encuesta sobre Capacitación en Empresas Industriales, Buenos Aires, December, 1965 (mimeographed).

23. José Luis de Imaz, op.cit., pp. 154-163.

24. Dirección Nacional de Estadística y Censos, Censo Industrial de 1954 (Buenos Aires).

25. M.A. Almada, M.A. Horowitz and E.A. Zalduendo, Los Recursos Humanos de Nivel Universitario y Técnico en la República Argentina. Centro de Investigaciones Económicas, Instituto Torcuato Di Tella (Buenos Aires: Editorial del Instituto, 1963).

26. The study being referred to clarified that the classification of personnel in the executive, professional and technician categories was left to each individual firm studied. It also defined a "professional job" as one which required college education, whether the individual actually performing it had attended college or not.

27. I.D.E.A., Instituto para el Desarrollo de Ejecutivos en la Argentina, Indice de Costo de Vida para Ejecutivos. Metodología e Información Estadística, Buenos Aires, 1966.

28. The I.D.E.A. study also indicated that 90% of these middle managers were Argentine-born, which is then far away from the immigrant era. It is perhaps worth noting, in addition, that the same survey showed that 60% of the wives of the middle managers had attended high school (whether graduating or not), while 12% of them reached college level.

29. General Motors Argentina, S.A., op.cit., p. 28.

30. See also Oteiza, E.J., "La Ingeniería y el Desarrollo Económico, Centro de Investigaciones Económicas, Instituto Torcuato Di Tella, Buenos Aires, 1966 (mimeographed).

31. Frank Brandenburg, The Development of Latin American Enterprise (National Planning Association: Washington, D. C. 1964), pp. 52 and 54.

32. J. Fred Rippy, British Investments in Latin America, 1822-1949 (Minneapolis, Minnesota: University of Minnesota Press, 1959), p. 159.

33. United States Department of Commerce, Basic data on the economy of Argentina, World Trade Information Service, Economic Reports, Part I. No. 58-73, p. 12.

34. Chamber of Commerce of the United States of America in Argentina, "Directory of American Business in Argentina," Comments on Argentine Trade (Buenos Aires: April, 1964).

35. The author is indebted to Executives S.A. and Indotec for the information given on this matter.

36. See Carlos F. Díaz-Alejandro, Stages in the Industrialization of Argentina, New Haven, Conn., 1965 (mimeographed).

37. Frederick Harbison and Charles A. Myers, Education, Manpower and Economic Growth, Strategies of Human Resource Development (New York: McGraw-Hill Book Co., 1964), p. 48.

38. Morris A. Horowitz, La Emigración de Profesionales y Técnicos Argentinos (Buenos Aires: Editorial del Instituto, 1962).

39. F. Harbison and C. Myers, op.cit.

40. For the sake of brevity, only main locations are mentioned.

41. M.A. Almada, M. A. Horowitz and E.A. Zalduendo, op.cit., p. 290.

42. Presidencia de la Nación Argentina, Consejo Nacional de Desarrollo, Plan Nacional de Desarrollo, 1965-69 (Buenos Aires, 1965) p. 339.

43. All of these are undergraduate schools, as explained later in the chapter.

44. Enough has been written about the traditional inclination to study "traditional" or "prestige" careers such as law, liberal arts or medicine. For this reason, the analysis given in this section focuses on the development of managerial resources. For a sociological study of students at the University of Buenos Aires, see Inéz Izaguirre de Cairoli, op.cit.

45. Furthermore, the frequent hiring of Argentine technicians from businesses located elsewhere in Latin America may indicate their "quality" is high.

46. Presidencia de la Nación Argentina, Consejo Nacional de Desarrollo, op.cit.

47. The main difference is that in the United States the C.P.A. status is administered by the American Institute of Public Accountants, while in Argentina an accountant has the privileges of a C.P.A. immediately upon graduating from college and complying with certain administrative requisites.

48. Obviously, and as is the case in other countries, the civil service also absorbs individuals with degrees in various fields of specialization.

49. The analysis of the problems of Argentine universities is complex and would require a lengthy study. The reader should bear this in mind when reading the synthesis that follows.

50. The effects of this problem are difficult to measure. For example: how much has it affected the decision of potential faculty members to become full-time professors? How much has it affected the emigration to the United States of potential faculty members, or their decision to return to Argentina?

51. As opposed to professors under a special contract or "ad interim" professors, which are not regular faculty members and, therefore, have no voting power in Faculty meetings.

52. Between 1958 and 1965, a total of 410 scholarships were awarded to graduate students.

53. Source: Ministry of Education and Justice, and La Nación, May 5, 1965.

54. It is worth noting that the Córdoba Catholic University is starting to develop its 200-acre campus, where the first building, the School of Engineering, is under construction.

55. It might be also added that the School of Industrial Engineering of the Northern University "Santo Tomás de Aquino" opened its doors in 1965 with a total enrollment of 106 in its preparatory and first year courses.

56. "Las provincias y sus universidades", La Nación, June 25, 1966, p. 6.

57. As a matter of fact, the Deans of the Schools of Economics of the National Universities issued a statement, in their 12th meeting, pointing at confusion and the danger created by the proliferation of private institutions that adopt the denomination of "university," without holding to any academic standards in their teaching activities (La Nación, April 26, 1966).

58. Although no data were obtained from the other institutions listed in Table 14, the number of those enrolled in them was probably smaller than these figures.

59. Congreso de Organización Científica de la Empresa, "Antecedentes de Racionalización Administrativa," Revista de la Universidad Argentina de la Empresa (May, 1964), pp. 87-90.

60. General Motors Argentina S.A., Departamento de Personal, op.cit.

61. Several men had been sent abroad by 1965 for graduate training in public administration. Upon their return, they would engage in research activities in their field of specialization.

62. This institution channels in Argentina Scholarships awarded in the United States through the Institute of International Education.

63. Initially, the department was mainly staffed with men with an accounting background, plus their own personal experience and informal training in management concepts.

64. Previously, the National Rationalization Agency ("Dirección Nacional de Racionalización") and the Advisory and Technical Studies Service for Public Administration ("Servicio de Asesoramiento y Estudios Técnicos en Administración Pública") had existed.

CHAPTER IV

MANAGERIAL RESOURCE DEVELOPMENT IN BRAZIL

by

Dole A. Anderson

<u>Social-Economic</u> <u>Environment</u> <u>for</u> <u>Managerial</u> <u>Resource</u> <u>Development</u>.

The Brazilian environment for managerial resource development is the result of the impact of the nation's recent leap into the modern industrial world on its cultural norms and attitudes regarding business and administration which developed over the history of the country. In modern Rome, the coexistence of the architectural past and present adds charm without significantly affecting the substance of life. But for a nation undergoing the strain of rapid economic development, the co-existence of the cultural past and present <u>is</u> the substance of life. Thus, one must begin with the still visible roots in any description of the present environment.

The peopling of this half of the South American continent began with the arrival of a richly diverse base stock from Portugal, consisting of groups with a tradition of agriculture and nobility from the North of that country, and those of the urban areas with a commercial tradition, many with Jewish strains. To this base stock, and a small number of Amerindians already on the land, there was added the importation of African slaves, whose impact on the culture persists to this day. Beginning in the 19th century, the flow of immigrants from Italy, Spain, Germany, and later Japan, began. Although relatively small in numbers in comparison with immigration to the United States, these immigrants to Brazil concentrated in a few areas of the country and became of great social and economic significance for her modern development.

Until recently, the land supported an economy based on monoculture for the European metropolis. Originally, it was sugar cane in the Northeast which dominated the economy based on the plantation system and slavery. With the loss of the world market and the abolition

---

The author acknowledges his heavy debt to Flavio Penteado Sampaio who has given unstintingly of his time in clarifying and interpreting Brazilian society and higher education. Professor Sampaio was director of the São Paulo School of Business during most of its first decade. Also most generous in their help and critical insights were Paulo Ernesto Tolle, of the São Paulo State Council on Education and Luiz Carlos B. Pereira of the São Paulo School of Business. Responsibility for the final product is, of course, exclusively the author's.

of slavery, the Northeast became and remains today the economically decadent region of the country, now being revived by a massive rehabilitation plan. Later, coffee in the Central South, and especially in the state of São Paulo, became the profitable export crop which generated capital for the beginnings of the current leap into industrialization.

The proportions between the two -- the people and the land -- constitute a third element in the environment. There have never been enough people to even physically occupy the tremendous land area, much less exploit it economically. Thus, the "March to the West" exists as a national theme, but with a hollow, rather than solid, frontier which leaves ghost regions in its wake.

The Two Brazils

Although the preconditions were evident at the end of the 19th century, the "take-off" of the Brazilian economy into rapid growth began in the South in the 1930's. This rapid growth revealed the coexistence of two Brazils. In the words of the French sociologist, Jacques Lambert -- one modern, the other archaic, "equally Brazilian but separated by centuries."[1] The Northeast typifies the archaic Brazil, although not coextensive with it, just as the states of São Paulo and Guanabara (which consists of the city of Rio de Janeiro) typify the modern. Although the population of the seven northeastern states equals that of these two southern states, the latter, with only a fourth of the area of the former, contributes over four times as heavily to the national product. Although the Northeast may be generalized as the archaic and traditional region of Brazil, it contains pockets of relative modernity, including the third largest city of the nation, Recife; similarly, pockets of the archaic can be found almost within sight of the skyscrapers of São Paulo and Rio de Janeiro. If the Northeast typifies the archaic Brazil, then the prototype of its economic and social structure is the sugar plantation of Colonial time, paternalistically structured to protect the worker and his family rather than produce. Lambert has described its effects as follows:

> "The traditional Brazilian fazenda is bad, not because
> it is inhuman and brutal but because it is insufficiently
> economic. In other countries, the large land owners
> expelled the miserable ones, obliging them to find employ-
> ment where they were needed and where they could educate
> and elevate themselves; in Brazil the fazenda aided them
> and multiplied their number, thus contributing to the
> growth of an unproductive and under-employed rural popu-
> lation."[2]

On the other hand, the prototype of the economic and social structure of modern Brazil is, as in any economically advanced area, the steel mill or factory producing automobiles, typewriters, or television sets. It is located in, or near, an urban area and employs a skilled labor force which is relatively mobile, now thoroughly dependent on the amenities of urban life, enjoying a steadily expanding standard of well-being, and consequently heavily in debt on installment purchases of consumer goods. Most important, of course, it is structured on production and not protection.

Inevitably, the vestiges of the archaic Brazil must disappear under the inexorable diffusion of the modern. The Brazilian revolution will be aided by the fact that the nation has one language, basically a common national origin, and a sense of national political unity. It will be impeded by the country's tremendous land area and great distances, which hinder the formation of a single national market, by the great and presently widening disparities in regional levels of development and by the persistence of institutions and attitudes surviving from the old Brazil.

Cultural Attitudes Towards Management

One of Brazil's greatest students of its contemporary culture, Alceu Amoroso Lima, has described the national character as humanistic, reflecting the "predominence of man over land and institutions." Among the aspects he finds in the national character are the "ascendancy of of sensibility over reason ... the precedence of the abstract over the concrete ... a preference for the extemporized over the prepared, and ...a reliance on talent rather than on scholarship..."[3] While these very characteristics give Brazil its special essence and its great contribution to the community of nations, many are at variance with the aims and methods of modern management of public and private enterprises.

Similarly, the nature of the national economy until very recently was also inimical to the attitudes required for modern management. The successive cycles of the primary economic activities of agriculture or mining which formed the nation's economic history -- first, Brazil-wood, then sugar cane which enjoyed world dominance for three centuries, minor cycles of tobacco, cacao and cotton, then gold, coffee, and rubber (with all but gold and coffee originally carried out in the Northeast) -- were pursued in an exploitative fashion with extensive patterns of land use. The result of this preoccupation with the primary, extractive activities, and of the successful imposition of mercantilist policies by Portugal on Brazil, was that the beginnings of industrialization were delayed until the second half of the 19th century. Thus, since the economic base was agriculture for export and the more simple forms of commerce, pressures for the development of managerial capabilities were not felt until recently in Brazil's economic history.

As the Dean of Brazilian sociologists, Gilberto Freyre, has observed:

> "There seems to be no doubt that the plantation system
> in Brazil, with its whole structure based on slave work,
> developed in many Brazilians a peculiarly aristocratic
> attitude toward manual labor and also toward trade,
> business, and commercial or industrial activity."[4]

While these attitudes have largely disappeared today, vestiges can be observed. But in that pre-industrial society, the careers appropriate to a gentleman included the Army or Navy, government, diplomacy, law, the Church, and, for the most progressive, medicine.[5]

With independence, and the withdrawal of the Portuguese, it became necessary to organize and staff the new governmental structure. But even then, a career in public administration apparently did not imply status in the society. Of course, the most cultured and intellectual members of the society were and still are attracted to public life, but as amateurs, in the best sense of the word, and not professionals.[6] Those who made their careers in public administration were governed by other rules. They were the minor officials and functionaries who were a part of the middle class in its beginnings. Even today, "job seekers were primarily interested in public employment as a sinecure and not in [the value system of economy, efficiency and rationality]."[7] So, while the public servant and the society pay lip service to the merit system and civil service examinations in getting an appointment, the public functionary falls back on paternalism through the regional power figure who is the modern counterpart of the plantation owner.[8] Thus, the parallel is complete between the archaic plantation system and public administration, both predicated on an institution of protection rather than production. However, the recent rise in the public corporation, which often finds itself in direct competition with the private corporation, is creating an exception to this rule as will be shown later.

The Beginnings of Professionalization in Education

Higher education in colonial Brazil was, basically, religious education controlled by the Jesuits. It was "... neither popular nor vocational, for it only had in view the humanistic and Catholic formation of the ruling classes."[9] With the Age of Enlightenment and conflicts between the church and state in Europe, Portugal ordered the expulsion of the Jesuits from Brazil in 1759, thus ending the emphasis on the study of the Latin classics and religion in the preparation of a gentleman. Higher education turned toward the professions, with the first faculties of medicine founded in 1808 at Bahía and in Rio, of law at Olinda and São Paulo in 1827, and the first beginnings of the discipline of engineering in the military academies in the 1830's, which later became the Polytechnic School in Rio in 1874.

Unfortunately, what thrived most was the least practical, and the "cult of the Bachelor of Laws", as Azevedo calls it, began. According to this author, the efforts of Don João VI (the King of Portugal who moved the seat of his government to Brazil from 1808-21 to escape Napoleon) to stimulate technical education failed, by and large, because of the agricultural, slave-labor economy and the "...discursive and dialectical propensities of the Brazilian mind...more inclined to letters than to sciences, more to the liberal professions than to the useful professions."[10]

At the beginning of the Republic in 1889, there were five schools of higher education in Brazil: two law schools with a total of 1329 students, two medical schools with 800 and one engineering school with 161 students.[11] Apparently, the intellectual elite formed in these schools turned for employment to the new government; while this was especially true of the law graduates, it included even those in medicine and engineering.[12]

The first three decades of the Republic -- from 1889 to the end of the First World War -- saw a conjunction of factors which stimulated the beginnings of industrialization. Among these were a protectionist tariff, the arrival of European immigrants, and the development of a railroad network and hydro-electric energy. As a result, the number of industrial establishments increased from 636 in 1889 to 13,336 in 1920. Thus, a base was created for increasing professionalization and for the demand for trained professionals.

The results of these developments, carried down to the present for comparative purposes, are shown in the percentage distribution of enrollments in higher education by profession:[13]

	Law	Medicine Dentistry Pharmacy	Engi- neering	Eco- nomics	Phil- osophy Science Letters	All Others
1889	58%	35%	7%	--	--	--
1907	41	48	7	--	--	4%
1912	27	48	13	--	1%	11
1933	33	46	9	1%	1	10
1953	26	25	14	6	15	14
1961	24	18	12	9	23	14

From the beginning until very recently, the law schools provided the most "liberal" education available and their function was broader than their name implies. More recently, the faculty of philosophy, science and letters has taken over this role; these faculties are roughly equiv- alent to a liberal arts college and to the college of education for the preparation of secondary school teachers in the United States.

The Emergence of a Managerial Elite

International and domestic adversity were principally responsible for breaking down the traditional agricultural economy of Brazil and introducing the industrial revolution. The two World Wars impeded the importation of manufactured goods and the Great Depression brought a drop in export earnings when the coffee market collapsed. Finally, government promotion of industrialization clinched the trend to "self- sustaining economic growth" which now seems to be established.[14]

In the fifteen years from 1949 to 1963, the indexes of real product (based on 1949) grew to 326 for industry, against 177 for agri- culture, 218 for commerce, 272 for transportation and communication, and 152 for services. By 1960, approximately one quarter of the population was employed in industry, as against only 10% in 1920. In the two decades from 1940 to 1960, food processing and textiles dropped from 58% of the total value of industrial production to 37%. In 1940, 31% of the population was classified as urban; by 1960, the urban population had grown to 45%.

Generalizations on the nature of entrepreneurship in Brazilian economic history are hazardous until more research has been done on this subject. However, two students of this subject -- Bresser Pereira and Cardoso -- have attributed leadership in industrialization to a new elite, largely with foreign backgrounds, who challenged the traditional centers of economic power. Bresser Pereira summarizes this development in the following terms:

> "In the upper class, the industrialists appeared to take their place beside the planters and merchants. Originating primarily in the middle class -- particularly from Italian, German, Jewish, and Lebanese immigrants -- and in the old upper class, their power and prestige increased rapidly with the industrialization process. Today, they may be considered the dominant group in Brazil. Their rise, however, was not easy. For years and years, they waged political and ideological battle against the planters and the old merchants, who represent the traditional and non-progressive sector of the Brazilian economic and social system. Today, this conflict is ending. The position of industry in the Brazilian economy is now an established and definite fact."[15]

Within the group of industrialists, Cardoso distinguishes between the traditional and the modern.[16] Apparently the traditional industrialist transferred agricultural or merchandizing profits into industrial undertakings as well as into banking and real estate, partly as a reflex to the poor earnings associated with the coffee collapse. Also in this group would be most of the owners of the textile and food processing firms dating from the first World War or earlier. Since this group came out of aristocracy and was well-connected politically, it "...used every means possible to influence decisions which would assure government concessions and loans."[17] Clearly this group, with its roots in exploitative agriculture or in the export-import trades, contributed to the proclivity of the business class for rapid payout and large rates of profit, although continual and substantial inflation in the Brazilian economy has had the same effect.

Cardoso's "modern" industrialist, on the other hand, is more concerned with the technical aspects of production, expects mid-term rather than short-run profits, manifests pride in the quality of his product and a competitive spirit, and is preoccupied with the modernization of his equipment and the reorganization of the firm's administrative organization.[18] Certainly, this description is of a type in its pure form.

The Foreign Influence in Brazilian Business

Although Brazilians of traditional families are to be found in the group of "modern" industrialists, the importance of the foreigner among the Brazilian entrepreneurial class which has given the principal impetus to industrialization since 1930 is borne out in a recent study by Bresser Pereira of the São Paulo entrepreneur.[19] Approximately 50% of these entrepreneurs were themselves immigrants, an additional 23% were sons of immigrants, and an additional 11% were grandsons of immigrants for a total of 84% with foreign origins, leaving only 16% as Brazilians of the third generation.

With respect to the social origins of these entrepreneurs, only 4% came from traditional families of the Brazilian "aristocracy" (the fazendiros and exporters), although this group controlled most of the capital at the beginning of the industrialization period.[20] Some 50% of the entrepreneurs came from the middle and lower levels of the middle class and another 22% from the upper class which was rich but not of the aristocracy. Finally, some 18% came from the lower classes. Apparently, the majority of the entrepreneurial talent came from families where the father, with no more than a secondary education, was at best in small business or the middle levels of the military or of public administration.

In addition to the predominance of immigrants among Brazilian entrepreneurs, the foreign influence is apparent in the importance of foreign firms in the structure of the nation's industry. One of the most spectacular achievements of recent industrialization was the creation of an automobile industry by an ingenious government policy of stimulation which, in the nine years to 1964, achieved an annual output of 180,000 units of passenger cars, buses, and trucks by eleven companies, nine of which had foreign origins. A most significant by-product of this effort was the creation of an industry of some 1,600 firms supplying new car components and replacement parts; many of these started as a one-man, one-machine operation in a garage less than a decade ago. Quality and cost standards imposed by the large auto assembly firms on these suppliers has achieved a wide diffusion of modern business methods. Outside the automobile industry, the foreign firm is also an important element; probably one-third of the thirty largest corporations in Brazil today are foreign-owned.[21]

The Rise of Middle Management

Parallel with this dramatic change of the Thirties and Forties in the upper classes of the industrial south of Brazil is the change in the middle class. To the old, small middle class of the liberal professionals, public functionaries and rentiers is being added a great new middle class of small businessmen and middle management of the large private and public enterprises. Evidence of the characteristics of the middle management group is found in a recent survey by Flavio Sampaio of the composition and mobility of 125 middle managers in the São Paulo area.[22] Clearly a young group of middle management professionals has come into being with industrialization. They are 86%

Brazilian born, in contrast with the high percentage of foreign entrepreneurs cited earlier. One-third are college graduates, of whom 47%
have degrees in engineering, 35% in economics or accounting, 7% in law
and 2% in business administration. Increasingly, they describe themselves as specialists in the various areas, such as marketing or financial managers, rather than simply as business administrators. They
show a high professional mobility, with three-quarters having worked in
other than their present firms and most of those in different industrial
sectors. Finally, two-thirds of these middle managers thought it likely
one could rise to the top management (director) level in their firm
without family or close personal ties with the directors. Of the 125
middle managers interviewed, 69% worked for national companies and 31%
for foreign companies; the replies show substantially more "professionalization" for managers employed by foreign firms than for those in
national firms. Thus, foreign firms appear to place a higher value on
knowledge and experience and less on family ties, contacts, and loyalty;
employ substantially more college graduates; and have led their managers
to believe they have better chances to rise to top management in the
company.

It seems clear that the very rapid industrialization of the past
few decades, especially in the São Paulo area but also throughout the
industrial traingle of São Paulo-Rio de Janeiro-Belo Horizonte, has
required quantities of professional managerial talent far beyond the
supply available. The shortage of managers has become a concern of the
National Confederation of Industries which, in a statement of criticisms
and suggestions to the revolutionary government on its first anniversary
in March, 1965, noted that one of the economy's bottlenecks was the lack
of administrative talent and qualified labor. The statement went on to
criticize the government for inverting the problem by giving emphasis to
literacy and and primary education when "...it is the development of
technical and higher university education which will create the conditions indispensible for the eradication of illiteracy in Brazil."[23]
Even the efforts to strengthen the nation's economic problem area -- the
Northeast -- suffer from this shortage. Southern firms interested in
investing in branch plants in the Northeast with the significant tax
advantages now made available by the federal government complain of the
lack of managers who can be entrusted with these investments far from
the direct supervision of the home office at the same time that Northeastern firms try, often futilely, to recruit managers in the southern
labor market.[24]

Before turning to a consideration of the role of Brazilian higher
education in supplying this demonstrated need for managerial talent, we
should examine briefly the extent to which managers have been trained
abroad. Brandenburg has observed that it is not uncommon to discover
that two or three generations of a Latin American entrepreneurial family
have studied abroad.[25] Brazilians of the aristocracy have gone abroad
for university study since the 17th century, for long to Coimbra in
Portugal, later to universities throughout Europe.[26] In more recent
times, foreign training has extended to graduate students of all classes
and it has been estimated that a minimum of 1,200 Brazilians are abroad

each year in all types of training programs or graduate study.[27]
However, the principal areas of study have been the pure sciences, medicine, and engineering.

It seems likely that the number of Brazilians trained abroad in the
managerial sciences is extremely limited. Confirmation of this was
sought through a survey of all schools in the United States offering
Master's degrees in Business Administration. During the five years,
1960-1965, only eight MBA degrees were granted to Brazilians by schools
other than Michigan State University, which has had an AID contract to
develop schools of business.[28]

Data which would permit a serious estimate of the size of the
Brazilian managerial class today are not yet available. However, an
idea of the order of magnitudes is possible. The Census of Industry for
1960 shows the total number of persons employed as 1,797,000; this
figure includes owners and partners, whether full or part-time as well
as non-remunerated members of owners' families. The number of workers
participating directly in production, including supervisors and foremen,
was 1,423,000, leaving 374,000 persons in managerial, administrative,
and non-production activities. Of these, some 207,000 are in firms with
less than 100 employees and some 167,000 in medium and large firms.
Census results for Commerce, Finance, and Services have not yet been
made available.[29]

It is clear, however, that the infinitesimally small number of
Brazilian managers trained abroad and the limited number of foreign
managers in the employ of foreign firms operating in Brazil can be dis-
regarded as a supply of managerial talent for growing industrialization.
The training of the nation's future managerial resources must come from
her institutions of higher education.

MANAGERIAL RESOURCE DEVELOPMENT: CONCEPTS, COMMITMENTS, AND STRATEGIES OF HIGHER EDUCATION

The Structure of Higher Education and Its Role in Economic Development

Over a century passed between the creation of the first Brazilian
faculties in the early 19th century and the formation in Rio de Janeiro
of the first university by joining faculties in law, medicine and
engineering. In contrast with other Latin American countries where the
university has a long history, only since 1931 has Brazil had legislation which permits the founding of a university by bringing together
a minimum of three faculties. As yet, therefore, the university is more
a loose federation of separate and autonomous faculties than an institution with overall goals and a coordinated program.

The faculty, or "establishment of higher education" as it is known
in the official statistics, is thus the basic unit of organization in
Brazil today. During 1960, there were 438 faculties in existence, of
which 206 were components of 25 universities, and the remaining 232
establishments were isolated faculties unattached to any university.

The following table shows the distribution of 128 faculties in the four areas of law, engineering, economics, and administration which were in existence during 1960, by the period of their creation.[30]

Number of Faculties Existing in 1960
by Date of Creation

Periods	Law	Engi-neering[1]	Eco-nomics[2]	Administration[3] Business	Public
Before 1900	6	6	–	–	–
1900 to 1919	7	5	2	–	–
1920 to 1939	5	3	9	–	–
1940 to 1949	5	3	16	1	–
1950 to 1959	23	12	15	1	1
during 1960	5	2	–	– 1	–
Total	51	31	42	3	2

Grand Total   128

[1]Includes Faculties of Industrial Engineering, Chemistry, and Industrial Chemistry.

[2]Includes Faculties of Political and Economic Science.

[3]The school between the columns for 1960 is the joint business and public School of Administration at the University of Bahía.

From this table, it will be seen that the most recent decade of the 1950's saw the creation of the greatest number of establishments of higher education in these four disciplines. In view of the often-heard criticism that the nation is vastly over-supplied with lawyers, it is interesting to observe that more new law faculties have been created in the past two decades than have faculties in the other disciplines shown, which are presumably more intimately related to the needs of industrial-ization. However, other factors than the prevalence of the law degree as a status symbol are involved in the creation of new faculties. In the majority of cases in Brazil, both student and professor in higher education are part-time. With many obstacles to mobility, such as inadequate transportation systems and strong family ties, most students live at home and the typical faculty serves a local market. Among the law faculties created during the 1950's were three located in cities with 1960 populations of less than 50,000. Since the creation of a law faculty involves a minimum investment in building and library and has a local faculty readily available from the professional and government class in the community, a city can in this way bolster the evidences of its cultural life at a low cost.

Within the faculty, the traditional organization is by cátedras, or chairs, rather than by departments. As a result of a public competition which is required by an article in the Brazilian constitution, the holder of the chair or catedrático acquires not only life tenure but also executive rights to his subject matter. The cátedra may cover one course in the curriculum, or more than one, or even less than one sub-ject.[31] While the system is justified as providing essential security and assuring academic freedom, it is also subject to the abuses of part-time activity, stagnation of the discipline, and the creation of king-doms where young assistants do most of the teaching while the professor is free to engage in other pursuits within or outside the academic world. A result of this now highly controversial catedrático system is low student-professor ratios in Brazil, perhaps the lowest to be found anywhere.[32] For all disciplines in 1962, the average was four students per professor. By disciplines, the ratios varied substantially; law had a relationship of 17.5 students per professor, while engineering had only 2.2 students. The low ratio for engineering apparently results from the complexity of the course; at a typical university with approxi-mately the same number of students in each program, the engineering faculty is offering three times as many courses as the law faculty with a corresponding need for a large number of professors. When to this need for a large faculty is added the investment in buildings and laboratory required for engineering, the slow growth of faculties in this area is understandable.

The tradition of viewing education as a consumer good that is as a protector of status or, more recently, as a vehicle for achieving status through social mobility has its effect, of course, not only on the sub-ject matter of higher education but also on its quality.[33] Although there is criticism of the quality of law being taught, this is perhaps not so crucial since so few graduates will practice law. However, in the case of engineering and economics, which are more intimately related to industrialization and to the new society based on production rather than protection, criticism of the quality of the courses is serious. Thus, a government report on university training and economic development found the traditional schools of engineering and economics, in the main, to be turning out graduates with badly taught and obsolete knowledge of limited value to the society today.[34] Although a few excellent schools have developed within the university system, we must look outside the traditional structure of higher education for points of educational inno-vation and for examples of efforts which are clearly aimed at satisfying the needs of the new society. Two examples may be cited -- that of the Engineering School created by the Brazilian Air Ministry in 1947 and the Schools of Administration created by the Getulio Vargas Foundation in the mid-1950's. Both illustrate innovation from outside the traditional educational structure of Brazil; both are aimed at the development of managerial and technical resources which would find immediate and effec-tive employment in the industrialization process. Finally, both have had a multiplier effect on other institutions with traditional back-grounds and structures.

Federal Government Control Over Higher Education

It is on the level of higher education in Brazil that the federal government, through the Ministry of Education and Culture, exercises most control. Universities and faculties are of either federal, state, or private organization and administration; although all receive federal

103

subsidies, the degree of control by the Ministry is most detailed in the case of federal universities. In addition, the Ministry registers the diplomas issued by all schools after verifying that minimum standards have been met, thus giving legal force to the document and enabling its holder to practice his profession.

The organization of an aeronautical engineering institute by the Air Ministry made it independent of the Education Ministry, even extending to financial independence. The Getulio Vargas Foundation is a quasi-governmental economic and educational institution financially dependent on the federal government, although only in part through the Education Ministry. Thus, it too gained substantial freedom to experiment educationally. In both cases, federal recognition of programs and diplomas came only some years after the first students were graduated. The price of such freedom from the rigidities of federal control was uncertainties over financial support, especially in the case of the Foundation's schools. Although all higher education has suffered in recent years from inflation and the demands on the federal budget from infrastructure investments required by the nation's economic development, it is clear that the Foundation's schools, and especially the Business School, have been particularly hard hit.

Three Examples of Innovation

The Aeronautical Technical Institute (Instituto Tecnológico de Aeronáutica or ITA) was organized in 1947 and began immediately offering a five-year undergraduate program with specialization in either aeronautics, air transport operation, or electronics. Entering students selected in nationwide examinations were given full scholarships including living costs, were predominantly civilians, and had no obligations to the Air Force upon graduation. Since it was recognized that the young Brazilian engineer often becomes as much or more involved in administrative functions as in purely technical functions in local industry, various business administration courses were required in his program such as cost accounting, industrial production, and personnel administration. The Institute began with a faculty of some twenty Americans, mostly from M.I.T. and an American Reitor or president; over its history, an increasing proportion of its foreign faculty was contracted in Europe. In 1962, the University of Michigan began supplying technical assistance through a contract with AID for developing the program in mechanical engineering. The Institute was located near the small city of São Jose dos Campos some 50 miles from São Paulo; this decision by the first American Reitor was intended to insure that both faculty and students would be full-time by their distance from job and consulting opportunities in São Paulo and also to develop a campus atmosphere.

In 1952, the Getulio Vargas Foundation inaugurated the first Brazilian School of Public Administration (Escola Brazileira de Administração Pública or EBAP) at the Foundation premises in Rio de Janeiro, then the national capitol. For five years, the School operated under an agreement with the United Nations which provided a faculty of foreign visiting professors, a program for training Brazilians abroad, and scholarships for students from other Latin American republics. After the termination of the agreement, the School continued for $2\frac{1}{2}$ years with no external support until mid-1959 when an AID agreement brought in the University of Southern California to provide technical assistance.[35]

In 1954, the Getulio Vargas Foundation inaugurated the São Paulo School of Business Administration (Escola de Administracão de Empresas de São Paulo, EAESP).[36] From the beginning, this School had a technical assistance mission from Michigan State University under a series of contracts with AID and its predecessor agencies.

The agreement of 1959 between the Getulio Vargas Foundation and AID which brought the Southern California technical assistance mission into EBAP also created the so-called Expanded Program, which provided for introducing schools or programs in both business and public administration at two other locations -- the federal universities of Bahía in the Brazilian Northeast and of Rio Grande do Sul at Porto Alegre in the southernmost state.[37] In this expanded effort, representatives of the two American universities worked side by side, and the "parent" schools in São Paulo and Rio were designated national training centers, with obligations to provide technical assistance through making their Brazilian professors and teaching materials available to the new schools and training teacher candidates from the new schools prior to their departure for Master's degrees in the United States. It will be recognized that the total program of AID technical assistance in introducing Public and Business Administration into Brazil offers a rich case study in institution building; first, the introduction in isolated, new and flexible institutions, followed by a transfer and adaptation of these experiences into the more rigid and tradition-bound federal universities.

We shall now examine the results of the activities of these schools in each of three functions they have performed: the introduction of new courses or disciplines in university education, the building of new educational institutions, and the implantation of innovations in educational techniques and procedures.

The Introduction of New Disciplines

The Aeronautical Institute introduced a new area of specialization-- aeronautical engineering -- into the existing and thoroughly accepted discipline of engineering. Hence, it was not involved in selling its product. The "major" areas permitted a student were aircraft and engine design, airline and airways operation, and electronics; in recent years a fourth area of specialization was added in mechanical engineering. Although Brazil has no significant aircraft manufacturing activity, the nation has one of the largest commercial air transport systems in the world because of its large land area, and the people are highly airminded. A limited number of graduates have been absorbed by the Air Ministry and by private aeronautical activities, but the majority have been employed by private non-aeronautical firms which were quick to recognize the unusually high quality of their training. Although higher education in federal or state universities is virtually tuition-free, the full support provided by the Aeronautical Institute is an added attraction which helps explain the fact that the Institute has over twenty candidates for each vacancy in its entering classes of 130 freshmen.

In the case of the public and business administration schools, both were trying to introduce an unknown discipline on the university level. In the case of Public Administration, there was a lack of acceptance on the part of parents and students of the field as one which could provide suitable career opportunities and doubts among administrators themselves as to the role of specialized higher-level training for public jobs. In the case of business administration, rapid industrialization had created a more favorable environment, but the question of whether businessmen were "made" or "born" still remained. Thus, the first activity in every school -- at São Paulo, Rio, Bahía and Porto Alegre -- was nearly always the stimulation of local interest by offering intensive courses or week-end seminars for those already working in the profession. The first teaching activity at the São Paulo Business School in 1954 was a management development intensive course of thirteen weeks duration for people with a minimum of three years business experience. Since then, twenty-seven such courses have been offered to over a thousand managers who have come from all states of the nation and from most other Latin Republics under an agreement with the Organization of American States.

Institution Building

Faculties have been built in all institutions through a combination of local training under the guidance of the foreign professors and graduate work in the United States and Europe. At the Aeronautical Institute, foreign professors have been contracted from a number of countries. At the São Paulo Business School, the thirty-five Brazilians who constitute the "full-time" (as contrasted to the teachers contracted on an hourly basis) faculty have received MBA degrees in the United States and four of them have subsequently returned for their doctorates. In the Public Administration School in Rio, forty-five were sent to the United States for advanced work, most of them for Master's degrees. Similar patterns of building a faculty are being followed at Bahía and Porto Alegre. In the case of Porto Alegre, however, the programs in Public and Business Administration were introduced into an existing institution -- the Faculty of Economic Sciences -- and substantial use was made of the professorial resources already available.

Attrition in the Faculties of business administration has been quite limited. At São Paulo, all but half a dozen of the thirty-five trained in the United States over the past twelve years are still teaching in the school; while at Bahía and Porto Alegre, only one has resigned of the twenty-six trained abroad since 1960. However, this does not mean that the professors are engaged in these schools full-time by North American standards. Although at the urging of the American advisory missions full-time dedication has been a goal of all three institutions, practice deviates from this ideal because faculty salaries fall far short of compensatory levels for full-time service. Also, since salary increases have lagged behind the rapidly rising cost of living, professors have been forced to supplement their incomes from the school with varying amounts of other outside activities as the gap widened or narrowed. The São Paulo School has had significantly higher salary levels and more frequent adjustments so that it has been able to require that its "full-time" staff at least hold no other regular job. On the other hand, the professors at Bahía and Porto Alegre all have additional employment which takes as much or more of their time and contributes as much or more to their total income as do the schools.

As yet, the institutions we are describing have avoided the catedrático system, instead following generally a contractual relationship with the professor together with a departmental structure which joins related courses for purposes of internal organization. An exception is the Faculty of Economic Sciences at Porto Alegre where the professors upon their return from foreign training have often gone without salary for months until they could be nominated as assistants to senior catedrático professors. Despite the fact that the catedrático system is subject to increasing criticism, the expectation for the programs at Bahía and Porto Alegre is that they will both have catedráticos in business administration in the future; they now constitute exceptions to the rule within their respective federal universities and the temptation to join the system for the privileges it provides the professor are great.

Of all the institutions, the São Paulo Business School is unique in having a Board of Trustees consisting largely of businessmen as a policy-making body which operates within the frame set by the Getulio Vargas Foundation. This Board has carried out two financial campaigns among the business community -- almost unheard of in Brazilian higher education -- and is currently engaged in a campaign of continuing financial support to take advantage of a $500,000, four-year, equal-matching grant of the Ford Foundation. This grant is an element in an expansion plan of dramatic dimensions which began in 1966 and which began a new phase in the School's history. Since its beginning, space restrictions had limited enrollment to less than 500 students, including nearly 100 students annually in the thirteen-week management development programs. The imminent conclusion of a twelve-story school building begun seven years before confronted the school with the opportunity to better satisfy the demand for its courses and with the necessity to better utilize the new space which was over ten times greater than the school premises in the past. In March, 1966, an evening undergraduate program (requiring six years to complete as against the four-year day program) and a postgraduate program (of two years versus the eighteen-month day program) began. Together with a nearly doubling of vacancies for day students, the result was an increase of four times in the number of entering students over the preceding year.[38] An outline of the undergraduate program is given in Exhibit I.

The financial aspects of the expansion plan involved the creation of a student loan fund by which the cost of each year's tuition and fees could be paid in annual installments beginning one year after graduation. This plan of the administration of EAESP was founded on two premises: the first was that the costs of professional education at the university level in Brazil ought to be borne increasingly by the individuals who

107

benefit by the higher future earning power resulting from that training. Although secondary school students pay the costs of their education in the private institutions which predominate at that level, students in the federal and state universities pay virtually nothing and, in recent years, have resisted by strikes and other pressure attempts to impose even minimal charges. Private university-level schools, such as the São Paulo Business School, charge tuition which for all but the rich can be an important factor in the prospective student's choice of a school and which can only be compensated for by a demonstrably higher quality of education. Thus, the second premise of the plan was that without some mechanism for borrowing against the future, any attempt to cover all or a large part of the true cost of education through tuition would be undemocratic in that it would limit the student body to those with substantial resources.

At the beginning of the school year in March, 1966, tuition levels were increased over 100% and this, together with the increases in enrollment, resulted in the estimate that tuition and fees would account for nearly two-thirds of EAESP's total operating costs in 1966 as against approximately one-fifth in the preceding year. The facilities of the student loan fund were made available to both old and new students and 8% of them arranged total financing, 38% chose the plan of 60% financing of tuition, while 54% of the student body requested no financing. Based on present tuition levels and on the average starting salary of an EAESP graduate, it was estimated that monthly repayment charges would equal 8% of the graduate's salary in the case of 100% financing. The promissory notes signed by the student include a provision for monetary correction of the debt.

The loan fund was created by contributions from the business community which indirectly are matched by the Ford Foundation grant. The financial campaign is soliciting contributions in units which represent the annual cost of educating one student, and multiples thereof, with adjustment for anticipated bad debts. The slogans of the campaign, such as "Help us grow from the 400 students now trained for private enterprise to 2,000 by 1970," together with the emphasis on the revolving nature of the fund which provides for training one man annually in perpetuity gave the campaign a positive tone and an enthusiastic reception by business people. Finally, the initial success of the campaign permitted immediate substantial faculty salary increases and the attracting of new faculty members.

There is little doubt that the institutions and the programs which have been described are viable and a permanent part of Brazilian higher education. The only reservation is in the case of the Aeronautical Institute which in recent years has suffered from serious conflicts between the military direction of the Center and the civilian faculty and administration of the teaching Institute. Paradoxically, but not surprisingly, the subordination to the Air Ministry, which gave the Institute the freedom to innovate so dramatically in educational matters in its early years, becomes the constant threat to its future.

Finally, some comment is in order on the experience of joining programs in Public Administration and Business Administration at Bahía and at Porto Alegre in view of the different points of view on this subject in North American academic circles. At Bahía, a new School of Administration was formed with a Public Administration and a Business Administration Division. The undergraduate course outlined in Exhibit I has a common curriculum for the first two years, with the student opting for one or the other program at the end of his second year. In fact, however, the student indicated his preference at the time of taking the common entrance examination. From the beginning, approximately three-quarters of the candidates requested the program in Business Adminis-tration, reflecting, of course, the feeling that job opportunities were likely to be more attractive after graduation.[39] At the time of select-ing the second freshman class in 1961, a quota system was introduced making 2/3 of the openings available for Business Administration majors and 1/3 for Public Administration but with the proviso that unfilled vacancies on either side might be filled by any excess of candidates on the other. Since equal number of prospective professors were being trained in the United States in the two areas, it was feared that there might be few or no students in the upper class levels if the Public Administration programs were not protected. The quota system has since been abandoned but the problem remains. The alternatives which have been discussed have ranged from the separation of the courses from the first year to separate entrance examinations and even to the abandonment of the undergraduate course in Public Administration. The Public Ad-ministration Division meanwhile has concentrated with great success on the shorter programs for the development of those already committed to careers in government -- in-service training programs, intensive courses, and postgraduate courses.

In the case of Rio Grande do Sul, an Institute of Administration was created in 1959 within the existing Faculty of Economic Sciences which had for years been offering four-year undergraduate programs in economics, accounting, and actuarial sciences. In 1961, a program in business administration was introduced as an option along with the three above-mentioned existing options after the first five semesters of a common program. The curriculum is outlined in Exhibit I. In 1966, a proposal to introduce the additional option of public administration was accepted by the faculty. It must be borne in mind that the academic economists have viewed administration as a part of their area; indeed, the charters and even the names of some of the oldest economics schools refer to administration, meaning generally some courses in organization and finance.[40] While competition for undergraduates has thus not existed in Rio Grande do Sul, the Public and Business Administration sectors have again done different things.

Educational Innovation

The Business and Public Administration Schools have pioneered in the use of dynamic teaching methods to replace the traditional emphasis on the students' rote learning of lecture materials. The case method, student research, business games, apprenticeship or intern programs com-bined with classroom work have been used extensively in all institutions and are now being widely imitated throughout the country.

Similarly, both programs realized at an early stage the lack of local teaching materials and have made research and publication programs an essential part of their efforts. Although the Basic Law on Education of 1961 and even the Federal Constitution of 1946 refer to the importance of research activity in higher education, a number of obstacles exist. The part-time devotion of a professor to a career where continued productivity and growth often need not be demonstrated is conducive neither to research nor publication. The case of the São Paulo School of Business illustrates the difficulties. Although as mentioned above, full-time service has been and continues to be the philosophy of the School, the erosion of the professor's purchasing power, as the spiraling cost of living outstripped the occassional and inadequate salary increases, forced the faculty to seek out sources of additional income. During 1962, a grant from the Ford Foundation enabled the School's Research and Publications Center to program the writing of five basic textbooks by departmental teams of from three to seven professors who were compensated as their completed chapters were approved for classroom testing and subsequent publication. During the four years to 1966 when this project was completed, with a total of ninety-six chapters in use, most of the "full-time" professors took advantage of this means to supplement their incomes and reduce the extent of their part-time activities outside the School. Grant funds were used under similar systems of "extra compensation for extra effort" to continue the publication of the School's quarterly journal which was threatened during these difficult years, the collection of business cases, and the preparation of monographs resulting from a special research project on the problems of Brazilian small business firms. Fortunately, the improvement in 1966 in the financial situation of the School and in salaries, which has been described earlier, relieved the economic pressures on the faculty just as this research and publications project was being completed. It is interesting to note that at Bahía and at Porto Alegre, the faculties in Business Administration, with similar American training and orientation but without the financial stimulus of São Paulo's Ford Foundation grant, produced almost no research or writing during this period.

The development and use of business cases at São Paulo is a subject which merits a thorough evaluation rather than the mere impressionist treatment which is now possible. The first team of American advisors advocated strongly the case method and the first management development courses relied heavily on translated American cases. About twenty of the senior Brazilian professors had the additional exposure of participation in the International Teachers Training Program at Harvard after completing their master's degrees. Over the years approximately 160 Brazilian business cases have been collected; however, this output is largely the result of the efforts of perhaps half a dozen of the faculty. Apparently, the use of the case method is similarly concentrated in a few of the professors who use it extensively and with good success. Among the course programs, its widest use is in the intensive Management Development course. It is to be hoped that in the future a thorough evaluation of the Brazilian experience with the case method will be made.

The Multiplier Effect

The institutionalization of the disciplines of business and public administration has clearly been achieved in Brazil. There are now more than a dozen university-level programs in public administration in Brazil. In business administration, six schools in the city of São Paulo alone are offering undergraduate programs in competition with EAESP. During April, 1966, the first Congress of Brazilian Schools of Business was held in São Paul with fifteen institutions represented. Of course, many of these programs would have sooner or later come into being in the absence of the three model AID-supported institutions simply in response to the needs of the rapidly developing business sector. However, these new institutions clearly look to the pioneer schools for technical assistance. The latest government data show that slightly over 1,000 students were enrolled in business administration undergraduate degree programs at the beginning of 1964 and nearly 700 in public administration. Given the great discrepancy between these small numbers and the demand for managerial resources, additional new schools and programs can be anticipated, in most cases with inadequately prepared faculty, library, and other resources. Meanwhile, the demands on the time and energies of the trained personnel of the pioneer schools grew geometrically. In 1964, by international agreements, both the São Paulo and Rio schools were named Latin American centers for training personnel and research programs in their disciplines, which not only attests to their leadership but also poses problems of the maintenance of their quality in the light of all their other obligations.

During 1965, legislation regulating the profession of business and public administration was passed by both houses of the Brazilian Congress. This bill limited the practice of administration, including the top management of private firms, to persons holding undergraduate degrees of business or public administration, or those with at least five years administrative experience as administrators at the time of passage of the law. This legislative bill had been limited to the practice of public administration when it originated but grew to include business administration during its course through the Congress. As finally approved by the president, business administration was eliminated from the regulation, perhaps in part because of the strong stand in opposition taken by the faculty of the São Paulo School of Business. In any event, the roots of the past are still visible in a society in dramatic transition such as Brazil.

EXHIBIT I

SELECTIVE BRAZILIAN UNDERGRADUATE CURRICULA IN ADMINISTRATION, 1966

	The Federal University of Bahia School of Administration[1]	The Federal University of Rio Grande Do Sul Institute of Administration[2]	São Paulo School of Business Administration
First Year 1st Semester	Intro to Economics Mathematics I Intro to Administration Economic Geography Brazilian Institutions English	Mathematics I Financial Math Legal Institutions Intro to Scientific Methods	Intro to Economics Mathematics I Intro to Administration Intro to Psychology Intro to Sociology Money and Credit
2nd Semester	Micro Economics Mathematics II Communications I Productive Resources Sociology English	Mathematics II Intro to Administration General Sociology	Micro Economics Mathematics II Communications I Productive Resources Psychology
Second Year 1st Semester	Macro Economics Communications II Acct. Administration Labor and Social Law I Intro to Statistics Industrial Equip. & Processes Anthropology	Intro to Economics Mathematics III General Accounting	Macro Economics Communications II Commercial Law I Political Institutions I Intro to Statistics Industrial Equip. & Installations
2nd Semester	Communications III Acct. Administration Commercial Law Labor & Social Law II Applied Statistics Industrial Psychology Brazilian Industries	Micro Economics Cost Accounting Gen. & Applied Statistics	International Economics Commercial Law II Political Institutions II Applied Statistics Industrial Sociology I Industrial Processes

EXHIBIT I (Continued)

	The Federal University of Bahía School of Administration[1]	The Federal University of Rio Grande Do Sul Institute of Administration[2]	São Paulo School of Business Administration
Third Year **1st Semester**	Acct. Administration Organization Production I Intro to Marketing Financial Institutions	Psychology of Human Relations Personnel Administration Production Administration I	Acct. Administration I Gen. Administration I Aux. Functions to Production I Intro to Marketing Labor Law I
2nd Semester	Cost Accounting Obstacles to Communications Production II Marketing Administration Finance I	Marketing Administration I Production Administration II Tax Law	Acct. Administration II Industrial Relations Aux. Functions to Prod.II Marketing Administration Labor Law II Industrial Sociology
Fourth Year **1st Semester**	Personnel Administration Finance II Marketing Research Production Planning & Control I	Macro Economics Business Finance Marketing Administration II Commercial Law	Human Relations Financial Admin. I Marketing Research Prod.Planning & Control I Tax Law I
2nd Semester	Administrative Policy Analysis of the Firm Production Planning & Control II Retailing Administration	Administrative Policy Analysis of the Firm Social Law	Administrative Policy Financial Admin. II Prod.Planning & Control II Marketing Strategy Tax Law II

(Note: In addition 10 optional seminars are offered in the last 2 yrs., 6 of which must be completed to graduate.)

[1] The program is common for students of Business and of Public Administration through the second year.
[2] The program is common through the first 5 semesters for students of Economics, Accounting, Actuarial Science and Business Administration.

NOTES AND REFERENCES

1. Jacques Lambert, Os Dois Brasis (Rio de Janeiro, INEP-Ministerio da Educação e Cultura, 1959) p. 107.

2. Lambert, op.cit., p. 120.

3. Alceu Amoroso Lima, "Men, Ideas, and Institutions," Perspective of Brazil. An Atlantic Monthly Supplement (Intercultural Publications, Inc., 1956) pp. 24-25.

4. Gilberto Freyre, New World in the Tropics (New York, Alfred A. Knopf, 1959) p. 8 .

5. Freyre, op.cit., pp. 87-88.

6. Amoroso Lima, op.cit., p. 25 observes that "...the Brazilian is by nature an amateur and not a professional. He does things because he likes to, not because he has to. One feels that, by contrast, men in the United States are more professional... People are identified by their occupations...[and] vocational training has become an exceedingly prominent part of education in the United States. In Brazil, on the other hand, professional nomadism is the rule. Brazilians wander from occupation to occupation, putting off -- sometimes indefinitely -- the time when they must choose a permanent profession."

7. Gilbert B. Siegel, "Administration, Values and the Merit System in Brazil," in Robert T. Daland, ed. Perspectives of Brazilian Public Administration (Rio de Janeiro, Getulio Vargas Foundation, 1963) p. 9.

8. Siegel, op.cit., p. 10. It is estimated that only about 12% of the over half million jobs in federal service covered by the examination process have in fact been filled through examinations.

9. Robert J. Havighurst and J. Roberto Moreira, Society and Education in Brazil (Pittsburgh, University of Pittsburgh Press, 1965) p. 56. The chapters of Prof. Moreira in this book give a thorough development of the history of education in Brazil against the background of the nation's political and economic history.

10. Fernando de Azevedo, Brazilian Culture. An Introduction to the Study of Culture in Brazil (New York, The Macmillan Company, 1950) p. 174.

11. Havighurst and Moreira, op.cit., p. 76.

12. Azevedo, op.cit., p. 180.

13. Havighurst and Moreira, op.cit., p. 200.

14. Lincoln Gordon and Engelbert L. Grommers, United States Manufacturing Investment in Brazil. The Impact of Brazilian Government Policies, 1946-1960 (Boston, Harvard University, Graduate School of Business Administration, 1962) p. 4.

15. Luiz Carlos Bresser Pereira, "The Rise of Middle Class and Middle Management in Brazil." Journal of Inter-American Studies, IV, No. 3 (July, 1962) 316.

16. Fernando Henrique Cardoso, Empresario Industrial e Desenvolvimento Econômico no Brasil (São Paulo, Difusão Europeia do Livro, 1964) pp. 133-156. He uses the terms "captain of industry," and "businessman" to describe the traditional and the modern respectively.

17. Cardoso, op.cit., p. 134. And further, "If it can be manipulated, the patriarchal State becomes the ideal government for these defenders of private initiative."

18. Ibid., p. 140. This description fits very well a group of small business owners surveyed in 1963 who, of course, have no political or financial power. See the studies in Problems of Brazilian Small Business now being published by the Research Center of the São Paulo School of Business (Escola de Administração de Empresas de São Paulo).

19. Luiz Carlos Bresser Pereira, "Origens Etnicas e Sociais do Empresario Paulista." Revista de Administração de Empresas IV, No. 11 (June, 1964), 83-106.

20. Ibid., pp. 95-104.

21. No measures of sales or revenue is yet possible for all of the principal corporations (Sociedades Anónima); registered capital is admittedly a defective measure although recent obligatory asset revaluation makes it less so. The following table classifies the thirty largest corporations by type of majority ownership:

Distribution of Thirty Largest Firms
by Type of Ownership

	Government	Private National	Private Foreign
Ten largest firms	6	3	1
Next ten largest firms	3	1	6
Next ten largest firms	3	4	3
	12	8	10

Source: Banas-Brazil, 1965, pp. 69-75.

Of the three national companies among the top ten, one is Industrias Matarazzo, the industrial complex begun by an Italian itinerant peddlar and now controlled by his sons, the second and third have Japanese and American origins with majority ownership now held by Brazilians. By type of activity, the twelve government companies include the Federal Railroad System, Petrobras (the national oil monopoly) six hydro-electric companies and three iron and steel companies. Of the ten foreign companies, three are in the automobile industry, three in food and agricultural products, two in petroleum distribution, and one each in textiles and steel.

These data confirming the importance of private foreign capital correspond approximately to those shown by Frank Brandenburg, The Development of Latin American Private Enterprise (Washington, National Planning Association, May, 1964) p. 55.

22. Flavio Penteado Sampaio, "A Profissionalização do Administrador Paulista." Revista de Administração de Empresas, IV No. 12 (Sept. 1964) 93-110.

23. O Estado de São Paulo, March 27, 1965, p. 16.

24. Cardoso, op.cit., p. 104.

25. Brandenburg, op.cit., p. 35.

26. Azevedo, op.cit., p. 344, 169n.

27. Americo Barbosa de Oliveira and Jose Jacarias Sa Carvalho, A Formação de Pessoal de Nivel Superior e o Desenvolvimento Econômico (Rio, CAPES, 1960) p. 58. During the 7 years 1953-59, CAPES, the federal agency for the development of university-level manpower, granted 790 scholarships for graduate study abroad; of these, only 16% went for the social sciences, including economics, law, education and administration.

28. During this period the MBA was granted to one Brazilian by each of the following universities: Arkansas, Chicago, Harvard, Kentucky, Michigan, Pennsylvania, Rhode Island, and Utah.

   In contrast, Michigan State University, which has had the AID contract to develop Brazilian Schools of Business Administration described later in this chapter, granted 28 MBA's during the five-year period and a total of 56 MBA's since 1956 under that program.

29. Quem Dirige os Negocios no Brasil, (São Paulo, Editora Banas S/A, 1962) is a simple listing of the names of all "directors," i.e., presidents, vice-presidents, general managers, of all corporations (Sociedades Anônima) which by law must publish annual reports of their activities. It showed 37,000 names in 1962, comprising the top management in industry, commerce, finance and agriculture.

30. CAPES (Campanha Nacional de Aperfeicoamento de Pessoal de Nivel Superior) Estabelecimentos de Ensino Superior, 1960.

31. For example, in a Faculty of Economic Sciences, two chairs may exist for the parts of Value and Price Formation, Part I and Part II. See Paulo Ernesto Tolle, <u>Reexame e Redefinição do Conceito de Cátedra no Ensino Superior</u>, 1964, São Jose dos Campos (mimeographed).

32. Brazil's President Castello Branco has observed that the student-professor ratio is the lowest in the world and that in certain "branches of teaching," the number of professors equals or even exceeds the number of students. Speech at the Universidade Federal de Santa Maria, reported in <u>O Estado de São Paulo</u>, March 13, 1966, p. 8, 10.

33. Rudolph P. Acton, "The Latin American University," <u>Die Deutsche Universitaetzeitung</u>, February, 1962. Despite his acerbity, Acton draws a picture all too faithful still of many aspects of Brazilian higher education. See also, Howard S. Ellis, Benjamin Cornejo and Luis Escobar Cerda, <u>The Teaching of Economics in Latin America</u> (Washington, Pan American Union, 1961).

34. Americo Barbosa de Oliveira and Carvalho, <u>op.cit.</u>, pp. 97-100, 131-134. The authors cite (p. 90n) the following criticism of Ernesto Luis de Oliveir Junior, Ensino Técnico e Desenvolvimento, (Rio, Editora ISEB, 1959): "The academic efforts of our schools do not receive the stimulus of new problems, arising directly out of productive activities or our national life. Such schools tend to fall into routine, forever preparing the same technicians, with the same courses, the same curricula, the same lectures, the same exercises, the same examination system. It is not surprising that men who progress in their work, each day facing new problems created by different conditions of production, look with a certain suspicion at these institutions which intend to remain unaltered in a civilization of rapid change."

35. Much of the material for the description of public administration education comes from the various reports to AID of the Southern California Group, especially its final evaluation report of June, 1965.

36. Although this was the first school in Brazil to offer a four-year integrated program in Business Administration, the Escola Superior de Administração de Negocios, organized in São Paulo in 1941 as part of the Catholic University, gave isolated night courses in Business which were integrated into a four-year program some years later. In the table on page <u>15</u> this is the school created in the 1940's which is shown in the column Business Administration. EAESP and EBAP are the schools in Business and in Public Administration created in the 1950's.

37. In addition, the program in Public Administration included assistance to the school inaugurated in 1958 by DASP, the National Administrative Department of the Public Service, which functions as the federal civil service agency.

38. During the period 1955-1960, an annual average of 109 candidates applied for an average of 43 vacancies in the entering class of the undergraduate program; during the period 1961-1965, the average of applicants was 365 for an average of 69 vacancies.

39. The preferences of the first entering class were twenty-eight for business administration, six for public and four undecided. A survey at the end of the first semester of this class, which had a median age of twenty-three years, showed sixteen full-time students and nineteen students also holding "full-time" jobs, of which eleven were employed by public agencies, either federal or state, and eight by private firms, equally divided between banks and other business. Thus, some students who were currently working in government agencies intended to major in business administration. Since "full-time" employment in Salvador normally involved a noon-to-six work schedule, regular attendance at a school with daily classes from eight a.m. to noon was possible.

40. The subjects taught in a typical medium-sized Faculty of Economic Science offering only a course in Economics (Pelotas, Rio Grande do Sul) are: Administrative Science, Science of Finance, International Trade and Foreign Exchange, Mathematics*, Introductory Accounting*, Political Economy*, Economic Statistics, Statistical Methodology, Structure and Analysis of Financial Statements, Structure of Economic Organizations, Comparative Economic Systems, Business Cycles, Economic Geography*, History of Economic Doctrines, General and Brazilian Economic History, Private and Public Legal Institutions*, Money and Credit, Financial Policy, Principles of Sociology Applied to Economics, Income Distribution, Value and Price Formation*. One of the smallest Faculties of Economic Science (Espirito Santo) offers the courses indicated with an asterisk. CAPES, "Estabelecimentos de Ensino Superior," 1960.

CHAPTER V

MANAGERIAL RESOURCE DEVELOPMENT IN CHILE

by

Jorge Riquelme Pérez

In Chile, and possibly most Latin American countries, managerial resources are of extrordinary importance due to the increasing efforts of these nations to overcome their economic and social underdevelopment and the strategic position of the executives in this task. As the multiple factors related to underdevelopment are too numerous to take up here, we will only concern ourselves with one of the apparently critical factors which has constituted an important obstacle in the normal process of development: managerial resources.

Distinct historical factors have determined a special composition to Latin American societies different from the known European and North American societies. We can, for example, point out the differences in the attitudes and types of organization of the colonizers of the United States and those of Latin America. While the former principally formed communities for production, the latter formed theirs for exploitation. While the North Americans based their preoccupations on technology (discounting the exploitation of the Negroes and the Mexicans in the South), the Latin Americans based the value of their properties on the number of "subdued Indians" they owned. While those exploited in the United States have always constituted a minority, in Latin America they have always constituted a majority.

From the beginning, manual labor was expensive in the United States, while in Latin America it still remains a far less valuable commodity. While the North has demanded strong technological advances, the Southern continent has maintained a policy of intensive utilization of cheap manual labor. In order to compensate for the superior quality and lower price of Northern products, it has invariably been necessary in Latin America to resort to tariffs and monopolies which have artifically defended its proprietors from these economies of scale and technological progress.

These developments are reflected in differences in attitude and ability between the managers of the North and the South. While some Latin Americans demonstrate a certain pioneer spirit, frequently overly aggressive, others exhibit a more resigned, conservative and even fearful attitude.

Certain sociological factors can also serve to clarify differences between these two groups of managers. While the United States, and, in general, the most economically developed nations live in a social framework of modern design, many Latin American countries still exhibit characteristics of pre-industrial societies. Possibly, the principle characteristic of the former nations is the development of principles of specialization within a political, economic and social order, both adequate and favorable to change. The institutions in the United States are adaptable to the requirements of development, and the individual and social values generally have more relation with developed capacities rather than with familial or group rights. On the other hand, traditional societies can be characterized by the significant value assigned to the familial relations, little value to the principles of specialization and delegation, little interest in change, and considerable preoccupation with conserving rights, privileges and, of course, control of economic, political and even religious power.

Even though it would not be possible to place all the Latin American nations in the category of traditional societies, neither could it be assured that all have been able to overcome these social characteristics.

It is clear that an impresario schooled in a society of modern design would not be the same as one from a traditional society. Each is confronted with a different challenge, and the instruments, systems, goals and evaluation of results also vary even though theoretical administrative terms do not always reflect the difference. The situation is different and is presented by varying shades in each Latin American country; in fact, the social structures, ethnic composition and economic resources differ, and it would be inexact to arrive at any generalization. Chile is ethnically one of the most homogeneous countries, where the characteristics of the traditional society are being lost steadily due to the powerful pressures brought by political, cultural, academic and even religious groups. Even though land value appraisal by the number of "subdued Indians" never existed, probably due to the fact that the Araucanian Indians could never be subdued, it is not difficult to recognize the strong influence of a society of traditional design through a system of landholding and the administration of enterprises. Since we Chileans do not like to recognize these facts and always prefer to attribute these characteristics to other more underdeveloped countries, we will cite a foreign publication:

> Chile is at a disadvantage in its business development because of traditional reasons as well as circumstances. Even though its political tradition is democratic, its social structure is, configuratively, an aristocratic philosophy, authoritative and paternalistic, which in terms of business administration, represents a high degree of concentration of authority at the top. As for the selection of personnel, undue emphasis is placed on familial factors instead of ability, and as for labor relations, instead of accentuating democratic values, an excessive paternalism is insisted upon.

> Also, a sharp inflation during two decades has produced little concern for costs, improvements of methods, quality and productivity.[1]

Pioneers in Latin America face not only a lack of social sensibility and opportunities, but other characteristics of underdeveloped countries in the form of reaction to change, fear of challenge and government protection. According to William F. Whyte and Alan Holmberg:

Social relations in Latin America are rigidly structured and adhere more to the relations of interindependence and submission than to those of interdependence and liberty. The socio-economic structure, therefore, is based on domination and subordination.

The above relationships are not as significant in Chile if, simultaneously, one observes the extensive public, as well as private, activity which is presently being carried out with the intention of remodeling this structure. With the exception of those groups threatened by change, Chileans are dedicating themselves to a vast program of action including the improvement of academic education and the design of new extensive executive training programs.

The educational structure in Chile, until recent years, had favored little change but, rather, cultivated ancient values of traditional design. The formation of the elite has been, implicitly, the final objective of the entire system which has not been capable of retaining more than 10.1% of its students from the first grade through college. Nevertheless, today it is possible to observe a rapid turn-about with goals oriented toward technical and scientific training and the needs of managerial resources for socio-economic development.

MANAGERIAL RESOURCES

There still is little agreement in Chile concerning the significance of managerial resources; moreover, the meaning of the terms manager and executive are not necessarily understood in a homogeneous and unequivocal manner. For the purpose of this study, we will define the term managerial resources as an occupational group represented by the professionals of university origin. There will be included, therefore, within this definition, the majority of the professionals and specialists trained by the university, such as administrators, engineers, economists, lawyers, doctors, dentists, agronomists, etc. These men will assume many middle and top management positions in all sectors of national activities, coordinating resources in commerce, industry, hospitals, agricultural business and every type of private activities as well as public service.

In another more restricted sense, the term managerial resources could define those professionals who have total or partial training in administration. In this case, the university preparation would not necessarily be a decisive factor, since the preparation could be partially based on other sources such as actual experience or informal training. In this case the reference would be directed to the group of persons charged with what is understood in Chile as executive functions, which are different from directive functions. The latter is more closely associated with the owners of financial and material resources, and the former related to the concept of "professional manager."

In more industrially advanced countries there would be no problem in dichotomizing both concepts and in referring to them separately. Nevertheless, in Chile, as an example of a traditional society attempting to modernize itself and an economic system which is undergoing industrialization, it is still not possible to establish clearly the difference since very important elements prevail which impede speaking with propriety of such a distinction. A sociological study carried out by the Institute of Administration (INSORA) further clarifies this point.[2]

When speaking of managerial resources, we will refer occupationally to professionals, university technicians, managers, higher administrators and directors as seen in Chart I, while, educationally, we will refer to the university graduates. In fact, we will compare both concepts to see that they do not correspond and will analyze this difference in detail.

HIGHER EDUCATION IN CHILE

Within the terms of our definition of managerial resources, we will quantitatively summarize those significant areas of higher education which constitute the principle source of this manpower for all national activities.

There are eight universities in Chile, two of which are public. The remaining six are private, even though 80% financed by the state. The total number of students registered in 1964 was 32,959 and was distributed as shown in Chart II.

There are an additional 2,000 students registered in the regional high schools of the Universidad de Chile, the adaptation courses in the Universidad Technica del Estado and the courses in the "special plan" of the Universidad del Norte. It is calculated that for 1967, the total university enrollment will be approximately 41,000 students.

The enrollment distribution in higher education by field of study is as shown in Chart III.

Even though the concentration of high percentages in careers necessary for the economic development of the country is obvious, the situation regarding the preparation of basic scientists is lamentable. These scientists constitute the base of technological growth which is an indispensable element for development.

COMPARISON OF HIGHER EDUCATION WITH OTHER COUNTRIES

Chart IV indicates the percentage relationship between the total population of nine Latin American countries and the total number of students enrolled in universities. It also shows the percentage of graduate students in the schools of law, economics, finance and the total number of students enrolled in the universities. The comparison between the total enrollment and the graduates of law, economics and finance was included because of the supposition that managerial resources

CHART I

ECONOMICALLY ACTIVE POPULATION OF 15 YEARS OR MORE, ACCORDING
TO THE PRINCIPLE OCCUPATIONAL GROUPS (IN THOUSANDS)

Principle Occupational Groups	Total	Men	Women
1. Professionals, Technicians and Related Occupations	121.3	61.8	59.5
2. Managers, Administrators and Directors	40.9	35.2	5.7
3. Office Employees and Related Occupations	161.9	112.6	49.3
4. Farmers, Fishermen and Related Occupations	632.1	610.3	21.8
5. Salesmen and Related Occupations	164.4	121.4	43.0
6. Miners, Stone Masons and Related Occupations	57.3	57.2	0.1
7. Transportation Conductors and Related Occupations	77.7	77.6	0.1
8. Craftsmen and Operators	534.5	428.9	95.6
9. Day Laborers	119.3	113.0	6.3
X. Personal Service Personnel	301.8	82.7	219.1
Y. Other Personnel	154.8	137.1	17.7
TOTAL	2,356.0	1,837.8	518.2

Source: Dirección de Estadística y Censos: "Algunos resultados del
XIII Censo de Población y II de Vivienda", Abril, 1962.

123

CHART II

ENROLLMENT OF HIGHER EDUCATION INSTITUTIONS IN CHILE

State Universities	Men	Women	Total	%Total
Universidad de Chile (1)	9,582	6,601	16,183	49.1
Universidad Tec. del Estado (2)	2,743	962	3,705	11.2
Private Universities				
Pontificia Univ. Cat. De Chile	3,184	2,125	5,309	16.1
Universidad Católica de Valparaíso	887	869	2,756	8.4
Universidad del Norte (3)	336	232	568	1.7
Univ. Tec. Federico Santa María	339	21	360	1.1
Universidad de Concepción	1,394	1,204	3,138	9.5
Universidad Austral	359	244	603	1.8
Other Institutions				
Schools dependent on the National Health Service (4)	21	352	373	1.1
TOTAL ENROLLMENT	20,385	12,610	32,959	100.0

Notes: (1) Without considering regional high schools
(2) Without considering course of adaptation
(3) Without considering "special plans"
(4) Schools dependent on the National Health Service have yet to attain university status. They have been included since they impart teaching on a higher level. These schools are under the guidance of the Universidad de Chile and the Universidad de Concepción.

Source: Boletín De La Universidad de Chile, Instituto de Investigaciones Estadísticas, Universidad de Chile, No. 56 (May, 1956).

CHART III

ENROLLMENT DISTRIBUTION BY FIELD OF STUDY OF HIGHER
EDUCATION IN CHILE

Major Field of Study	Per cent of Total Enrollment
Education	29.5
Technicians	13.6
Engineering	9.2
Law	8.7
Medicine	6.0
Economics and Administration	6.0
Social Service	3.3
Architecture	3.1
Dentistry	2.5
Political and Administrative Sciences	2.3
Nursing	2.2
Agronomy	2.2
Chemistry and Pharmacy	2.0
Journalism	1.4
Psychology	1.2
Veterinary Medicine	1.1
Applied Arts	0.8
Obstetrics	0.8
Medical Technology	0.8
Liberal Arts	0.7
Library Science	0.7
Sociology	0.6
Forestry	0.5
Geology	0.3
Music	0.3
Physics and Sciences	0.1

Source: Boletín de la Universidad de Chile, No. 56 (May, 1965).

CHART IV

COMPARISON IN NINE COUNTRIES OF THE RELATIONS BETWEEN THE TOTAL
POPULATION AND UNIVERSITY ENROLLMENT AND THE ENROLLMENT IN LAW
ECONOMICS AND FINANCE

ARGENTINA

Years	A	B	C	D	E
1955	145,158	19,110	0.76	1,300	0.90
1956	138,916	19,470	0.71	1,670	1.2
1957	135,944	19,858	0.68	1,895	1.4
1958	136,208	20,256	0.67	1,647	1.2
1959	135,982	20,614	0.66	1.854	1.4
1960	160,600	20,959	0.77	1,900	1.2
1961	164,931	21,338	0.77	2,000x	1.2x
1962	160,371	21,726	0.74	2,100x	1.3x

COLOMBIA

Years	A	B	C	D	E
1955	--	13,441	--	320	--
1956	--	13,828	--	278	--
1957	14,769	14,223	0.10	349	2.4
1958	17,122	14,627	0.12	320	1.9
1959	19,383	15,042	0.13	350	1.8
1960	20,687	15,468	0.13	409	2.0
1961	24,371	15,908	0.15	474	1.9
1962	27,410	16,360	0.17	473	1.7

COSTA RICA

Years	A	B	C	D	E
1955	2,247	951	0.24	23	1.0
1956	2,179	988	0.22	35	1.6
1957	2,474	1,033	0.24	24	0.97
1958	3,111	1,076	0.29	25	0.80
1959	3,672	1,126	0.33	32	0.87
1960	3,828	1,173	0.33	30	0.78
1961	4,053	1,255	0.32	32x	0.79x
1962	4,419	1,305	0.34	34x	0.77x

CHART IV, CONTINUED

CHILE

Years	A	B	C	D	E
1955	16,971	6,761	0.25	387	2.3
1956	--	6,944	--	211	
1957	--	7,121	--	159(2)	--
1958	19,084	7,298	0.26	--	--
1959	21,681	7,465	0.29	210	0.9
1960	24,663	7,627	0.32	212	0.9
1961	25,612	7,802	0.33	208	0.8
1962	26,840x	7,987	0.32x	--	--

ECUADOR

Years	A	B	C	D	E
1955	5,697	3,691	0.15	94	1.6
1956	5,942	3,800	0.16	107	1.8
1957	6,448	3,929	0.16	97	1.5
1958	7,143	4,049	0.18	90	1.3
1959	8,040	4.169	0.19	--	--
1960	8,912	4,298	0.20	--	--
1961	10,245	4,455	0.23	108	1.0
1962	10,928	4,579	0.24	--	--

EL SALVADOR

Years	A	B	C	D	E
1955	1,126	2,108	0.05	13	1.2
1956	1,525	2,166	0.07	10	0.7
1957	1,336	2,231	0.06	17	1.3
1958	1,898	2,298	0.08	3	0.2
1959	2,134	2,367	0.09	14	0.7
1960	2,241	2,242	0.09	13	0.6
1961	2,536	2.520	0.10	16	0.6
1962	2,941	2,601	0.11	12	0.4

CHART IV, CONTINUED

PANAMA

Years	A	B	C	D	E
1955	2,226	914	0.24	41	1.8
1956	2,563	940	0.27	23	0.90
1957	2,929	967	0.29	26	0.92
1958	3,320	995	0.33	31	0.93
1959	3,419	1,024	0.33	23	0.67
1960	3,915	1,053	0.37	22	0.56
1961	4,227	1,084	0.39	29	0.69
1962	5,056	1,114	0.45	47	0.93

PERU

Years	A	B	C	D	E
1955	17,867	8,902	0.20	464	2.6
1956	20,188	9,130	0.22	481	2.4
1957	23,234	9,364	0.25	497	2.1
1958	22,438	9,604	0.23	--	--
1959	26,616	9,850	0.27	--	--
1960	29,270	10,098	0.29	--	--
1961	31,170x	10,365	0.30x		
1962	33,070x	10,642	0.31x	--	--

VENEZUELA

Years	A	B	C	D	E
1955	7,325	6,049	0.12	154	2.1
1956	8,834	6,309	0.14	161x	1.8x
1957	10,270	6,569	0.16	168x	1.6x
1958	16,126	6,829	0.24	419	2.6
1959	21,292	7,080	0.30	395	1.9
1960	24,320	7,331	0.33	571	2.3
1961	29,142	7,588	0.38	772	2.6
1962	31,692	7,858	0.40	774	2.4

CHART IV, CONTINUED

Meaning of the Columns:

(A) Total number of students enrolled in the university
(B) Estimated population of the country (thousands)
(C) Percentage relation between enrolled students and estimated population
(D) Number of graduates in law, economics, commerce and finances(1)
(E) Percentage relation between the number of graduates and students enrolled

Notes:

(1) Included the following professions: Law (Law and Jurisprudence), Economics, Commerce and Finances (Commercial, Banking, Public and Private Finances, Business Administration)

(2) From that year the figures refer only to the graduates of the Universidad de Chile, which comprise about 40% of Chile's university production

(x) These are estimated figures

Source:

1. Boletín Estadístico de América Latina, Volume I, No. 1, Cepal, Santiago, Chile, March, 1964.

2. Department of Statistics, Pan-American Union, Interamerican Institute of Statistics, Secretary General, O.A.S., Washington, D.C., 1964.

are developed by way of these disciplines. It is easy to appreciate from the charts the obvious differences existing between the nine Latin American countries.

When Chile is compared to countries not in Latin America, the situation is promising for an underdeveloped country of scarce financial resources. In fact, comparing the country's total population in the 20-24 age group with university enrollment figures for 1966, the percentage in Chile is 4% enrollment as contrasted to 13.2% in the United States, 9.4% in the Soviet Union, 5% in France, and 5.1% in the United Kingdom. It is estimated that in 1967, the total university enrollment in Chile will be approximately 41,000. All figures are estimates based on information obtained for the period 1957-1970, with adjustments made on the figures up to 1966.

UNIVERSITY CURRICULUM

Chart V presents the curriculum offered by the schools of economics, with a major in administration of the Universidad de Chile and the

CHART V

CURRICULUM CONTENT FOR A MAJOR IN ADMINISTRATION
AT TWO CHILEAN UNIVERSITIES

Universidad de Chile			Universidad Católica	
		First year Major Courses		
Semester 1	Semester 2		Semester 1	Semester 2
XXX	XXX	Economic Theory	XXX	XXX
XXX	XXX	Mathematics	XXX	XXX
XXX	XXX	Administration	XXX	
		Accounting		XXX
		Humanities Courses		
XXX		Introduction to the Social Sciences		
		Contemporary History	XXX	XXX
		Religious Culture	XXX	XXX
	XXX	Systematical Sociology		
		Second Year Major Courses		
XXX	XXX	Economic Theory		
		Money and Banking	XXX	
XXX	XXX	Mathematics	XXX	XXX
XXX	XXX	Accounting	XXX	XXX
	XXX	Administration	XXX	
		Price Theory		XXX
		Commercial Law		XXX
		Statistics		XXX
		Humanities Courses		
XXX		Social Psychology		
		Religious Culture	XXX	
		Third Year Major Courses		
XXX		Economical Development		
XXX	XXXQ	Statistics		XXX
XXX	XXX	Accounting	XXX	XXX
XXX	XXX	Labor Law		XXX
		Price Theory	XXX	
		Mathematics	XXX	
		Administration	XXX	XXX
	XXX	Chilean Economics		
		Monetary Theory		XXX
		Humanities Courses		
XXX		Political Science		
	XXX	Sociology		
		Religious Culture	XXX	

130

Universidad Católica de Chile, the most influential universities in the country.

From analysis of the course titles it is apparent that in spite of certain changes and modifications in the study plans, they are not adequate to effectively combat the needs peculiar to a country that wishes to break barriers impeding its development. The school directors point out that the plan of studies of the Universidad de Chile has taken into account the basic considerations contained in the studies by Robert Gordon and James Howell[3] and Frank Pierson and others[4] who have elaborated on the important elements needed for the development of modern executives.

The analysis of the curriculum shows that there is a preponderance of functional specialties over the courses in the humanities. Even though this does not confirm the fact that instruction in the schools of administration is more oriented toward the teaching of things than to the development of the individual, neither does it convince us that the result is totally different.

Other important elements that cannot be deduced from the study plans are the quality of the professors, course content and teaching methods. With regard to the first point, it should be indicated that both schools maintain permanent programs abroad for the development of faculty, even though there does not exist an effective method of utilizing these faculty upon their return. With reference to the course content and teaching methods, there exists a constant concern that a majority of the professors are employed on a part time basis.

In spite of these constraints, management education in Chile is improving. One of the principle disadvantages in the teaching of administration is the lack of comparative detailed analysis of the experiences of other countries such as is available to the fields of medicine and engineering. The preparation of the administrative leadership necessary to develop a country's organizations and institutions is much more complex and difficult than that required to train its scientists.

Still, there remains to be considered the pressing problems of developing entrepreneurs, which for Chile, as well as other emerging countries, is of vital importance. The development of entrepreneurs is not, by any means, the exclusive responsibility of the university. The entrepreneur can emerge from any educational level or specialty, and if by chance his success has some relation to his academic training, it may be fundamentally due to the merit of innate qualities which are complemented and improved by intellectual development.

David McClelland[4] associated managerial development with the type of education received, and it appears that the relation does not depend so much on the level of education, but on the degree to which the total education experience, in or out of school has been able to sufficiently activate the individual's needs for achievement.

BUSINESS AND MANAGERIAL RESOURCES

We have previously considered several aspects of managerial resource development relative to curricular origin. In this section we will analyze the point of view of several owner-managers and professional managers concerning the personnel for their firm's management positions.

The overwhelming majority of managers believed that the university preparation of their management employees was excessively theoretical in nature. The managers interviewed in the survey[5] indicated that the university student should better prepare himself to render practical solutions to the most common business problems. With this concept of their future management's needs, they felt administrative training should be increasingly oriented toward current concrete functional skills.

We might also conclude from the above managerial viewpoints that they do not anticipate utilizing management employees in the definition of policies, especially those policies concerning organizational structures more conducive to the encouragement of individual development.

Managers approve the short courses of executive training which emphasize specific administrative techniques such as personnel administration, accounting, finance, production, etc. They believe that these seminars are excellent for overcoming the inadequacies of university preparation and the hiatus existing between university theoretical education and their practical problems. This accounts for the great popularity of the short courses given by specialized institutions such as the Servicio de Cooperación Técnica e Industrial, an institution dependent on the Production Development Corporation, the Institute of Administration (INSORA), the Universidad dè Chile, and other institutions similar in character.

The Instituto Chileno de Administración Racional de Empresas (ICARE), an outstanding representative of this type of activity, currently offers the following program for executives:

1. Seminars related to the problems arising from the changes brought about by new government proposals or projects.

2. Small group seminars dealing with such subjects as production, finance, commerce, industrial relations, and general administration. These programs last approximately five days.

3. Seminars and courses concerning the same general topics, but of a longer duration, currently fluctuate between one to two months and eventually will involve full-time study. In the last six years, ICARE has sponsored 285 seminars of this type with approximately 8,000 participants. To this figure we must add at least 50% to reflect the total of such activities in Chile today.

4. To the above activities of ICARE, we must add seminars dedicated to specific sectors of industry, closed seminars

limited to specific firms as well as conferences, and forums and publications which complete their operations.

It is also interesting to point out that these extension services have been increasingly carried abroad. According to the data supplied by the Servicio de Cooperación Técnico e Industrial, during the years 1956-1966, more than 1,000 executives were trained in Paraguay, Honduras, Ecuador, Venezuela, Uruguay, Peru, and Panama.

Besides its consultation and investigation services to business, INSORA has extended its information service through Latin America by way of direct agreements with Colombia, Uruguay, El Salvador, and Argentina. More recently at INSORA, through an agreement with the Organization of American States, an administration program has been developed for students from all parts of the continent. INSORA also maintains a graduate administration program.

It can be generalized that the Chilean manager's concept of his executive employees' needs involves university training but with an orientation toward the development of middle management skills. There was little indication in the survey that a scarcity of higher level personnel for top management responsibilities existed. The above appears reconcilable with the previously cited information concerning management in Chile and is further supported by the following investigation.

THE DEMAND FOR MANAGERIAL RESOURCES: SOCIOLOGICAL ASPECTS.

In the first part of this work, mention was made of sociological characteristics which were believed to affect the selection and promotion of employees to higher executive levels in Chilean and Latin American firms. A recent investigation carried out by INSORA helps clarify and support the previous observations concerning these human problems in Chilean industrial development.[6]

A survey was made of 182 executives of Chilean businesses, statistically selected so that, in effect, over 300 businesses were represented. The questions principally dealt with how the individual achieved his high position in the business and his education. The analysis of this survey indicates that 35% of the executives possess college degrees. Of these, only 43.4% hold degrees directly related with administration. The rest of the degrees are distributed among other professions, not typically related to administration. It also concludes that approximately 80% of the executives attained their present position through family ties, personal relations or ownership in the business. The maximum education of 61% of these executives was not beyond the secondary level. The data further indicated that, in general, the highest educational levels were achieved by those executives whose familial ties did not influence their employment or promotion. In this group, 57.5% have completed their university education.

Those individuals prepared by the university to undertake executive functions may not only find their careers impaired by the different

133

conceptions and values of managers and the universities as to what should be taught, but by an alarming lack of social mobility in the private sector itself. This study does not postulate that simply because an individual has completed university studies he is thereby necessarily capable of assuming executive responsibilities. However, it seeks to point out that today in Chile higher education, talent and experience is often not sufficient to qualify him for many upper executive positions. In fact, the existing extended familial selection process, in our judgment, is retarding Chilean aspirations for achievement and must be considered as a major constraint to social and economic development.

NOTES AND REFERENCES

1. Investment in Chile. Basic Information for United States Businessmen, U. S. Department of Commerce, 1960.

2. "Pensamiento Político y Acción del Ejecutivo Industrial en Chile," INSORA (Unpublished).

3. Robert A. Gordon and James E. Howell, Higher Education for Business, New York: Columbia University Press, 1959.

4. Frank C. Pierson and others, The Education of the American Businessman, New York: McGraw-Hill Book Company, Inc., 1959.

5. "Pensamiento Político y Acción del Ejecutivo Industrial en Chile," INSORA (Unpublished).

6. Ibid.

CHAPTER VI

MANAGERIAL RESOURCE DEVELOPMENT IN MEXICO

Stanley M. Davis

Development is revolutionary, and revolution, in the true sense, must be social, political, and economic. Political goals and economic activity must be translated into social reality. Social change, beyond welfare benefits, better health conditions and more education, means a change in the organization, institutions, and values of men. In a rapidly growing urban-industrial nation, commerce and industry result in the development of complex forms of social organization. They also reflect newly differentiated systems of values appropriate to particular roles which parallel an extensive division of labor.

The thesis of this chapter is that the development of managerial resources occurs more truly through these generalized processes of social change than through specific advances within the field of formal management education itself. In order to understand how these processes occur, we must enter into the industrial enterprise and examine change and development at this level. Our efforts, therefore, will concentrate on changes in the social environment and their effects upon managerial development and performance at the workplace. We will examine the stratification system within industrial firms in Mexico, paternal relations between managers and workers, and the characteristic system of authority and control. The concluding section will discuss the relation of our findings to the future development and performance of management and to some implications for business management education. A brief historical review will help set the stage for the analysis, and those already familiar with Mexican history may want to proceed directly to page 139.

Social Change and Mexican Development

Spanish domination of Middle America began in 1519.[1] The aims of the Conquest were economic, religious, and political; or more colloquially, gold, souls, and subjects. The attainment of these goals ultimately rested upon the management and control of the indigenous population, but by 1650 six-sevenths of the Indian population--over ten million people--had been wiped out. The utopian hope of the Conquest turned into a catastrophe. The Indians suffered defeat, exploitation, biological collapse, and deculturation. Partly in consequence, trade also suffered, and by the seventeenth century Middle America had relapsed into a system of rural isolation and restricted markets.

At this time, two new patterns of social integration emerged: the hacienda, the large and privately owned landed estate of the colonist, and the república de indios, the tightly-knit Indian peasant communities. These two systems of social organization lasted well into the nineteenth century, never achieving a synthesis of the conquering and the indigenous cultures. Instead, there existed a perpetually hostile symbiotic relationship between the two forms, and the new social and economic order was based upon a fixed dichotomy of a small number of landlords and a large number of peons. Relations between the two were paternal. They involved reciprocal obligations of responsibility and subordination, respectively, and they were highly personalized even though they existed for basically instrumental reasons.

Although this form of organization and the values which supported it have undergone great changes in the past three centuries, its essential features still permeate much of Mexican society today. For the mass of peasant communities, economic activity is deeply imbedded in the social framework and has little or no intrinsic meaning outside of it. There is a minimal utilization of technology; production is for subsistence and a means of securing one's place in the religious-political system, rather than for capital accumulation and exchange in far-flung markets. The scheme of life is considered natural and unchanging, and one's position in it is determined by birth. Activities are not separated into distinct spheres; rather, there is a common set of values appropriate to most aspects of a man's life, and highly prescribed means of fulfilling them.

Despite the resurgence of mining, trade, and production for export, when Spanish colonialism ended in 1810, Mexico was forced back into a reliance on the countryside. With continual increases in population, however, the subsistence Indian community produced a surplus population which moved off the land and into the city, out of a tightly knit community and into the mushrooming urban mass. This movement did not create a middle class or a proletariat, but rather an alienated mass of individuals who learned to live by their wits. The rootless mestizo, not the white landlord or the Indian peasant, became the true child of the future Mexico.

The period of early nationalism was characterized by severe political instability and the violent rule of regional caudillos (strongmen). Force and economic power were wedded together, while the leaders of the country searched for a national identity and sought to overcome the basic social and economic polarities of Indian and European, feudal and capitalist, worlds. Economic development was still an unheard-of and impractical notion, but the economic stranglehold of the Church was broken during this period.

The dictatorship of Porfirio Díaz (1876-1910) brought political stability, national unification, and the awakening of economic progress to Mexico. It also brought paternal and despotic rule, the suppression of the peasantry and of any labor organization or agitation and, ultimately, provocation for the Mexican Revolution. During this time, foreign investment was encouraged and protected, and Mexico's foreign credit rating soared as the expansion of exports created a favorable balance of payments. Internal transportation was improved, particularly through the development of the railroads, domestic incomes rose, and domestic markets broadened. The state played a largely passive role, keeping adverse elements in line through patronage and privilege, and guaranteeing security and stability to large private enterprise.

136

The Revolution exploded in 1910 and called for social and political reform. The power of the landbarons, the generals, the Church, and the foreigner had to be curbed. The psychology of Mexican rule called for "all power or no power," and the leadership embarked upon a course of either incorporating diverse interest groups into the revolutionary party or, if that failed, crushing them. Under Plutarco Calles (1924-1928), special interest groups such as labor unions and government employees were granted a legitimate role in the party structure, and by the reign of Lázaro Cárdenas (1934-1940) no major group was either cut out completely or strong enough to dominate the central government. Cárdenas, however, differed significantly from Calles on two important matters: land reform and the role of organized business.

While Calles favored small private farms, Cárdenas preferred the communally-owned ejido. The Cárdenas program dealt the coup de grace to the hacienda system and signaled revolutionary change in landholding principles. By 1940, half the crop land and half the rural population of Mexico were included within the various communal units. The flaw in the program lay in the unproductive size of the small units; the ejido has been a political success and an economic failure.

Following the policy of co-optation, Cárdenas also drew organized business into the political system. All enterprises above a minimum size were required to be members of a national trade association chamber, whose job it was to maintain a bridge between government and business. The Mexican business entrepreneur was now given a public role. Simultaneously, the role of foreign capital was brought under harness; foreign investment in the development of Mexico was welcomed, so long as it was on Mexican terms. The expropriation of the oil industry in 1939 represented the triumph of economic nationalism. In 1944, Avila Camacho consolidated the transformation by decreeing that 51% Mexican ownership was required in companies where foreign investment was involved.[2]

Mexico sustained its economic growth, and in an anomalous fashion, the revolution was about to become an institution: the Party of the Mexican Revolution became the Party of the Institutionalized Revolution (PRI). Mexicanism became part of the revolutionary creed, as did racial and religious tolerance. The mestizo came into prominence. Public education, literacy, social security, and medical care were to be available to everyone. A tremendous sense of optimism spread over Mexico.

The loosening of traditional ties to the land swelled the ranks of migrants coming to the cities. Rapid population growth, due to a reduction of the death rate and a continuing high birth rate, added to the rural overflow into the cities. In 1910 Mexico was 22% urban, by 1950 it was 43% urban, and today the figure is well over 50%. Between 1910 and 1950, urban population expanded 153%, compared to a 37% rise in rural population. Mexico's rate of national increase has been sufficient to double its population in less than twenty-four years, and the growth rate of the Federal District (Mexico City) alone doubles its population in less than twelve years. Almost half of Mexico City's workers are migrants from rural areas and from small towns and cities.

Traditional Mexico was rapidly becoming a modern urban and industrial society. Economic activity was now explicitly oriented toward
expansion and pecuniary reward rather than directly subordinate to the
social order. Occupation was replacing kinship and property as the
major index of social stratification. Holders of "middle class" occupations, such as skilled workers, clerks, government employees, small
businessmen, and professionals, were growing more rapidly than the
population at large. The total labor force increased from 53% of the
population in 1940 to 62% in 1960; and of this figure, agricultural
workers declined from 64% in 1940 to 52% in 1960. The percentage of
women in the labor force went from 8 in 1940 to 17 by 1960. Of all
the changes, those in manufacturing were the greatest. By 1960, the
industrial sector (including petroleum and electrical power industries)
accounted for one-quarter of the gross national product. Moreover, the
relative importance of salaried employees, as opposed to wage laborers,
has increased significantly.

Despite these advances, however, it is frequently argued that
increased wages for the labor force were sacrificed in favor of capital
accumulation and forced savings.[3] The controversy between increased
purchasing power for the worker versus increased production with a lid
on wages has been perhaps the major economic issue in Mexico for the
past twenty years.[4] Miguel Alemán (1946-1952) turned decidedly to
rapid industrialization. World War II had provided considerable opportunities for manufacturing entrepreneurs, under the cover of inflation,
and Alemán sought to continue this industrial development. The private
sector (including foreign capital) was encouraged under the protective
guidance of the state, which reduced risks and removed bottlenecks.
Mexicans became willing to invest in Mexican industry, even in commercial agriculture, and foreign investors now sought to sell their
manufactures in the Mexican market.

Devaluation of the _peso_ to its present-day parity of 8 cents
brought about a period of economic restraint in the 1950's. To Adolfo
Ruíz Cortines (1952-1958), therefore, fell the job of simultaneously
avoiding inflation while raising the purchasing power of the Mexican
worker. On the production versus consumption issue, he still favored
the former; but the lot of the people was to be bettered, not through
direct pay raises as much as through indirect welfare benefits--better
social and job security, clinics, irrigation projects, and price ceil-
ings on basic commodities.

The debates in Mexico between production and consumption, between
more egalitarian distribution of incomes or capital accumulation and
forced savings, between price controls or principles of demand and
supply, between public ownership or private enterprise, and between
industrialization or agricultural reform, have raged in Mexico since
the 1940's. They have been particularly prominent during the period
of Adolfo López Mateos (1958-1964). The debates are reflected in the
positions of two groups: the _técnicos_ who urge increased industrialization and the extension of government powers into economic affairs,

and the _políticos_ who hold to a more middle-road position and seek a broad popular consensus of the various public and interest groups.[5]

The ups and downs of the Mexican economy are variously identified as outcomes of the seesawing differences between these points of view, and future growth hinges largely in the balance. Despite the variations, however, the success of Mexico's development remains an irrefutable fact that has been of great interest to all the underdeveloped and developing nations of Latin America, Africa, and Asia. With this background in mind, we now turn to the analysis.

Values and Stratification

In this section, we will examine the social stratification of the Mexican firm. Most theories of change from traditional to modern societies include the development of a highly differentiated and open system of _social stratification_. In traditional societies, social stratification is portrayed (in ideal-type form) as a fixed dichotomy of a small number of landlords and a large number of peasants. Modern society, on the other hand, is said to have a complex division of labor where there are many intermediate strata, where the distinctions and separations between them are not so sharp, and where passage from one stratum to another (vertical social mobility) increases.

From the perspective of the social sciences, the key questions have then focused on analyzing the transition from one to the other. Taken from the outline of this model, for example, how do intermediate strata develop, what are the bases for differentiation between them, and what are some of the conditions for passage? Understanding impediments to this process can be equally instructive: what inhibits the growth of a complex, equalitarian, and open stratification system? From the perspective of business management, on the other hand, the hierarchy of job functions within an enterprise may be seen as a reflection of the social hierarchy in society at large. The corresponding questions for management study therefore become: how do middle levels of supervision develop; what are the bases for differentiation between workers and first line supervisors, and between upper, middle, and lower levels of management; are first line supervisors considered members of the lower level of management?

Also characteristic of theories of modernization are changes in the _values_ of a culture. From a traditional emphasis on acceptance of things as they are and a common set of values appropriate to most aspects of a man's life, the values of modern society stress choice and change, and differentiated values appropriate to particular social roles. The utility of the general model thus rests upon its ability to specify the core values in one historical time and place, the conditions under which they are most likely to change, and the factors impeding such change.

A third topic of theories of change is _industrialization_, the growing dominance of industry as the basis for social organization. The industrial enterprise, here, serves as a reflection of the changes occurring in society at large. This section treats two features

139

central to models of social change, values and social stratification, within Mexican industrial firms. It analyzes some of their key elements and focuses on how they influence one another. The theme is the relation of organizational structure to general values and common aspects of social stratification in Mexican society. From an understanding of this relation we will be better able to assess the development of Mexican managerial resources.

Empleados and Obreros. The most basic distinction made in the stratification system in all Mexican industrial firms is between empleados and obreros. In English, this distinction is variously known as that between non-manual and manual, salaried and wage earner, white collar and blue collar, office worker and factory worker, non-union and union, respectively. The distinction between these two groups in Mexico, however, has greater significance than the English terms can suggest. It is essential for understanding this culture's system of social stratification in factories and society. It draws the basic line of division in the hierarchy of a firm and reflects the social hierarchy of the society at large.

One way of describing the difference is that empleados generally earn more, have greater prestige, and occupy superior authority positions. From another point of view, however, the difference does not evolve around these common indices of social stratification. These are seen as reflections of a general cultural implication that empleados and obreros are different kinds of people. The former, more democratic, interpretation implies that the differences are of degree, not of a kind, and that mobility is a definite possibility. The second statement, on the other hand, is more tradition-bound and more authoritarian. It implies that the differences are natural and fixed, or at least ought to be; they are "ascribed." In reality, there is a mixture of both views involved in the distinction between empleados and obreros.

In a firm stratified according to traditional distinctions, management rules because it is "entitled to rule," as one respondent put it. Acceptance of this rule on the part of the workers also implies a traditional mentality; each party knows his place. Indeed, the barrier between the two groups is rather caste-like.

In traditional firms, especially large ones, one may think in terms of two stratification hierarchies. These two are the worlds of the empleado and the obrero. Since there is usually little possibility of crossing this line, in the traditional firm it is more meaningful to think of differences within each group as class differences, and between the two groups as caste differences. Vertical mobility within a firm is generally limited within each of the two hierarchies, and although this barrier diminishes with modernization, it simultaneously acts as an inhibitor to such open hierarchies.

The caste differences, however, are basically economic and cultural, not racial, and no "pure" caste system is implied.[6] They are manifested in various ways. In one firm, for example, there were separate but equivalent bathrooms for employees and for workers, side by side; in another firm, there were separate dining rooms, also side by side, which operated identically; in a third firm, some employees refused to ride in the same company bus that brought workers to their jobs, feeling that it was beneath their dignity and status.

In less traditional firms, the separation between empleados and obreros is less sharp, and distinctions are more a matter of degree. The general notion is that management rules because it has achieved a higher level of skill, education, preparation, and the like. This is similar to, but not identical with, the conceptual contrast between "ascription" and "achievement." What is achieved is a kind of education, not an amount of education. The Spanish term educación refers to a general quality of culture and breeding, not unlike the Greek word paideia, meaning both culture and education. A very common criticism of workers is that they are mal educado or mal preparado, meaning that they have no breeding and not that they are technically untrained. The implication here is that if they had received or assimilated the broader sense of education, then their technical training would not be a problem.

Whether the difference, then, is considered one of degree and amenable to change, or one of kind and appropriate as such, in both cases there is a sense of qualitative difference between empleados and obreros. In one view the quality is considered immutable; in the other it is not.

This sense of the qualitative difference between employees and workers is well illustrated in the case of a traditional firm headed by a very authoritarian owner-manager. This owner nostalgically looks back to the days before the Revolution, "when the worker unconditionally loved the man who paid him," and then looks with disdain upon the situation today, where "the lower class people think they can get away with murder in the labor unions." There is a considerable degree of antagonism between management and labor, in general, and this is manifested in a variety of ways: the workers on each shift are searched before leaving the "mill"; there is a high rate of absenteeism, and a management-directed shake-up system to fill the empty slots; some of the workers are machine breakers and others are "stool pigeons" for management; no worker is completely trusted, and if he has joined the union, he is not trusted at all.

Forms of worker protest, such as absenteeism, theft and sabotage, are characteristic of early periods of industrialization and are common among uncommitted workers.[7] Although the workers in this case are generally committed to earning a livelihood in industry, however, management's attitudes and practices have created a situation more typical of mill life 150 years ago in Britain, 100 years ago in North America, and fifty years ago in Mexico.

The example of this company is instructive because of the way in which it differentiates empleados from obreros. It is well expressed by one of the lower level managers who distinguishes between a moral and a material sense of confianza. To have confidence in a man in the moral sense is "to honor and respect his human rights and internal values," while to have confidence in a man in the material sense "involves a sense of the right of property and a trust in his workmanship."

141

In this traditional firm, management applies the moral sense of <u>confianza</u> to <u>empleados</u> only, and when it exists at all, applies only the material sense of <u>confianza</u> to <u>obreros</u>.[8] Again, we see the notion of qualitative difference.

From another perspective, the difference of quality is an artifact of a difference by definition. In this case, <u>empleado</u> is a shortening of the term <u>empleado de confianza</u>, often simply <u>confianza</u>, which translates "trusted employee." Apart from the translation, there are two different meanings attached to the term. The earlier and more literal meaning derives from the time when virtually all management was by the ownership. An empleado de confianza, then, was a non-related employee in which the owning-management had a degree of confidence and trust. This feeling and relationship had developed over a very long time, was often of a pseudo-familiar nature, and was limited to very few people. Sometimes these <u>confiados</u> were part of a limited managerial structure; others may have been at lower levels such as the cashier or night-watchman. But they were not ordinary workers because a degree of personal responsibility was involved, something which was absent in an <u>obrero's</u> role. This meaning still exists in the more traditional firms today.

The second definition of <u>empleado de confianza</u> gained relevance vis-a-vis the existence of unions. It refers to anyone in the firm (where there is a union) who is <u>not</u> a union member. In firms without unions, this meaning has less relevance, but is rapidly gaining ascendancy. The theoretical legal status of an individual has less meaning than the personal assessment given by the head of the organization. Still, this latter definition, made formal by the government, has affected how people think of informal status differences. Rather than emphasizing the different nature of each group, it defines <u>empleados de confianza</u> only by the feature of not being union members. It creates a legal distinction from what had been a traditional one. While previously there had been employees, a few of whom were <u>de confianza</u>, the law recognized no such distinction and thus helped strip the term of its earlier and more literal meaning. By differentiating only between <u>empleados de confianza</u> and <u>obreros</u>, the effect swelled the ranks of the former and thus reduced its traditional significance proportionately.

The change, then, from a fixed status difference to a difference by changing degree and definition had two results. Reducing the meaningfulness and expanding the membership of the <u>empleado de confianza</u> category had a democratizing effect; by weakening the traditional barriers it nourished the openness necessary for industrial advancement. By making the difference formal and legal, on the other hand, it strengthened in some cases the barrier between the two groups, thus minimizing mobility. This latter effect, however, was both weaker and more delayed. Moreover, it may be argued that it sped up the awareness, independence, and strength of labor as an organized and legitimate force.

Once the difference rests upon role definition, and is not considered within the "nature of things," basic indices of stratification are pertinent to the analysis, for they are then more determining of

one's station than they are determined by it. Apart from the clear
cases of true _empleados_ and of unionized _obreros_, there are large numbers of people whose positions in the industrial hierarchy are not crys-
tallized; each has a disproportionate mix of class, status and power.

Let us illustrate some of these distinctions by looking at a number
of examples within a single firm, the NORSA company. The case of one
worker is exemplary. He was with the firm a number of years and did his
job well. Management wanted to reward him, and so he was promoted to
the rank of _empleado de confianza_. His work remained exactly the same
and he still punched a time clock, but he no longer wore the union
coveralls and he could eat in the _empleado_ dining hall although he felt
more comfortable with his co-workers. His earnings were now salaried
rather than based on a daily wage, and he was given a slight raise. Most
important of all, he gained a considerable amount of prestige by just
being of _empleado de confianza_ status.

When the union contract was renegotiated (every two years, by law),
the disproportionate aspects of his position rose to the fore. He
found that his fellow workers, who were still in the union, received a
10% wage increase, while he was only given an extra 200 _pesos_ yearly,
equivalent to less than one week's salary (less than 2%). Through time,
his salary slowly increased in an absolute sense, but decreased relative
to the cost of living and to the gains made by his co-workers. He went
to the personnel department to complain and got nowhere; he could no
longer go to the union representative. He was odd man out, and truly
represented by neither major power group--labor or management. In
effect, he had traded money and power for prestige, and he began to
feel that he could not eat prestige.

Another example from the same firm points up the disproportionate
mix in power which may occur between _empleados_ and _obreros_. This was
the case of a fifty-year old laborer whom we shall call Díaz. Díaz had
an excellent record of long standing, and several years ago had been
promoted to _empleado_ rank. One day while in the company shower room, he
found two _obreros_ who had started a fire and were taking torches to burn
down the factory. Because the company dealt with highly explosive sub-
stances, this action was doubly dangerous. Fortunately, Díaz was able
to put out the fire and stop the two men from going further. This incident eventually found its way back to the head of the personnel department, who immediately brought charges against the two men in order to
have them fired. The personnel manager then told Díaz that he would
have to appear at the Labor Legislation Board in three days to testify
against these men and hence justify the company's petition for dismissal
without indemnity payment. What he failed to tell Díaz, however, were
the reasons why these men should be punished and why his testimony was
required.

Hearing about these developments later that day, the two _obreros_ in
question stopped Díaz and asked him not to say anything that would make
them lose their jobs, telling him that they have families to support and
that they didn't know what they were doing. Díaz agreed and, at the
trial, changed his story around. Lacking evidence, the men were acquit-
ted of the charges, and the company could not fire them. Shortly

thereafter, one of the two men ruined $16,000 (dollars at cost price) of a substance, which represented a serious loss to the company.

Angered by these events, the personnel manager then decided that he was going to fire Díaz for having changed his story. For months, at the time of the interviewing, Díaz had therefore been under pressure; and the more nervous he got, the poorer his work became. Because he was in an _empleado_ he did not have the support of the union on his side; and he was in an even worse fix than the worker in the first example.

The implications of this case went far beyond the concerns of the three men involved. It reflected a general dissatisfaction in management-labor relations and, for our purposes, pointed up the important differences between _empleados_ and _obreros_. Díaz had saved the company from a disaster, and he was seen as a good and brave man in the eyes of his co-workers, while the other two men were generally considered undesirables. Still, it was Díaz that the company was now trying to fire, and no longer the two men. A strong sentiment therefore developed among the workers that it was better, and safer, to be in the union than out of it; perhaps you would not get promoted, but at least your job was secure. The incident reflected the interplay between the changing values of the personnel and the changing system of social stratification in the industrial firm.

These cases are by no means unique to Mexico, and other examples of disproportionate indices of stratification reveal the similarities to universal trends. Office boys, for example, have very low pay and no power whatsoever, yet by their position as _empleados de confianza_ they have begun above the basic dividing line of the industrial hierarchy, and are therefore able to rise. More than likely, their fathers are from the _obrero_ class, earning more than their sons and holding some power because of their seniority among the workers, but frozen at the top of the bottom half of the structure. Secretaries, too, are above the line, yet their major prerequisite as _empleados_ is prestige. The foreman is the classic example of the man caught between in the process of stratifying a firm, and we turn to him next.

In sum, the most striking distinction in the stratification of Mexican firms is the dichotomy drawn by the line between employees and workers. Although the line is not always clear, it is basic. While its roots are in the traditional social structure, it nonetheless represents an adaptation to the developing industrial structure. Finally, it suggests that stratification dichotomies are real, rather than over-simplifications and that they severely restrict the potential develop-ment of manpower resources. It should be noted, however, that they are more applicable to earlier periods of industrial development and become less sharp through time.

The _Problem_ at _the_ Middle: The _Foreman_. In some senses the distinc-tion between _empleados de confianza_ and _obreros_ is coterminus with the separation between management and labor. One may ask if foremen are _empleados_ or _obreros_, or he may ask if foremen are lowest-level manage-ment or highest-level workers. The two questions carry the same impli-cation: are foremen above or below the basic dividing line? Answering each question by the general pattern, they are supposed to be _empleados_, but for most practical purposes are not, and they are in almost no sense management.

Foremen are officially considered empleados, yet it is common to find them punching a time clock, hanging their clothes in the same place as the obreros, being paid by a daily wage, and receiving wage increases proportionate to union gains. They are not union members, but many of the indices of obreros status are applicable to them. In many senses they are like the workers discussed above who were promoted to employee status. The major difference, however, is that they are supervisors; their job is to see that the work is carried out, but they do no physical labor themselves. As the immediate link between management and the work force, they are the key figures in maintaining a smooth rhythm in factory operations.

In the overwhelming majority of Mexican firms, supervisors are promoted directly from the ranks of the workers, and in many this is written into the requirements of the union contract. Management's attitude about this is usually the same: when you promote a worker to foreman, you lose a good worker and gain a poor foreman. By taking a good worker and rewarding him with this promotion, you have changed his position but not his person. Clothes alone do not make the man.

Regarding their person, foremen are generally described as being of two types. For simplicity, we will call them duro (hard) and humilde (humble). The "hard" type is young and aggressive. He has little experience in leading men, perhaps some formal education, but no general educación or style of behavior with which to generate respect. To all around him, his entire manner, his way of life, is the same as that of his fellow workers. He has been placed in a higher role, but has not been socialized to it. His job is to see that the workers carry out the orders passed down to them, but with no preparation on how he is to do so. His position has given him power, but not the knowledge to carry the orders out. In consequence, he is too rough with the men.

The most common remark about the trouble with a foreman is that "he doesn't know how to give an order;" indeed, he orders (ordenar) rather than requests (pedir). Emphasis is seldom placed on a lack of technical knowledge, but rather on how he treats people. Above all, a manager must know how to handle people, how to treat each one according to his station in life. When a supervisor lacks this knowledge two things are known: he is of worker origin, and he can never be a manager.

The "humble" supervisor is older and completely non-aggressive. He has a great deal of experience, perhaps no formal education, but a little general educación. He gets on with the men in his work group much better than the "hard" supervisor. He is not at all rough on his men; he doesn't have to be. He has generally won their respect, and they call him maestro. He began as a worker and life has rewarded him; he has gained the respect of both superiors and subordinates. He knows how to treat people, each according to their station, but he is also well aware of his own station. Humility is a virtue, and one which he has. But virtue in excess becomes a vice, and for those above he is too humble to be an effective leader. He, too, is still a worker and can never be a manager.

The distinction between these two types is important because, as different as they are in some respects, both bring characteristics from their background which distinguish them from management and prevent their becoming part of it. Despite this marginality, however, foremen are generally not the group most dissatisfied with their job; indeed, they are often among the more satisfied. Unlike the worker who is promoted from the union to employee rank, the man who is promoted to the level of foreman has made real gains. Still, he measures the gains with the yardstick of the worker, and from this reference he is not likely to make a dent on the managerial structure.

Given an increased division of labor and a loosening of traditional social structures, the divisions between social classes become less sharp but more numerous. Taking the hierarchies of an industrial firm and of society at large as reflections of one another, then general industrial development presages the more complex stratification of both. Following this line of reasoning, one would expect the rapid development of middle levels in the society at large. But our analysis of one such middle level, the development of the foreman role, does not support this line of reasoning. The growth of industrial enterprises seems to reflect a growing gap in education and cultural background between management and labor. The result is a bigger gap in the middle, and as it grows the foreman has thus far fallen to the side of a glorified obrero.

The situation, however, is neither dismal nor unique. It reflects a lag between needs of an industrial structure and the time and resources available to fill them. Lack of qualified foremen, and the treatment of foremen as nothing more than senior laborers, is common to early periods of development. It is a reflection of the general lack of managerial resources at all levels.[9] Literature about the foreman as the forgotten man in industry overlooks the fact that he must be created before he can be forgotten. A highly differentiated and developed managerial structure is the luxury of a considerable industrial heritage. The lack of adequately prepared management at lower levels presupposes the need for such management, and this need is only beginning to realize itself.

Scattered instances where foremen are hired directly from technical schools, where elementary management practices are mixed in with basic technical training, reveal strong identifications with management and few complaints about the appropriate treatment of subordinates. However, union regulations in some firms and industries require that foremen must be men promoted from obrero ranks. This renews the problem of an hiatus in cultural backgrounds, and creates poor rapport between the foremen and his immediate superior. It limits the freedom of management to look outside the enterprise for qualified managerial personnel. It also emphasizes investment in the human factor which brings no immediate or specifically quantifiable returns, factors which are very salient to businessmen in general and particularly in Mexico. Moreover, it forces the realization that if supervisors are to occupy a meaningful place between labor and management they must be developed; they cannot be created by a role definition.

In sum, the idea that good supervisors are an important key to a smoothly functioning plant, but that this key group does not exist in any developed form, is largely a result of rapid and recent industrial growth. What makes the development of the supervisor's role particularly important for our analysis is that it represents the most difficult transition to make because it is the one which must bridge the greatest cultural gap in the traditional social structure. The real problem in this regard, or rather its solution, still lies in the future.

Terms of Reference and Address. The analysis thus far has led us to examine ways in which general cultural values affect the organization of some Mexican industrial firms and, in consequence, their system of social stratification. Of particular importance have been the meanings attached to actions and manners appropriate to each place in the organization. One form of behavior particularly important to Mexican organization, though it has received minor attention in the analysis of U.S. organizations, is the way in which people address one another.[10] Terms of reference and address provide ways of analyzing relations in an industrial structure which are, at the same time, simple, informative, and intrinsic to the social context. The most meaningful for us are the ones that workers use in addressing and referring to the boss and vice versa, for they get more at the content of the relationship involved.

The title of address for the head of an enterprise varies in each Latin country, and in Mexico three terms predominate: jefe, gerente, and patrón. Gerente is sometimes reserved for the top few managers, and jefe used for those at middle levels. The gerencia, moreover, generally refers to ownership aspects of management, while jefes are usually employed management. These terms are purely instrumental labels; patrón is not. The meanings and appropriate usage of patrón are more numerous and complex.

A patrón is an employer. The term is therefore closely tied to ownership, if not in fact then in the mind of the user of the term. The man who uses the term patrón does not separate the man from the office or the company. If you have a patrón, you work for him personally. So there is also an element of strong personal identification. "Anybody can be a jefe," said one manager, "but to be a patrón you have to be liked, or perhaps disliked. I mean, they have to feel something emotional about you." The feeling is usually positive and thought of by the boss as a compliment. If it is not taken favorably, the term will almost never be used to address the man directly and seldom used to refer to him either. Not only must the subordinate want his superior to play the role of his patrón, but the man must also want to assume this role.

When patrón is used expressively,[11] it is the result of a relationship built over a long time. "If a new man replaced Don Ramón, people would speak of him as the jefe; after they'd known him a bit, and got to like him, they'd think of him as patrón too."

The production manager of one plant had recently been brought in from the Far East. In his previous job, the men used to call him twan, "lord," while they called the head of the company, whom they didn't like very much, "sir." This new manager was called and referred to as jefe at the time of the interviewing, but there were already predictions that he would gain acceptance and be called <u>patrón</u>.

Whereas <u>jefe</u> means boss, <u>patrón</u> means both boss and benefactor. The <u>patrón</u> has the responsibility to protect and help those who consider him such. When the term is used, there is a constant interplay between this instrumental function and the expressive nature of the relation involved. There are occasions, however, when an individual will employ the term for strictly instrumental reasons. "He will only address me as <u>patrón</u> when he feels that he really has to impress me."

A similar, though less commented upon, difference exists in the way that managers refer to workers. Managers who refer to them as <u>obreros</u> or <u>trabajadores</u> define the workers in terms of the functional service they provide. Other managers, however, refer to workers as <u>muchachos</u> (boys) and some address them as such. The use of <u>muchacho</u> involves three things. It is a paternalistic term, considering the worker like a child, regardless of his age. It is expressive; there is an affectionate quality relating to the paternal; he is a person, a whole being, and not just a productive unit. It may be used demeaningly in the way that racial discrimination has the upper-caste boss referring to the lower-caste worker as "boy." Which aspect predominates over any other depends upon the individual and is reflected in the structure.

It would be misleading to assume that management of a firm in Mexico is paternal and/or authoritarian, or that expressive or instrumental characteristics predominate, on the basis of terminological preferences alone. A portrait of Mexican managerial values and the basis for a firm's stratification does begin to emerge when one jointly considers the manner of distinction between <u>empleados</u> and <u>obreros</u>, the consideration of the role and personality of the foreman, and the choice and content of terms of reference and address.

Minimizing qualitative distinctions between types of men, emphasizing role functions, and avoiding invidious patterns of address are likely to develop concurrently and are indicators of a decline in the traditional basis for Mexican industrial stratification. But the development of modern organization, run by industrial man, and led by professional management still contains the Mexican character which its culture has imbedded in it. The implications of these changes in stratification patterns for social relations between managers and workers are analyzed in the following sections on paternalism and on authority and control.

Paternalism

<u>Paternalism</u>.[12]   Paternalism, here, broadly refers to the reciprocal relations of responsibility and subordination between manager and worker, respectively. In its fullest formulation, the security and welfare of the worker is taken care of in return for the latter's willingness to take orders, owe allegiance, and work hard. The hierarchical element involved in the superior-subordinate relationship suggests something comparable to a father's behavior toward his son, and also reflects Mexico's earlier social structure and cultural tradition.

Bennett and Ishino describe the general phenomenon of paternalism in the following way:

> Two features appear to characterize paternalistic economic organizations wherever they are found: (1) There is a hierarchy which is greater than the minimal amount that any employer-employee relationship should display. That is, the status difference between employer and employee is not purely a matter of instrumental necessity, but contains a cultural or ideological element which suggests that the employer is more than just an employer: he is a 'superior' person in control because of his superiority. (2) The second general characteristic is the concern showed by the employer over aspects of the lives of his employees which have nothing to do with the actual work performed, or the organization in which it is being performed. That is, he is responsible in some way for his workers and, in most cases, for their families.[13]

Eric Wolf traces the roots of this cultural or ideological element in Mexico to the system of colonial rule imposed by the Spaniard upon the Indian.

> Upon the twin foundations of landownership and peonage, the colonists thus erected their new edifice, the mainstay of their new social order.... The peon was dependent on the owner, both economically and psychologically. He abrogated his right to decide his own fate; the owner of the hacienda became his guardian and judge, as well as his employer.
>
> The hacienda achieved this end by elevating the hacienda owner to the role of a stern and irascible father, prepared to guide the steps of his worker-children, ready to unleash his temper and anger upon them when provoked. As long as the worker remained dependent and submissive, he received his just reward: a sum of money, a draft of pulque, a plot for growing corn. When he rebelled against authority, or provoked its anger, he was tied to the whipping post, possessed by every hacienda, and cruelly lashed. Thus the hacienda bound men not only through debts or through force, but also through ties of love and hate. ...Given the appropriate social conditions, men make peons of themselves.[14]

The disappearance of a feudal landlord system in Mexico "was not due to the advent of more business-like managers or absentee owners, but rather to the fact that the management of the plantation no longer held the reins of power in the regional and national society."[15] It was killed by the Revolution of 1910, but its persistence for centuries created a distinct hierarchy of superiors and subordinates and produced a dependency mentality, a psychological vulnerability that still permeates much of worker relationships with management today.

Several other factors also influenced the growth of paternalism in Mexico. Geographic isolation and political regionalism, strong until well after the Revolution, added more importance to the presence of strong individual leaders than to institutionalized and impersonal structures of government control. The industrialization of Mexico is of rather recent vintage, and is concentrated largely around the central valley. Economic forms of organization, which are restricted to outlying regions and are associated with only indirect and local market competition, which utilize labor intensive techniques, and which have low levels of production and a scarcity of jobs, are other sources. Among the workers, low levels of education, skill, and wages, a marginal or subsistence existence, and a lack of alternative means for attaining a livelihood provide more reasons for the development of paternalistic systems, with a strong degree of hierarchy.

The strength of the hierarchical element conveys the expectation that, although mutual obligations do exist, the subordinate owes more to his superior than vice versa. This notion points up the two faces of paternalism: exploitation and benevolence.

The exploitative mode of paternalism is strong when the employer is considered superior as well as superordinate in relation to his employees. The economic and psychological power of the patrón, combined with the economic and psychological vulnerability of the worker, stresses the unequal distribution of rewards and tends to increase the exploitative quality of the relationship. This is particularly the case under conditions of potentially rising profits, and in the absence of countervailing checks by other organized groups such as the government, labor unions, or competitors.

The benevolent mode of paternalism, on the other hand, lacks the clear-cut features of dominance-submission and instead stresses mutual support and a reciprocity of favors. The superior accepts a generalized sense of responsibility for his subordinates, offering guidance, assistance, and support, especially in regard to the non-work matters. A common form of benefit and protection involves the role of patrón as an intermediary who can deal with other powerful persons (officials) and things (e.g., legal forms) which the worker cannot do himself. Other services and supplies may include housing, clothing, food, medical care, religious facilities, and many others. In return for these favors, the subordinate is expected to be loyal to his benefactor, and to perform services (often errands) for him at any time. These are generally limited in extent, though not in frequency. Despite the more positive connotation of the benevolent mode, however, it must be remembered that benevolence

> was not the expression of genuine sympathy or kindness, but rather a formal justification of the ruling function and the position of the superior. Therefore, it was meaningful only when considered in combination with obedience and fealty on the part of the inferiors.[16]

Paternalism may occur in many social contexts, including economic, political, religious, communal, educational, and marital.[17] Religious paternalism had been strong in colonial Mexico, but the extreme curbing of church power after the Revolution has all but eliminated this form except in small village parishes. Political forms of paternalism are still quite prevalent in Mexico today. They characterize the present official party and the government from the top on down to the lowest levels, and are often a strong mixture of both exploitation and patron-age.[18] In general, however, and Mexico is no exception, paternalism is most commonly associated with economic forms of organization. These extend from the traditional hacienda, which also included educational, marital, and other forms of paternalism, to business enterprises of all types, including large and modern ones.

Bennett and Ishino, as well as others, describe paternalism within such a single business enterprise as a "patron-client" system of employ-ment. "A vaguely hierarchical, vaguely paternal" relationship, which is rarely exploitative, manipulative, or authoritarian, and where benevolence and noblesse oblige "have a kind of sensible genuineness." This type of patron employer will pay his workers

> lower than standard wages, but in compensation he will
> protect them against emergencies like illness or minor
> disasters. He is a kindly paternal figure, but may
> regard his paternalistic behavior not as 'traditional'
> but simply good business sense.[19]

The labor contract removed the element of bondage or indenture from the employer-worker relationship, as it existed on the plantation, and therefore lessened the exploitative mode of paternalism. The pro-cesses of urbanization and industrialization, and more generally the entire modernization of Mexico, have weakened the pervasiveness of paternalism throughout the country. The persistence of some forms of "pragmatic paternalism," however, demonstrate the continuing importance of this system in the social context of present day Mexico. In order to understand why this patron-client system persists, how its form has altered, and what are the chances for its survival in the future, we must first understand the importance of personalism in Mexican society.

Personalism

> There is almost everywhere a distrust in the large and
> impersonal corporation because such an organization is
> regarded as being over and above the individuals who
> are members and employees of it. One cannot talk to,
> argue with, or deal personally with, banks, governments,
> or insurance companies. They in themselves have no life,
> no vitality, no souls. Only people are possessed of such
> characteristics, and these are the things in life that
> count.[20]

With these words, Whyte and Holmberg sum up the Mexican (and Latin) values on the importance of the individual and on personal re-lations between individuals. These personal relations are of a very particular sort, however, and are not of the kind which the North American has in mind when he speaks of personal relations. We have examined the greater importance given to an owner than to the top employee of an enterprise, and the stress on the owner as an individual rather than on the concept of ownership. We have also seen how the significance of face-to-face relations affected the entire organizational structure of Mexican enterprise. In comparison to the often characterized impersonal bureaucracy of industrial society, it would be tempting to assume that the paternal relationship between managers and workers reflects the intimate relations of a tightly-knit community.

Speaking of these personal ties as they existed in the hacienda and old style plantation, however, Wolf points out that these were "personalized relations, in which the relationship bears the guise of a personal relation but serves an impersonal function."[21]

> They retain the form of personal relationships, but serve different functions. When a plantation owner returns to the plantation at Christmas to give presents to the children of his workers, or when he lends money to the worker whose wife stands in need of medical care, or when in the past he supervised the flogging of a recalcitrant peon at the plantation whipping post, he is using the form of personal relationship, while carrying out functions which maintain the plantation as a system of labor organization.

> In these acts he carries out operations of a technical order (to use a phrase of Robert Redfield) which are still mediated through cultural forms that bear the personal stamp. He involves himself in relationships which carry affect, either positive or negative, in order to underline the dependent position of the laborer in contrast to his own status of dominance. He thus reinforces the managerial relation between the worker and himself.[22]

The superior-subordinate relations which existed in the hacienda system of colonial Mexico characterized the more exploitative mode of paternal relations, where the Spanish hacendado thought of his Indian peons as inferior beings. The Revolution and the heritage of its ideology, however, erased the exploitative notion of the peasant as some lower form of animal, and replaced it with a more benevolent interpretation of the worker as a child: someone whose subordinance is due to his lack of training and education, who must be taught as well as advised and protected, and who must above all be treated as an individual, a human being. The weakening of the traditional meaning of empleado de confianza paralleled this development. In this way, a strong sense of individualism is not incompatible with a readiness to subject oneself in a subordinate relation with a powerful and protecting individual. Notions of the unique personality and the dignity of the individual, albeit subordinate, are often found in harmony with strong paternalistic relations within Mexico today.

To better understand the nature of personalism in Mexican enterprise, then, it is useful to distinguish between instrumental and expressive roles.[23] An instrumental role refers to a pattern of behavior utilizing nonpersonal means to attain determined ends, such as the production and sale of goods in business enterprise; and an expressive role refers to a behavior pattern involving personal aspects of relations to others, such as the promotion of a common set of values, group solidarity, and mutual obligations. Both roles involve a distinct set of relationships between superiors and subordinates, and in Mexican enterprise both are legitimate parts of the organization; that is, expressive as well as instrumental aspects of the boss-worker relations are stylized, formal, explicit, and obligatory.

In the system of paternalism described above by Wolf, the owner's bestowal of favors to the workers involves the fulfillment of his expressive role, but these expressive relations exist to meet instrumental needs, the proper functioning of the economic organization. While the exploitative mode of paternalism involves more clearly instrumental activities, the benevolent face of paternalism stresses the expressive content of personal relations. The benevolence of the patron, however, and his workers' loyalty and service to him as an individual, characterize the formalized system of personal relations and the essentially instrumental nature of the expressive role.

How does a formalized expressive relationship, an impersonal personalism, develop in any one instance? When the manager of an enterprise first begins in his position, as anywhere, he is an unknown quantity. At this point, minimal respect is granted to the individual because of his position, but a "feeling out" period quickly takes place in which the subordinates make a judgment about him as a particular person. ("Anybody can be a _jefe_, but to be a _patrón_ you have to be liked, or perhaps disliked. I mean, they have to feel something emotional about you.") Once this has occurred, the element of personalism grows continually stronger.

One general manager expressed this growth with a complaint about the trouble he had in switching some of his department heads:

> The workers say they don't necessarily like him
> [the old superintendent] as much personally as they
> like you and me, but they're used to him. ...This
> intense personal loyalty is something which makes
> life much more difficult.

It is interesting to note in this regard that both managers and workers speak of the importance of the worker having _confianza_ in the manager, but not vice versa; workers, it will be remembered, are not held in _confianza_. The more trust a worker has in his manager, the more he will define his superior in personal terms. The same may be said for the notion of _respeto_ (respect). While both workers and managers talk of it, all use it primarily in reference to the workers having respect for their _patrón_. "They respect me more than they do their fellow workers," said one typical owner, "because of the difference that I am their _patrón_." This quality of respect is more relevant to vertical relationships, and is similar to what J. K. Campbell calls "honor" in the Greek patronage system.[24] More than a matter of heaping praise on one's superior, however, the notion of respect also involves a demonstration of deference to the person.

When the personal relationship between manager and worker has been strongly developed, the worker will carry out directives because they come from his patrón, and not simply because they come from above. The production manager of a firm in a small town, for example, had considerable contact with his workers away from the factory. He said that this outside contact helped him, "because anything that I tell them to do, they will do it. If I ask anyone to cut the grass, for example, they will do it; but if anyone else asks them, they will say that it's not their job."

The head of a foreign firm had not developed any such personal relationship with his subordinates, with the result that he felt "a Mexican will take an order more quickly and easily from a foreigner than from another Mexican, but how quickly and correctly he will carry it out is very different." In another foreign firm, the plant manager was well accepted as the patrón. In describing the effect this had in relations with his subordinates, he said:

> If I ask any of these people to do anything, they
> will just do it. But it doesn't necessarily affect
> the performance of their duties. If I asked one of
> them to come in and clean my shoes, for example, I'm
> sure he would do it without feeling that it was de-
> meaning in any way. If I said 'be sure you don't
> make a mess of this job or I'll be annoyed,' I don't
> think it would have too much effect.

In the same firm, the personnel manager, an elderly Mexican gentleman, said:

> We have to motivate the people so that they feel that
> they are working for an institution and not for you,
> personally. If they steal your wallet, they feel
> guilty; but if they steal from the company, they have
> the attitude, 'who is the company?' They have to
> associate the company with someone in order for the
> abstraction to be meaningful to them. People here
> need a caudillo (strong leader) and that is bad.
> Even I, for example, collaborate with my bosses
> because they are Mr. So and So, and Mr. So and So,
> and not because I am working for Company X.

These examples show that when a worker is bound by a personal relationship with his superior, he will carry out a request more quickly than when it comes from an impersonal source. They also show that a worker will carry out personal requests more readily than requests pertaining to the job. If a worker is asked to do something that is expected and required of the job itself, doing it will not bring any particular gratitude or extra thanks. The more personal a favor it is, however, and the more removed it is from what may legitimately be asked within the definition of one's job, the more it piles up credit for future favors to be returned. Because the worker is in the subordinate position, it is he who must seek to accumulate these "reciprocity credits," for without them he is not in a position to ask his patrón for anything, while the patrón may always ask him to carry out an order or a favor.[25]

The _patrón_, who understands this personalism, is also aware of these rules of behavior and develops a very formal set of expressive relations with his workers in order to get the job done. The plant manager in the last example volunteered the way in which he approached the matter:

> What you need to do is say, 'I want this done by tomorrow, if it's convenient for you to do it,' and with a lot of flowery explanation. And when you come back tomorrow and find it's not done, you say, 'You, my favorite son, you've hurt me deeply by not doing this; now come on, let's try and get it done by tomorrow.' And everyone goes away with a smile, and it's darn well done by tomorrow, because they wouldn't like to hurt you again. ...[To please you] people will promise to do things without having considered whether it's possible. If you get annoyed when you find it's not done, then you're finished.

Because of the emphasis on this expressive form of relations with subordinates, we see that authority and control are not only central-ized, they are also personalized. This further encourages by-passing, and all the other problems discussed in the previous chapter. Both superior and subordinate individuals prefer to deal directly with those whom they know and in whom they have the most _confianza_, and this in-volves a "ritual pantomime" of expressive sentiments. One of the most common and successful ways of insuring personal treatment in hierarchi-cal relationships is the Latin system of _compadrazgo_, the spiritual relationship between a child's parents and the godfather, in this case the worker and his patron, respectively.

While this system was once taken quite seriously,[26] it has lost a great deal of its original meaning in Mexico today. In its tradi-tional setting, it provided a moral bond between peón and _patrón_, and added stability to the local social structure. With greater freedom of movement, the job contract, and increased economic security, the economic protection afforded by the bond of fictive kinship became less crucial. The decline in its importance also spelled a decline in the expressive ritual which had developed around it. The _compadrazgo_ has become weaker, more consciously manipulative, and its religious quali-ties have yielded almost entirely to considerations of power and pres-tige. Where the traditional religious meaning still exists, the _compadre_ relationship occurs horizontally, between peers, and not vertically, in the framework of a power hierarchy.

Thus, the term _compadre_ has also lost most of its expressive connotations, and is now employed in more purely instrumental fashion: "When the workers start to get a little difficult, then I call them '_compadre_.' Perhaps they have noticed this, and perhaps they know that when I call them '_compadre_' it's because something is going wrong." In other words, when problems arise, the best way to deal with them is by invoking the personal bond, by handling an instrumental problem through the expressive role. Personalism, then, is a relation between, and treatment of, people based on intimate knowledge of the specific individual(s) involved, and not just on the positions which they hold. It does not seem to involve the presence of any real sense of friendliness or affection.

With this background, let us analyze some specific factors which affect the paternal relationship in enterprise: labor commitment and its relation to hiring preferences, the change from payment in kind to payment in cash, and the role of labor unions and government welfare programs.

Labor Commitment and Hiring Practices

During early stages of industrialization, the working forces may be largely uncommitted to industrial work and an industrial way of life. As industrialization proceeds, this situation becomes more problematical and enterprise managers are likely to look for means of committing workers in order to reduce such problems as turnover and absenteeism. They must simultaneously resocialize new industrial workers to adequately perform new tasks and to adopt norms of behavior imposed by the functional requirements of the production process. It has often been suggested that to accomplish this dual task, traditional patterns of paternalism, and its attendant system of authority, be maintained in the factory during early periods in the industrial transition.[27]

In Brazil, for example, Stein reports that "From the beginning... textile entrepreneurs maintained a paternalistic attitude toward the working force, the only way to reduce labor turnover."[28] Alexander states that the practice later took on political, as well as economic, functions:

> In Brazil, the extensive system of employer
> paternalism had its origin right after World War
> II and was quite frankly designed to help adapt
> to the new industrial economy and to prevent them
> from turning to the unions and the Communist party.[29]

In Puerto Rico, Gregory points out that paternalism was more common in the newer sectors of industry where workers were largely drawn from the rural population, and had previously been uninvolved in urban life and wage labor.[30]

Paternalism, as a strategy to develop disciplined and responsible industrial workers, is least necessary when the workers have no need or expectation of dependence. Argentina is a case in point. The early industrial working class was drawn largely from among European immigrants who had generally high levels of sophistication and education.

> When, after 1943, the industrialists began drawing
> their labor supply from the relatively backward
> agricultural masses of Argentina, the Perón govern-
> ment was in the process of seeking to channel all
> action on behalf of the workers through its own
> hands, and had little sympathy for paternalistic
> efforts by employers.[31]

In terms of the general level of preparation for an industrial life, Mexico resembles Brazil more than it does Argentina. Virtually its entire labor supply is indigenous to the country, and the vask bulk of it is from rural areas. Industry in outlying areas tends to be more traditionally structured and more directly tied to the larger social structure in its communal setting; thus strengthening the maintenance of paternal institutions. Most industry, however, is heavily concentrated around Mexico City, which has a population of over six million that doubles itself in less than twelve years. As a result, nearly half of its inhabitants are migrants from farms, towns, and smaller cities. And it is the migrant, semi-committed industrial worker who is most inclined to try and establish a paternal relationship with the manager at his new work place.

The paradox of encouraging paternal relations among these new industrial workers, as a way of softening the shock of change, is that the worker may develop a commitment to industry and the enterprise but, at the same time, develop or maintain a set of socially structured expectations which are more appropriate to feudal than to modern institutions. A short-term advantage may only create a long-term disadvantage. All of this is fine as theory, but what actually goes on at the enterprise level? How does a manager decide what type of relationship to establish with his workers, and what type of worker does he prefer to have? Is paternalism employed as a strategy to facilitate the process of commitment, and to be done away with at a later date? The answer to the last question seems to be "no." When paternalistic features do exist within an enterprise, they manifest themselves more as a permanent preference for a particular form of social relations than as a temporary strategy of management.

The clearest example of this is in the managers' preferences for hiring workers of rural or urban origin. Those managers who engage in paternal relations with their subordinates seek to hire workers of rural origin; indeed, the sooner off the farm, the better. The typical reasons offered are that these workers are more respectful, honest, polite, harder working, and more willing to take orders. Managers who want to avoid paternal relations, on the other hand, always look for workers of urban background. These managers say that the workers who come from the city are quicker, more educated, more intelligent, and more independent. One type of manager finds the worker of rural origin easier to train and commit, and the other finds this the case with the worker of urban origin.

The preferences of each are arbitrary and, under conditions of a sufficient labor supply, derive from cultural, rather than economic, sources. In other words, either men of rural or of urban origin may make good workers, and either paternal or non-paternal forms of organization may be used as a strategy to commit workers to the requirements of industry. Few managers seem to think in terms of using paternalism today in order to discard it tomorrow, and those who say "but one has to be a little paternal with the workers" are defending the benevolence of their practice in the face of its exploitative mode. Although it will vary in strength, managers at the enterprise level are either disposed to practice and encourage paternalism or not.

Payment in Kind and in Cash

Many services which are considered part of the paternal responsibility later come to be called fringe benefits, and what once depended upon the whim or discretion of the individual patron may be institutionalized into the management-labor relations system, or even required by law. Thus, the Government Social Security program attends to the medical care of all citizens, and soccer uniforms are written into many union contracts. The bestowal of a gift in the paternal manner, however, differs from the fulfillment of contract clauses, particularly in the sense that in the latter there is no personal and individual benevolence involved, either on the part of the giver or the receiver. This leads to the typical, and probably universal complaint of management that once workers have a fringe benefit written into their contract, they "take it for granted," i.e., there is no longer any reciprocity involved.[32]

While some managers prefer to maintain this paternal system of gift-giving, others find it more encumbering than helpful. One manager in the latter category expressed it this way:

> The workers do not regard their salary as what they get for doing their work. They regard it, instead, as pocket money. They feel, and it's a continual source of resentment, that we should be providing them with a house, food, clothes, and everything else. You will find that they are really more interested in the little bestowals, food or shoes or anything...[than they are in obtaining a raise in salary].

While workers are prone to place emphasis on payment in kind, and often to be received individually rather than across the board, management which is unwilling to play the paternal role has sought to replace payment in kind with payment in cash. The same manager, for example, continued:

> The company's attitude is that money should be given, not favors. ...Even if it costs more money, it's better than getting yourself mixed up in real estate, transport, education, and clothing, or any other thing that might be given.

Some managers feel that reducing all worker increments to the common denominator of cash will help teach the worker to be more independent. Others take a less benevolent attitude:

> 'We will give you more money,' I will ultimately say to the union, 'and if you pee it away in the canteen it's your problem, but we won't give you food and clothing and beds and homes.'

Some managers are indirectly deterred in changing payment from kind to cash because of the government indemnity law. This piece of labor legislation provides that if a man is fired, the company must pay him an indemnification of three months wages plus twenty days wages for every year he has worked for the firm. The same is true for all employees, union or nonunion, labor or management. The government is very strict on this payment, and the courts usually favor the dismissed individual over the company. The law was instituted for the protection of the worker, and with the idea that management would be less prone to dismiss a man, and more likely to place greater emphasis on training present personnel.

As one observer wryly commented, in this way a worker with many years in a firm may become a capitalist overnight if he is fired. While this, of course, is not a common occurrence, many enterprises are nonetheless faced with the problem of maintaining a large cash reserve to pay the indemnización in the event of lay-offs or bankruptcy. While this does not present a very great problem to large firms, it is more serious in medium and small-scale enterprises, particularly those which are labor intensive.

A common way of handling this problem has been through the increasingly instrumental use of an originally expressive action: the gratificación. The gratificación is a gift, given by the head of an enterprise to his subordinates, in order to show his gratitude for the work they have done. Originally this gift was in the form of food, clothing, and the like, but in recent years it has become a predominantly financial offering. It usually varies with each individual, and is seldom identical for people at the same job. When there are too many people for the head of the enterprise to know the merits of each one personally, then someone at a middle rank makes the decision which is then passed on to the top for the actual doling out. What makes the gratificación different from the universal Christmas or year-end bonus is the sum, for it is often as large as one-third of the man's yearly wages or salary.

In the more formally organized firms, the gratificación may be an acknowledged set amount, in which case it may be included as part of total earnings in the figuring of the indemnity payment. This is not usually the case, however, and the amount may never accurately be shown on the books, or else it may be shown as a lump sum for the company but not for each individual payment. If two hypothetical men were fired, for example, one who was earning 10,000 pesos per year and receiving no gratificación and the other earning 8,000 pesos per year plus 2,000 as gratificación, then although their total income is the same, management would figure the second man's indemnity on the basis of only 8,000.

Besides being a financial safeguard for management, this system ties the personnel to management in the same way that the personally bestowed gift creates a stronger mutual debt than does the fringe benefit. This is more particularly true for empleados than for workers, for the ratio of gratificación to total earnings generally rises as one climbs the organizational hierarchy. While the gratificación, then, has lost most, if not all, of its expressive content, its instrumental quality works more in favor of management: without paying any more salary, it succeeds in making the employee more financially dependent upon the benevolent dispensation of those at the top.

While the indemnity law reduces the exploitedness of the worker by giving him greater job security, it also creates a protective atmosphere which some observers feel may work against a growing sense of independence on the part of the worker. Through several laws such as these, the government in Mexico, like the employer in Japan, has introduced a tenure system into enterprise. While it is undoubtedly true that some individuals use their access to an indemnity payment as an excuse to relax on the job, the law more generally has reduced the workers' dependence on the will of his employer and has thus weakened the paternal bond. In another sense, as a way of counteracting the effects of the indemnificación, the gratificación has somewhat strengthened the dependent tie to management, but in a far more formal and instrumental way. Even here, however, it has reduced it to the form of an impersonal cash payment which, in its ultimate formulation, is no longer paternalism.[33]

Labor Unions and Government

It has often been held that the growth and strength of labor unions and government security programs are directly related to the decline of managerial paternalism. Speaking of Guatemala, for example, Adams points out that the rise of labor unions after the 1944 revolution, combined with national governmental programs of labor security and agrarian reform, brought about the "effective forced deterioration of paternalism."

> The laborer now had access to rights and goods from other sources than the patrón; the labor unions promised things, the political parties promised things, and, of course, the agrarian reform program promised land. As might be expected, the response of the finquero in many cases was also a rejection of the older employer-employee or patrón-mozo relationship. The finquero too began to take refuge behind the laws and to try to defend himself in the local political arena.[34]

In Hawaii, Norbeck states that strong paternal traditions have declined in the sugar and pineapple industries partly because of the introduction "between boss and worker [of] a theoretical impersonal body, the union itself."[35] A similar development took place in Japan, where boss-organized dock workers deserted the paternal system when outside agencies such as the public employment offices began to supply medical care and unemployment relief.[36]

A converse example comes from Brazil, as mentioned earlier, where employers used paternalism as a means of preventing new industrial workers from turning to the unions. In Mexico, however, the trade union movement was sponsored, nurtured, and in many senses co-opted, by the ruling political party.[37] Labor unions and government welfare programs have weakened the hold of the employer paternalism on a national scale. While the character of paternalism in Mexico has changed considerably from the time of the traditional hacienda to the present-day industrial enterprise, distinctive paternal forms nevertheless continue to exist. The conditions for this process of social change are well stated by Bennett and Ishino:

When government takes over some of the security
guarantees provided by paternalism, and does so
efficiently, such organizations may wither or
change, although the response is never immediate,
and paternalistic systems can adjust in many ways
to a change in conditions. ...Paternalistic
organizations, in either their benevolent or
cynically exploitative phases, arise to meet
needs for security not provided by other means;
when government provides these, a good part of
the functional basis for paternalism is removed
or modified, but not necessarily all. Cultural
traditions, persisting social inequalities, and
other factors, may continue to exert their influence. Moreover, paternalism can have a psychological appeal quite apart from any 'objective'
security the workers may or may not possess (the
'escape from freedom,' or the dependency relationship...).[38]

Because the Mexican trade union movement has been incorporated into the
state party organization, the role of the union at the plant level in
any one case is contingent foremost upon the overall position of trade
unionism in the Mexican scene. Trade unions, in general, operate with
very restricted autonomy, and this is especially so for individual
plant units. This has important implications for the possible trans-
ference of paternal activities from management to labor. In order to
understand how the basis for paternalism has been modified, and in what
ways it has not been affected, it would be helpful to turn from the
national to the enterprise level of analysis.

Whyte and Holmberg point out that:

We know a good deal about the union in its relation
to government and political life. We know almost
nothing about the day-to-day relations between
union officers and workers in the industrial situation. ...What does the worker expect from his
union? How does he bring his problems to the
attention of union officials?[39]

One study which focuses on the union at the plant level, and its role
as an agent of social change, had been carried out by Juarez Lopes in
two towns in the interior of Brazil.[40] In the more traditional town,
Sobrado, workers who turned to the union lost all their rights in the
factory, and their requests were only attended to if they followed the
traditional form of being delivered to the patrones and not to the
union. In the second town, Mundo Novo, the union was ultimately
accepted as the legitimate voice of labor, and here management curtailed most of their paternal relations.

Many informants, in speaking of the large concern
which the owners used to have for the workers in
earlier times, attribute this change in attitude
to the appearance of the union. One of the leaders

> in Mundo Novo says that in the past the patrons
> have all kinds of medical assistance, 'a function
> which diminished with the founding of the union
> and which subsequently, after eight months of
> operation, disappeared.'

> By turning to the union, the patron's traditional
> obligations to protect the worker, and the loyalty
> to the patron derived from it, were less each day.
> It is not surprising that the worker organization
> sought to assume the paternal role towards the
> worker. [41]

Instances of both types may also be found in Mexico. Threatened with the impending unionization of their work force, managers who wish to maintain the traditional paternal system of social relations often set up a puppet "company union" which they can effectively control. Even when this cannot be done, some managers find other ways of maintaining the paternal bond. One manager in a very traditional city had started a program to build homes for the workers. Whenever the union made a demand, he would then take the position, "Look at me, I'm your benefactor. Look at all I'm doing for you, and you ask me for such a demand." By using this carrot and stick technique he was able to minimize the union's role as an intermediary between himself and his workers.

A striking example of the way in which a <u>patrón</u> may seek to maintain his traditional hold over his workers was given by a very authoritarian manager in a small city in the provinces. This man said that if a worker delivered a legitimate request through union channels, he would never grant it to him,

> But if he comes in by himself, I'll give it to
> him, and by so doing I am showing him that he
> does not need those other bridges to get what
> he wants. <u>He does not have the right to come
> to me and that is why I give it to him.</u> But if
> he goes to the union he thinks that it <u>is</u> his
> right, and that he therefore has it coming to
> him.

In a very exploitative way, this manager was simultaneously trying to emphasize both the advantage and the obligation attached to the paternal route. One can also see from this example how the union, as well as foremen and department heads, are by-passed in the hierarchy of authority.

Lopes also suggests that the union takes over the paternal role from the manager. At the plant level, in Mexico, this is not the case. Since the strength of the unions on a national scale is largely dependent upon the President of the Republic,[42] an indirect sentiment of the national leader diffuses into the labor organizations. This is weak, at best, however, and rarely seems to affect daily relations at the plant level. At most it maintains a sentiment, a psychological prop, but not an actual program of paternal actions.

Speaking of new industrial workers in Puerto Rico, Gregory makes a similar comment on the inability of the unions to make use of the paternal role:

> One notices a rather strong residue of values and expectations associated with the traditional paternalistic relationship between patrón and obrero. Workers were commonly found to identify with the employer as a person and to desire recognition directly from him. At the same time, the employer was expected to be the arbiter of the worker's job problems, if not his personal problems as well. Thus workers tended to look to the employer for the dispensation of 'justice.' Assuredly, 'justice' was not always forthcoming, but this did not appear to stimulate moves for common forms of action. Beyond the employer, workers tended to look to the government, as personified by a charismatic governor, as the protector of their interests. ...Where unions have been organized, they are generally weak and ineffective.[43]

When workers object to the union on its own merits the most frequent reason given is corruption. The sentiment that the leaders are only watching out for themselves, and will sell out the rank and file, again adds emphasis to the sense of distrust. One traditional worker expressed his lack of trust in a very fatalistic manner:

> The union is not good because, if the ones who head the union see an error or something, they get the workers together and make a strike; and during that time the workers go hungry. And anyway, in the end it is the enterprise or the firm who always wins out, probably because of a crooked move on the part of the union leaders. ...In this world everybody is trying to screw each other up; the only person who helps me, without wanting something in return is the mother. Is that not true?

This man went on to say that unions are only necessary when one's employer was no good. In other words, so long as the patrón did not transgress beyond a reasonable limit, there was at least some mutual obligation, some reciprocity, involved in the paternal bond and this was absent in worker-union relations. Más vale malo conocido que bueno por conocer.[44]

Nevertheless, the union does act as a wedge between the traditional patrón-obrero bond, impersonalizing many social relations within the enterprise hierarchy. There are strong tendencies in Mexico to think of management as a person rather than as a function or a concept, to fail to distinguish between the owner and the organization (company), and to place an emphasis on personalizing rather than abstracting.[45] The union, as a formal organization, is also an abstraction in much the same way that the corporation in Mexico is an abstraction of the family firm. They are both organizations, run by officers to represent the constituency. In this sense, both union officials and executive-management act as separating agents in which the worker learns to distinguish between persons and positions.

If the worker's relationship with management makes no distinction between the corporation and the men who run it, then his getting along in such an environment depends largely upon the degree to which he can personalize his relationship with the man or men at the top. Within such a context, union development can succeed only to the extent that it, too, can personalize the worker's identification with the union leaders. Even then, the personalized bond of allegiance of worker to boss mitigates strongly against alternative forms of identification--namely those with union leaders--especially when those new paternal images would be in opposition to the old ones.

Moreover, the union head at the plant level lacks the _educación_ and the superior status of the _patrón_; he is often just one of many workers, perhaps selected by his fellow workers because of his honesty or because he had the most grievances. The power of the union leader at the plant level depends upon the strength of the larger association to which his local belongs. If it is a large and active organization, this gives the union secretary at the plant some more power. But if there is any serious trouble, then the union is likely to bring in its own officials higher up in the hierarchy. The local officer cannot compete with the _patrón_ beyond taking care of routine problems, and therefore he also cannot create a powerful image of himself among his fellow workers. While a union official at the central headquarters may have enough stature to approach the head of the enterprise, he is too remote a figure to assume any quasi-paternal role with the rank and file.

Thus, in terms of weakening managerial paternalism, unions have had little direct influence at the individual firm level for several reasons: a minimal emphasis on the preparation and training of leaders at the plant level; the general ease with which these leaders can be bought-off by management because of their low wages; the rotation of union officers within a firm which often prevents the development of, and identification with, any one leader; and the inability of these men to represent, or be seen as, a person of comparable power to that of the _patrón_, capable of giving workers the same protection and favors.

In sum, paternalistic management in Mexico has two opposing pressures: on the one hand, a background of cultural receptivity to this type of superior-subordinate relationship; and, on the other hand, the growth of labor organizations and government controls which challenge the employer's decisions about what should be done _for_ workers. While it is true that the growth of unions has contributed on a national scale to the weakening of paternalistic systems within industry, and has given labor more independent bargaining power vis-a-vis management,[46] at the individual plant level the local union group has done little to weaken the paternal bond between _patrón_ and _obrero_, and has certainly not taken it over for itself.

Change and Paternalism

To conclude this section, then, what may be said of the future of paternalism in Mexican enterprise and its influence on the development of Mexican management? The long-lived hegemony of the hacienda system has left its mark on superior-subordinate relations throughout Mexico today. Although many enterprise managers still try to maintain traditional patterns of relationship with their subordinates, paternalism has nonetheless declined in both the intensity and meaning given to it. The pattern of mutual obligations, arising out of a reciprocity of responsibility and subordination, has become less exploitative but more purely instrumental.[47] While the patron-client form of paternalism, found in business enterprise, is more benevolent, it has also lost much of its ritualized expressive qualities. Paternal relations have become less pervasive and more quantifiable. In more traditional form, "reciprocal favors are so dissimilar in quality that accountancy is difficult,"[48] but in present day form this is often no longer true. The tendency away from payment in kind in favor of payment in cash increases the element of calculability and destroys the more diffuse quality of the paternal relation.

Furthermore, no matter how weak the role of the union at the plant level, labor unions and government control on a national scale have strengthened the independent voice of worker demands. In many instances the union, as well as management, has attempted to translate prestaciones into increased wages, only to be held back by workers' dependency mentality. Each new contract negotiation brings about a re-evaluation of the workers' profits and losses from a paternal relation and, with the backdrop of continual economic growth, the system is slowly but surely fading.

Two contrasting views frequently have been advanced regarding changes in paternalism. One of them holds that as a traditional practice, paternalism is "nothing but a remnant of feudalistic relations between lord and retainer and of patriarchal family relations applied to the field of industry."[49] This reasoning proceeds along the line of the "logic of industrialization" and the inevitable decay and disappearance of paternal relations in the face of continual economic growth. The other opinion stresses that though these traditional practices may be remnants of a pre-industrial stage, they are imbedded in the local society and may be utilized, in slightly altered form, to achieve industrial development without any radical change in cultural or social continuity.[50]

Paternalism in Mexican enterprise represents a combination of these two theories. The trend in paternal relations is a decline in its intensity, expressiveness, and exploitativeness and an increase in its overt instrumentality and quantifiability. These are likely to continue with greater and greater rapidity. Personalism in the future will not be any less basic, but will, in time, become more dispersed through various members in the managerial hierarchy and not completely focused on the single dominant figure at the top. This change will be slow in coming, and because paternalism is so historically rooted in the culture, it will be even slower in spreading into the more traditional firms; but one may already see examples of this trend in a few companies. Before these new developments are explored, however, let us now turn more directly to an examination of the system of authority and control in management in Mexico.

AUTHORITY AND CONTROL

If management is to control and direct the activities of its workers and employees, it must have a strategy of organization and a system of values to support it. As societies develop and industrialization takes place, organizations grow in both size and complexity. The task of enterprise management increases proportionately and becomes a full-time concern. The coordination of men and machines by administration requires an ordering of positions and duties, an integration of a variety of functions in order to achieve a more or less defined set of goals. Sufficient managerial resources are therefore necessary in order to accomplish this task.

Since organization involves more than one person, it also means the delegation of various functions to different people throughout the organizational hierarchy. The larger and more complex the organizational structure, the more delegation there must be. Delegation may be either of tasks or of authority; it may refer to the increased division of labor and the specialization of job functions, or to the chain of command by which orders are passed down. Delegation of authority, or the decentralization of decision-making, involves a strategy of organization which gives increased discretion to subordinates, and has often been considered a logical consequence of organizational development. In this light, we turn to an examination of the system of authority within Mexican business organizations, to the characteristics of its development, the problems which it creates, and its relation to social change and the development of managerial resources.

Centralization

If the most basic distinction in the stratification system of Mexican enterprise is between _empleados_ and _obreros_, the most characteristic feature of the authority system is its centralization. In the more traditional Mexican firms, it is the centralization of _all_ power in the one top man who is simultaneous organizer, owner, manager, and sole decision-maker. Here, management is a person, not a position, concept, or function. Authority likewise resides in this person and is not spread throughout a managerial organization, for indeed no such organization exists.

The traditional entrepreneur of a small enterprise runs an operation in which the only division of labor is between himself and a few workers. Above this barest minimum, the introduction of an intermediate status creates the rank of _empleado de confianza_. _Maestros_, skilled senior workers, are usually among the first such _confiados_. The growing structural complexity, here, is an unplanned consequence of industrial expansion. These early _confiados_ are tomorrow's supervisors and department heads, and the important point is that their personal merits are established before their positions are defined.

Seen positively, the result is stability in the organization's structure, a general absence of the _empleado-obrero_ barrier, and little tension regarding the foreman role. Seen negatively, such entrepreneurially run firms tend to develop along lines of an increased differentiation from below, but with slight development, differentiation, or access to the top. Despite the natural evolution of an increased division of labor, however, all ranks are still subordinate to the top. What little authority is delegated is done so on the basis of confianza, not competence: you do not entrust a man with any authority simply because he has had training and is skilled at his job.

William F. Whyte and Craciela Flores report on this attitude in Peru as the reflection of a general cultural sentiment:

> The prevailing system of centralization of control seems to be based upon beliefs that you cannot trust your subordinates to do the right things unless you watch them closely. Delegation of authority and responsibility requires a degree of faith in people that is not common in Peru. ...The suspicious point of view [manifested by the Peruvian] would suggest that you had better not do something for the other fellow because he will just interpret that as a sign of weakness and take advantage of you in the future.[51]

In family-owned firms, fathers sometimes displayed this attitude of suspicion toward their sons, especially during periods of succession when the transfer of authority is a major issue. This may manifest itself in several ways. In one type, effective authority is completely denied to the son and is viewed as a threat to the power of the father. In a second pattern, authority is given to the son to carry on in his father's footsteps but not to expand on his own initiative; the ultimate authority still rests with the father. A third type of centralization involves the attempts of one branch in a family firm to wrest power away from another family group.[52]

The unwillingness to grant legitimate power to hired employees is even stronger than the hesitancy to delegate authority to other family members. This is most apparent in the firms which apply the more literal and traditional meaning of empleado de confianza, the small number of non-related employees who can be trusted.[53] Even when these individuals are given responsibility, however, they are less often given authority, and while they may formally be considered part of management, they have no decision-making powers. This prompted one observer to describe a Mexican manager as a man who "would delegate work but not authority."

No matter how highly placed a traditional employee may be, he still lacks the functional perquisite of his office, namely authority of his own. This is because of the intimate bond between ownership and authority in Mexican enterprise. The notion was well expressed by one engineer who simply said, "If the men who give the orders were not the owners, they could not give the orders." The owner is the ultimate, and often only, source of authority in the firm; hired management is there to carry out his directives. Thus, there is a distinct separation between the owner of a firm and his employee underlings. Charles

Myers reports on the same distinction in Chile:

> Few top operating managers are members of boards,
> for there is still a social distinction between the
> director of a firm and its hired manager. The latter
> is considered an 'employee'--no matter how highly
> placed.[54]

When one Mexican worker was asked about the difference between the
owners and the top-ranking employee in his firm, he said, "The differences
are great. The _patrones_ are _patrones_, but Sanchez is a servant, like
me."

The same gap seems to exist between the few above and the many
below in Brazilian enterprise. Pereira reports that this gap creates
strong disparities between production and managerial systems:

> Often, we find side-by-side the most modern machines
> and the oldest systems of management. More expressive,
> however, is the conflict within the typical small or
> medium-sized family enterprise, closed, paternalistic,
> working at a relatively low level of productivity, but
> using modern techniques, electricity, assembly line,
> [and] modern equipment. ...In other words, the forms
> of ownership and management of the enterprises are
> generally backward when compared to the productive
> system.[55]

Speaking of Latin America in general, Lauterbach sees the concentration
of authority in Latin management as due to the fact that:

> without the top man's political links and family
> standing little could be achieved in the conduct
> of _any_ of these firms, and informal conversations
> with friends or influential people take up a very
> substantial part of the top man's activity. Since
> the latter thus occupies a unique and authoritarian
> position, delegation of his major activities is
> considered impossible by himself and the others.[56]

This distinction between owner-management and executive-management,
as it relates to authority within the firm, is perhaps strongest in
Germany. In his study of German management, Heinz Hartmann distinguishes
between the _Unternehmer_ and the _Leitende Angestellte_.[57] The _Unternehmer_
are the top executives of individual industrial hierarchies, the traditional owner-entrepreneurs who have a strong set of values and an
image of themselves as the only true business leadership. The _Leitende
Angestellte_ are the members of upper management, including minor members
of the executive committee, heads of divisions, of departments, and of
important staff units.

Authority in German management is highly centralized in the
Unternehmer, even bordering on complete monopoly:

> In this extreme, the _Unternehmer_ will emphasize the
> subordination even of his immediate entourage of

upper management and high-level staff; he will make
an effort to control remotest details in the shop;
and he will leave his professional sphere of management and intervene in matters foreign to his skills
and training.[58]

The Unternehmer may consider it proper management strategy to retain the
function of leadership (Führung) for himself and delegate only authority
over routine operations (Leitung). When this is the case, the Leitende
Angestellte may be considered no more than the most skilled and most
trusted white-collar workers. Because of their lack of legitimate power
and their subordinate character, "the differences between a Leitende
Angestellte and a worker with regard to their subordination to the
Unternehmer are so small that the two may be put in one category."[59]
In these respects, the German case is quite similar to the Mexican
system.

David Granick reports on a similar, though not so pervasive,
phenomenon in English enterprise.

Owner-managers look down from on high at all lower
and middle managers; since the cleavage is great
and permanent, there is no need for them to make
major distinctions among these lower orders.[60]

The conjunction of ownership and management plays a critical role
in determining the authority system in Mexican enterprise, but it
cannot neatly be logged into the traditional category of one-man-rule
companies. Among entrepreneurs heading large, complex and modern industrial firms, some are characteristic of their traditional counterparts in smaller companies, while others hardly differ from executive
employees heading operations of all sizes. With the growth of an
enterprise, and an increase in its division of labor, the tendency to
concentrate authority in one's own hands also develops among middle
level management. The extent of this development depends upon the
nature of the man or men in the top position(s); the more they are
willing to delegate authority, the stronger becomes the control of the
department heads. Foreign firms, invariably headed by executive-
management, show a marked tendency toward this development of departmental autocracy. Unlike management in the German firm, there are two
loci of centralization: one at the top and the other at the middle.

In Mexico, the tendency of department heads to concentrate their
authority in their own hands, rather than delegate some of it to
subordinates, is in part a reaction to their lack of ownership. In an
attempt to legitimize their positions, middle level managers will sometimes turn to their technical competence as justification for their
holding of power. In all cases, and especially when the expertise is
lacking, department heads often attempt to impose a personal cast on
everything within their domain; they may try to create their own little
kingdoms.

One observer described the situation in his factory by showing me
an article from a Mexican magazine, entitled "Win Over Your Employees."

At the top was a cartoon in which a man with a crown on his head stood like a conqueror with his hands crossed over his puffed-out chest, and with one foot on top of a worker. To the right was another worker bowing down to the crowned man, and behind the man was a third worker sticking out his tongue and waving his hands from his ears. The respondent pointed to the drawing and said, "This is the problem we have here; the middle managers all want to be kings."

In a foreign company employing close to 1,000 people and having sixteen department heads, the General Manager described his problem with centralization at the middle:

> We have to restrain the tendency of the departmental managers to make their own little kingdoms because they may do something which sets a precedent. For instance, if the sweeper in their department comes to them and says, 'I need more money,' and they say, 'Sure, I'll give you fifty centavos an hour more.' Their attitude is that we've only got two sweepers, so that's only costing eight pesos a day, which can't affect the firm. But that would immediately mean that everyone in the plant had to have fifty centavos more. But they don't see it that way. They feel, 'Why do I have to consult with the Personnel Office on the matter of fifty centavos an hour? It's taking away my dignity to have to tell a man I can't decide, myself, on such a minor matter.'

The middle level manager is interested in protecting and enhancing every bit of authority that has been granted to him. The more authority he has, the more secure he feels in his position. The result is to create a hoarding effect:[61] the more authority you accumulate, the more indispensable you are; and as a corollary, abide by the rule not to grant authority to anyone when you can take care of the matter yourself. One of the key values of good management in the United States is the ability to delegate. In North America, the junior executive who is able to delegate authority is on his way up; in Mexico, however, the popular interpretation would be that this man is on his way out.[62]

Thus, for both owner-management at the top and executive-management at middle levels, hoarding of authority is part of the modus operandi of Mexican enterprise. Even in countries where decentralization is considered a positive managerial value, however, its implementation is proportionate to an increase in problems of control. Whether seen as a philosophy of management or as a logical part of industrial development, the delegation of authority involves a major paradox: "The more top management tries to decentralize decision-making, the more it must centralize its control of decisions."[63] Mexican management sees little efficacy in this distinction because it is the very fear of loss of control which prevents any decentralization from taking place. Authority and control are seen as identities. There is little or no distinction made between the two because of the feeling that you cannot maintain control unless you also maintain complete authority, and vice versa.

It should be noted, however, that centralization of one's business and of one's authority is not the same thing. Oriol Pi-Sunyer has shown how the heads of industrial enterprise in a rural region of Mexico prefer to diversify their business holdings in order to better maintain control:

> Rather than expand existing business to a size that
> would permit them to operate beyond the confines of
> the regional market, Zamora entrepreneurs prefer to
> launch another enterprise designed to tap a further
> segment of the regional market; expansion takes the
> form of multiplication.[64]

He goes on to suggest that:

> [the local] technique of multiplying the units of
> production rather than expanding a given unit is an
> attempt on the part of the entrepreneurs to increase
> total holdings while still retaining the organiza-
> tional advantages accruing from small units of pro-
> duction.[65]

A central part of these organizational advantages involves the system of authority. Zamoran entrepreneurs decentralize their business holdings in order to maintain better control, and at the same time increase profits by tapping other segments of the market. Diversification within a regional market, moreover, helps create enough places for relatives to hold positions of authority without jeopardizing too large a financial investment at any one time, in case the relative proves incompetent. Entering the national market, on the other hand, would require increases in size per unit and perhaps vertical integration. Besides concentrating the financial risk, this would increase pressures to establish middle layers of management, and thus threaten the direct control which the entrepreneurs can maintain within the regional context.[66]

It is worth noting here that Torcuato Di Tella, the great Argentine entrepreneur, faced these same problems, but resolved them differently. As his company (Sociedad Industrial Americana de Maquinarias) grew too big to maintain his own personalized control, Di Tella decentralized his operations into a large number of relatively small factories and affiliated companies. Unlike others, however, he did not place relatives in positions beyond their capacities or beyond the authority of a trusted circle of non-family hombres de confianza.

> This mixed group of a few relatives and a larger
> body of hombres de confianza provided a central
> control system for the extended S.I.A.M. enter-
> prises. ...As levels within S.I.A.M. were linked
> by personal contact, so the entire organization
> was integrated around the symbol of Di Tella in a
> way that would probably not have been effective in
> United States culture. The Consejo [board] ruled
> S.I.A.M. not only through formal positions of its
> members, but more importantly by virtue of their

171

inheritance of __confianza__ from Di Tella. After his
death, the __patrón__ underwent a process analogous
to canonization.

The seeming conflict between the theme of strong
individualism and the hierarchical management
system of a big company was resolved through both
the traditional __patrón-client__ relationship and the
individual's image of his place in the system.
S.I.A.M. maintained a symbolic configuration cen-
tering around the company 'family' and the Di Tella
tradition, and this was satisfactorily internalized
by most of its early personnel in terms of mutual
benefit.[67]

The history of Di Tella and S.I.A.M. are the exception in Latin American entrepreneurial development, but the case well illustrates the
interplay between economic necessity and Argentine cultural traditions.

Responsibility and By-Passing

The centralization of authority above creates problems of responsibility below. One of the most prevalent complaints by superiors about
their subordinate personnel is the latter's unwillingness to accept any
responsibility. In owner-managed firms, this complaint is often directed at middle level executive-management, if there is any; and when
centralization occurs at the middle level, the complaint is usually
registered at the foreman. Ordinary workers are almost universally
charged with a lack of responsibility by management in Mexico.

One personnel manager described a typical problem involving
responsibility. He said that if a department head gave an incorrect
order to a supervisor, the supervisor would carry it out without saying
anything, even if he knew the order was wrong. Later, when his department head would ask why he had carried out the order, he would answer
that he had been told to do so. A general manager in another company
reported the same phenomenon, saying:

> I have to be very careful what I say to people. If I
> say 'do something' and I haven't thought it out well,
> they will often go and do it, even though they know
> that it hasn't been too well thought out. There
> aren't many people here who would argue with me. I
> don't mean because they're unwilling to, or because
> they're afraid of me; they just feel that this is my
> factory and I can do what I like in it. And it's
> very difficult to get that attitude out of people.

An observer in another company reported that workers and employees
had adopted the attitude "knowledge is power."[68] Even if someone knew
how to do something which was expected of him, he would not do it unless
he was explicitly told to do so. A clear definition of job responsibility, in this case, would have established amounts of authority: no
one was willing to do this, especially at the top, and the result was a
continual power struggle which pervaded all levels.

In a third firm, a delivery date had to be decided. The department head in charge of the product in question said that delivery could not be made within a week, but the planning manager told the general manager that it could be done within five days. The boss was pleased with the early promised delivery date and displeased with the department head's estimate. After the meeting, the planning manager said to the department head: "Why did you tell him that? You know he wants to be happy. It would have been better to tell him we can have it in five days and then, when the time is up, tell him the machine is overloaded, or something like that."

While these examples reflect only part of reality, they are quite common, and hence influence behavior.[69] To the extent that the absence of responsibility does exist, it is largely a consequence of centralization at the top. When superiors are unwilling to delegate authority, subordinates do not want to accept responsibility. To the extent that the lack of responsibility at lower levels exists independently of management's efforts to centralize, however, it does reinforce tendencies in that direction. When subordinates are unwilling to accept responsibility, management will be hesitant to grant them any authority. Speaking of this vicious circle as common in most developing countries, Albert Waterston states that "a general reluctance to take responsibility on one hand and failure to delegate authority on the other lead to overcentralization and delays in decision-making."[70]

Another critical effect of the centralization of authority is by-passing. A major principle of organization theory is the necessity of an orderly transmission of information up and down the organization's hierarchy, through the maintenance of an explicit line of authority. According to this principle, effective control can only be maintained if an order from above is filtered through all successively subordinate positions until it reaches its intended recipient. In other words, if the director of a company orders a certain product to be made, he does not give the order directly to the workers who will make it. Instead, he transmits to his general manager, who in turn passes it on to the appropriate department head, who then gives the order to the foremen, who see that the workers carry out the original order. The same is true, holds the theory, for all upward communication. By-passing occurs when one or more levels in the organization hierarchy are jumped in the process.

By-passing is an extremely common phenomenon in Mexican organizations. It is particularly widespread in traditional systems of enterprise, which are small in size, and characterized by an informal and personal system of management. Here, it is easy for the head of the company to communicate directly with someone at any level, without the implication of thereby criticizing his immediate subordinate(s). This is especially true in a family firm, when his subordinate is a son or cousin. The informal and largely unstructured quality of lines of authority depend almost entirely on the discretion of the man at the top and his subordinates' personal loyalty to him.

Under the conditions described above, by-passing is rarely a problem. Formal lines of authority are seldom defined and both

superiors and subordinates have direct and frequent access to one another. What few individuals there are who occupy middle positions do so,
as we have said, because of their personal connections with the owner.
The relationship between a <u>patrón</u> and his workers is not something that
they are about to tamper with by trying to impose themselves as intermediary.

This relationship between the owner or owning family at the top
and the workers at the bottom and the consequent by-passing of inter-
mediates is something desired by both parties. When it is not desired,
then by-passing becomes a problem, and this change is usually instigated
at the top.

The owner-manager of a very centralized and very authoritarian
firm permitted frequent upward by-passing among his 150 personnel, but
refused to reciprocate by taking any direct action himself. His office
was in a secluded corner of the company, yet all sorts of people were
continually walking right in for various reasons. When queried about
this constant traffic, he replied:

> I let anyone come in. They don't even have to knock;
> you noticed that. They can walk right in, because
> if you always have the door closed, and they have to
> ask, they think you are too high up and that no one
> can talk to you. Even the guy who washes the car
> outside can come and talk to me. They know I can't
> decide anything. They tell me everything, but I'm
> just a wall. They tell me they want a raise in
> salary, they've been fired, they want some money;
> they tell me all sorts of things. I always write
> down everything they want and then I go through the
> ranks and say 'so and so came to me and told me all
> of this; what's it all about? '

In one family firm of several hundred people, the owners both desired and encouraged frequent by-passing. The General Manager, and
eldest son of the owner, said:

> When there's trouble inside the factory, say if
> someone gets hurt, well they don't go and see anyone
> else. They come right here to us and we take care
> of them. They have the personal feeling that we
> help them better than if they go to the one that is
> head of their department, their immediate supervisor.

This practice was looked upon favorably and encouraged by the Production
Chief, a first cousin of the General Manager: "The workers will not tell
their <u>encargado</u> (foreman), but prefer to come to me because they have
more <u>confianza</u> in me. This has developed after so many years that they
prefer to jump the <u>encargado</u> and come directly to me."

In this organization, workers were required to come directly to
the family managers for even the smallest request, such as a bandaid.
Immediately after one worker came in with such a request, the researcher
asked why this was done, and the family manager replied: "They like us

and that's why they come. When they have a problem, we feel we should help them because they're not completely capable of doing these things themselves." A similar occurrence took place while speaking with the Production Chief, and he said: "This is done so the workers can feel that the factory feels a responsibility for them, and also so they could acquire responsibility toward the factory." In actuality, this centralized and very paternal control discouraged independent action and developed a sense of loyalty and attachment to a set of persons, not principles.

The practice of dealing directly with the owners is often initiated by the workers, without any encouragement from those at the top. This was the case in a small factory, where an <u>obrero</u> was discussing why he liked working there. One of his reasons was "because here the owners and managers are the same people, so if you have a problem you can go and get it resolved right away, while this is not so when there is an intermediary." Middle managers, for him, blocked rather than helped a worker with his problems. Managers, therefore, by-pass middle levels in order to centralize their control, while workers prefer to by-pass middle levels because they feel that only the owner can take direct action.

The phenomenon of by-passing is not solely limited to internal relations. It is also found in relations between the enterprise and the general community, and the latter's influence on the authority system within the enterprise. The Sales Manager, and son of an owning partner in a large firm, described the following situation:

> We have a man whose job is to sell products at list prices. We found ourselves with a situation that whenever a customer went to him for some orders, <u>before</u> leaving the building he would come into my office and ask me to check the prices personally to make sure that he was getting the best deal. This happens in 99% of all sales, even though we will not change our prices.... [As a result], salesmen will generally come up to me, leave the order on my desk, and ask me to call the customer and verify the price.

This manager then went on to make a more general statement:

> People in Mexico have a very special feeling: they always want to talk to the <u>patrón</u>, you know. They always want to talk to the owner; a general sales manager is not enough. That, of course, helps me because when (someone) walks in here, he knows that I'm his last resort... That is very typical in Latin countries. People here are not accustomed to talking to an administrator, or a supervisor, or anybody like that. They want to talk to the man who owns the business because they feel they are important enough, regardless of their size, so that they should be taken care of by the boss.

Enterprises which are large in size, especially those run by executive-management, find the problem of by-passing aggravated. The more levels there are in an organizational hierarchy, the more opportunities there are to by-pass, and hence the more opportunity there is to disrupt the "normal" lines of authority. Because of the frequent concern of department heads to accumulate authority, and hence to centralize all decision-making within their domain, by-passing of the foreman in favor of direct relations with workers is a common practice.

We saw in the previous chapter how the growth of enterprise reflects a growing gap in education and cultural background between management and labor. To date, this gap still reflects a strong hiatus between department heads, above the major stratifying line, and foremen, below it. Because middle management view foremen as only glorified _obreros_, they are unwilling to entrust them with more than minimal responsibilities and will only delegate authority to them for routine operations. Given these attitudes, it is not surprising to find a department head by-passing his foreman in order to deal directly with his workers.

The middle manager is likely to practice and encourage by-passing of the foreman with his workers, if he makes few distinctions between the cultural and technical backgrounds of those beneath him, and if he feels a great separation between himself and all his subordinates in this regard. Likewise, if he is unsure of his position or his authority with respect to those above him, he is more prone to attempt to hoard his authority and control. He generally does this by establishing ties of personal loyalty to himself among the rank and file in his department. When this is accomplished, workers will carry out an order because it comes directly and personally from him, but are more reluctant to do so simply because it has come down an impersonal chain of command. Workers, therefore, more often by-pass the foreman on personal matters than on technical ones. Criticizing this development of departmental fiefdoms in his company, the General Manager of a Canadian-owned firm said,

> A good manager anywhere will try to give the
> impression to the workers and everybody else that
> he's available to discuss their personal problems
> when everything else has failed. But he can take
> damn good care that that never happens.

When the foreman is by-passed, however, this is not always done at the initiation of those immediately above or below him. If the foreman is unwilling to take responsibility, he often initiates the by-passing, himself. In the same Canadian-owned firm, this caused the General Manager to comment:

> There's also a certain encouragement to by-pass
> responsibility. [This occurs] when a man comes
> to a supervisor with a problem and the supervisor
> says, 'Hell, I don't dare touch that; I'd get
> chopped down about it. Why don't you go and see
> the departmental manager?' Now, the by-passing is
> being done there by the foreman, not by the worker.

It's quite a strong tendency for everybody. One of
the things you have to learn when you become a manager is to make sure not to by-pass things to the
man above you.

In sum, the tendency of upper and middle level management to centralize control discourages the acceptance of responsibility at lower
levels and encourages the practice of by-passing authority. This by-
passing occurs in both directions, and its locus depends upon such
factors as the size of the firm, whether or not ownership and management are separate, and the particular personalities of the individuals
involved. While the North American student of social theory and business administration classifies them as either traditional forms of
organization or deviations from modern organizational requirements, the
Mexican manager and worker is apt to consider them as natural and
legitimate features of the authority system in an organization's
hierarchy.

Communication

Despite problems of centralization at the top, unwillingness to
accept responsibility at the bottom, and by-passing at all levels,
communication up and down the organizational hierarchy does not seem
to create many problems. Communication along a horizontal axis, however, between members of different groups, departments, or sections,
at the same level, is often quite problematical. Natural divisions
between different departments exist in all organizations whatever the
cultural tradition. In Mexico, however, the patterns of authority in
enterprise make the separation between various branches in a firm particularly acute. This separation manifests itself in problems of communication, cooperation, and secrecy among those in equivalent positions.

The Mexican personality has been portrayed, on the one hand, as
being individualistic, suspicious, and closed; and, on the other hand,
as being tied to an authoritarian and/or paternal figure above and
manipulative of those below. These two sketches correspond to an individual's relations with peers and to his relations within a hierarchical system of authority, respectively.

When suspicion exists between people at the same level in an
organization, then communication or cooperation between them is difficult to achieve. Whyte and Flores found this a common problem in Peru
where "interdepartmental frictions have to be appealed up the lines of
authority until they reach a common superior who must spend a large
part of his time in arbitrating disputes instead of working out important plans."[71] The same situation appears in Mexico; and as one
manager expressed it, "I found that a 'fan' arrangement, with each
department reporting directly to the man at the top, worked better that
a coordinated pyramid-like hierarchy." In other words, the organization seemed to function better when people at any one level were not
asked to cooperate with one another, but instead communicated directly
with the boss. Observing similar examples, Whyte and Flores conclude
that

> where people are not bound by relations of
> authority, it seems difficult to get them to work
> together...in Peru, it seems very difficult for
> people to work cooperatively when they are not
> part of some previously established network of
> authority.[72]

In Mexican enterprise, this bond of authority seemed to have a
positive effect upon vertical communication in both directions, despite
whatever by-passing occurred, but imposed severe restrictions upon communications within any one rank. Thus, a worker will often trust his
foreman or department head sooner than a fellow worker in another department; a foreman will often cooperate more easily with his workers
below him or his department head above than with a foreman from another
part of the plant; and, similarly, department heads are more reluctant
to communicate freely with one another than with those above or below
them in a single line of authority. There is usually more than one
line of authority, and communication is more open and cooperation more
frequent within any one line than between them. Organizational hierarchies in Mexico thus seem to be determined by relations of vertical
trust and horizontal distrust.

The manner in which the vertical lines of trust are drawn depends
upon the relationships of those at the top, which is then reflected
downward throughout the entire organization. We have already seen how
these vertical divisions develop between opposing kin groups within a
single family firm. Lines of trust and communication also tended to
parallel natural divisions of labor, the breach between technical and
administrative parts of a firm being perhaps the strongest. This was
especially true when the factory and the offices were geographically
separated. Another common cause of vertical alignments was the growth
of national and foreign managerial factions at the top. Oldtimers and
newcomers were occasionally a cause, and others also existed. In all
cases, however, when a separation began at the top, it filtered down
to the very lower levels, and when little kingdoms developed among
middle management the same phenomenon occurred.

An interesting example of this occurred in a fairly new, North
American-owned firm which employed approximately 135 people. Within its
three years of existence, there had been four changes in the top manager (always a North American), and each change was the result of a
power struggle between the North American in charge and the top-seated
Mexican manager. Bitter rivalry developed and each party had lined up
their supporters. Soon there was talk of a "Mexican mafia" network
which was feeding information up one (Mexican) line of authority that
was detrimental to those at the top of the foreign faction. In another
foreign company, those who worked beneath North American managers were
called "The Untouchables," named after a popular television program,
by personnel who worked for Mexican department heads.

One day an _obrero_, working under the direction of a North American manager, told another man in his section not to trust a third
obrero from the same work group, saying that he was a spy for the
"Mexican mafia." When queried on this, the following story emerged:

The plant was located in the countryside, and all workers came from the nearby village where most of them still continued to farm some land and maintain some animals. The factory was surrounded by an open field which was also owned by the company, and workers who had a cow or two were permitted to bring them to graze while they worked in the plant. All that was necessary was to get permission from the plant manager, which was always granted, and which the third worker had done.

The plant manager was considered part of the "Mexican mafia," however, and so to his fellow workers this <u>orbrero</u> had transgressed the informal lines of authority. By going for permission to the Mexican plant manager, instead of his North American boss, he had acted disloyally in the eyes of his co-workers. He had also left himself open and beholden to the authority of the "other side" and therefore was no longer trusted by his own. A seemingly harmless and formally correct act had brought down a great deal of censure on this man because he had not abided by the informal barriers to communication across vertical lines of authority.

The North American manager, under whose direction he worked, also experienced difficulty in eliciting the cooperation of his fellow managers. He had lived in Mexico for many years, married a previous employee who was Mexican, and was generally well accepted. Nevertheless, standard information was often kept a secret from him. In one case, he had to know the number of kilograms of a material which the company had received, but the head of the accounting department would not let him see the billing sheets; the accountant, moreover, filed these sheets according to a code known only to himself and his few assistants. In a second instance, periodic government lists of duty-free imports were sequestered by one manager instead of being circulated around. A third example of secrecy was the hiding of new machine descriptions, especially by the technical personnel, with the explanation that "if you have a little more technical knowledge, then you have that much more power."

In sum, Mexican enterprise is generally controlled by a centralized system of authority, which is often reflected in the same tendency at middle levels. The effects are: a lack of responsibility at lower levels; inducements to by-pass up and down the hierarchy; conflict between two or more lines of authority; and problems of cooperation, communication, or coordination between these vertical lines. Given this type of situation, how relevant is the body of theory which stresses the necessity of decentralization of authority as a logical consequence of organizational growth? How adequately can it account for the system of authority in Mexican enterprise? How can the above data refine general organizational theory? And what implications do they have for the development of managerial resources? We turn now to these questions.

Change and Authority

One explanation of the characteristics that we have been discussing is that they are largely the effect of an early period of industrial growth, common in many countries. The beginnings of industrial enterprise are closely rooted in traditional social groupings, and the intimate bond between family and business puts a dual brand of personalism and ownership on early forms of management. A description of the centralization of authority in Egyptian enterprise is typical of these practices in newly industrializing countries:

> The great majority of Egyptian-owned private establishments...are organized closer to the pattern of the Abboud enterprises. Here the manager is a dominant individual who extends his personal control over all phases of the business. There is no chartered plan of organization, no formalized procedures for selection and development of managerial personnel, no publicized system of wage and salary classifications. The status of individuals in the managerial hierarchy is based not so much upon function as upon the nature of their relations with the owner-manager.[73]

Similar reports come from India, where the typical organizational structure in enterprise is described as centralized and personal. Myers,[74] and other writers, trace the roots of this to (1) a history of authoritarian relationships with subordinates; (2) a traditionally extended family system; and (3) a "managing-agency" system which was adopted from the British, which resulted in the concentration of control over many diverse enterprises, and which favored management on the basis of connection rather than competence. While such a situation is still common in India, since Independence it is gradually being replaced by trends toward non-authoritarian and non-owning, professionally oriented management. This is especially true in public enterprises.

The course of development in the United States, and to some extent in England, are offered as the exemplary cases of changes in the organizational systems of authority in advanced industrial societies. The use of authority by the individual proprietary capitalist of eighteenth-century England and nineteenth-century United States is depicted in similar terms as those used to describe the typical Mexican, Egyptian, and Indian entrepreneur. The separation of ownership from control, and the recognition of an independent body of trained professional management, led to the growth of the corporate system.[75] Intimately related to this process was the expanding size of American industrial corporations, production for a national market, and an increasingly complex technology. "Captains of industry" built large, vertically-integrated industrial organizations which were highly centralized under their own personal control. By 1900 these types were the dominant unit of business.

The decentralization of American management, both as value and fact, began primarily after World War II. Alfred Chandler summarizes this development as follows:[76]

> Diversification in multi-industry activities... helped to break down the huge centralized structures created to manage the vertically integrated corporations handling a single line of goods. The large functional departments have been divided into smaller

units based on products. This has permitted more
managers to become generalists, rather than specialists, and to become responsible, at an earlier age,
for over-all market and financial performance. The
shortening of the lines of authority, responsibility
and communication, the reduction in the number of
management levels, and the more explicit delegation
of decision-making have helped to make many a corporation less of a bureaucracy and more of an enterprise.

...While the decentralized structure has been the
normal organizational means to manage a diversified
product line, its creation has rarely come automatically.
In most cases its introduction required a change in top
management.

...The decentralized structure evolved, then, largely
to meet the growing complexity in all aspects of
development, purchasing, manufacturing, and marketing,
and to help assure the essential coordination between
these functions for the individual products within the
overall diversified line.

Today, the decentralization of managerial authority is often considered
a necessity as enterprises grow in size and complexity, and the United
States is considered the most advanced example of this development.
The earlier period of centralization, and the consequences for the
system of authority which followed, was interpreted as a logical stage
through which industrial organizations had passed.

On a national level, and in the absence of private ownership, the
recent changes in Russia offer yet another example in support of this
point of view. Here, centralization of all decision-making in the
state created problems of responsibility, by-passing, cooperation,
motivation, and the like, at the plant level. The illegal position of
tolkach, an individual hired by a plant to obtain necessary supplies
through bribery and other such means, became a permanent fixture in
most Russian firms as an institutionalized means of getting around some
of the problems caused by over-centralization.

In recent years, however, the death of Stalin, experiments with
private enterprise by Tito, the shift away from heavy industry, and
other important developments, have begun to bring about some decentralization of Russian enterprise under Gosplan, the coordinating committee
for all Soviet planning. There are indications that estimates of
growth are moving from an emphasis on total production to an emphasis
on efficiency of capital per unit invested. The Gosplan's changes mean
some delegation of authority to the individual plant level, and if this
increases, then the case of Russia may also be offered in support of
the notion that centralization of authority within organizational
hierarchies is more common to early industrial periods of growth and
is bound to be replaced by more decentralized systems at later periods.[77]

A major problem with the notion of a logical sequence of historical stages, however, is that it does not adequately explain why the

centralization of authority is only a temporary stage in the "development" of some societies, while it continues to persist in others; and why, within any one country, decentralization may occur more quickly in one firm than in another.

A second line of reasoning holds that the characteristics discussed in this chapter represent a period in the development of all organizations, regardless of time, place, or extent of industrial growth. According to this explanation, the organization is born from the idea of a man or a group of men. As its creator, the man is, in a sense, father to that organization. In the beginning the organization could not have survived without him; he made it a success. This is the situation described in Chapter II where the man who builds an organization must ultimately face the time when that organization becomes held back by its own creator. This course of events is universal and applies whether the organization is a business enterprise, a university, a hospital, a political party, or even a nation-state.

What makes this interpretation even more pertinent to the development of a business enterprise is the proprietary interest involved. Centralization and the consequence which follow are explained away as though by saying, "It's my business: I built it, I own it, and so of course I am the authority." When ownership is not involved, as with subordinates and in some cases successors, legitimation is the key issue.

A good deal of the theory of bureaucratization has developed around this problem of legitimacy. When a person's position in an organization is not legitimated by tradition, kinship, ownership, or the like, legitimation must come from more universal standards of competence. A growing division of labor and hierarchy of authority reflect a system based on these universal standards. The more complex this division grows, the more specialized are the particular bits of knowledge known by people at the middle levels; while the job of the few at the top concentrates on formulating general policies and goals, and coordinating all these bits in order to achieve such ends. Individuals at middle levels in a bureaucratic hierarchy thus legitimate their positions by virtue of their expertise in a limited field. Such knowledge tends to give power even without authority, and this may be guarded and kept secure by centralizing it within one's own person and by giving greater value to secrecy than to cooperation and communication.[78]

In order to control those who supervise the implementation of technical and administrative orders, as well as those who execute them directly, it then becomes incumbent upon top management to develop a strategy of organization. If organizations, governed by the founder-owner, can solve the succession crisis and divorce the person from the position at the top, then centralization may indeed only be a period in their history, a strategy appropriate to earlier organizational structure and needs. Even where ownership is not involved, as in political parties or universities, these steps may be part of a predictable change in the life of an organization. Regarding the problems of hoarding authority at middle levels, to the extent that those at the top are able to counteract these tendencies, they will be able to achieve a balance of decentralized authority with centralized control.

A major problem with this type of theory of organizational development is that it too often limits itself to an internal examination of a
single social system, and pays little or no attention to the influence
of the larger social structure. It is therefore unable to account for
trends within any one country, or to make substantive comparisons of
different trends in several countries.

A third approach to the question of authority and organization in
industry stresses the importance of the cultural setting. The more
closely centralization and personalization of leadership are related
to social and cultural tradition, the more one may expect to find it
existing, if not predominating, among complex industrial structures as
well as imbedded in traditional enterprise. Mexican history has been
a fertile breeding ground for just such a development, and the same is
true of many other countries.

The egalitarian ideology in the United States helps to explain
the acceptance of decentralized authority among its leadership. For
this reason, Philip Selznick has said that decentralization is seen as
a "halo that becomes especially useful in countries which prize the
symbols of democracy."[79] Similarly, a history of authoritarian state
control has been the basis for interpreting the centralized system of
authority in Russia.[80] Also, the traditional patterns of Japanese
feudalism and paternalism, the rigidly defined social hierarchy, and
the emphasis on loyalty, respect, and subordination, help to explain
why Japanese enterprise today is highly centralized and why even top
executives are seldom willing to take individual responsibility.[81]

A study of Italian management, for example, also points to the
importance of its cultural and historical setting.[82] According to
Ferrarotti, the early political disunity of the country, and hence
the lack of identification between the individual and the state, ex-
plains part of the emphasis upon absolute family loyalty and the over-
riding importance of the family in all aspects of Italian life. Moreover, the speculative quality of finance capitalism, after the
Renaissance, changed the old commercial families into a leisure class
and set the tone for essentially preindustrial forms of small family
enterprise. In 1951, over 70% of all industrial firms employed fewer
than three workers each, and less than one percent had more than 100
workers each. Ownership, control, and all top positions are family
centered and motivated. Italian managers are reluctant to delegate
authority and:

> they tend to think of their authority in terms
> of personal power rather than in terms of a neces-
> sary function related to, and coordinated with,
> other equally necessary functions within the enter-
> prise. The enterprise is seen as some sort of pri-
> vate kingdom.

Management is thus committed to "serving the basic interests of the
family even when and if those interests are not compatible with increasing production or expansion."[84]

In less developed countries, the relation of management systems of authority to cultural traditions is even stronger. Speaking again of the Abboud enterprises in Egypt, Harbison and Ibrahim state that,

> This type of system, where authority is associated exclusively with an individual, is quite compatible with the social and cultural traditions which stress the personal authority of the father or eldest son in the family and the individual prerogatives of the village or tribal leader. This is the kind of management which most Egyptians expect. Abboud is the kind of person most people have in mind when they discuss the successful Egyptian entrepreneur.[85]

The emphasis placed on centralized and personal leadership in Mexico may also be traced through its heritage of social relations. During the centuries of Colonial rule, there existed an extreme regionalism whose backbone was the self-sufficient agrarian hacienda. In an environment where the regional rulers were the sole arbiters of law, the only guarantee of one's rights rested either in his own power or in his ability to ally himself with a powerful protector. In return for this protection, the followers owed their subordination and fealty to this individual. These strong and paternal leaders permeated the entire fabric of Mexican life, and could be found in business, politics, religion, the military, and even in neighborhood social relations.

> Today, according to many observers, the tendency toward caciquismo [bossism] and paternalism is a great deal weaker. But it still lingers. The strong individual, posing as the father image and spreading his figurative mantle of protection still occupies an extraordinarily prominent place in the structure of Mexican society. Demanding unquestioning loyalty, he also undertakes to provide assistance and protection to those who follow his lead.[86]

Thus, the typical system of authority which has evolved in Mexican enterprise is firmly rooted in the traditions and values of Mexican society.

An approach which stresses the relation of national tradition to contemporary management systems, however, tends to emphasize cultural uniqueness and to minimize statements of more general applicability. It ignores general theory of organizational development and industrial growth, and does not attempt to isolate universal principles. Moreover, it is unable to account for those few firms which are attempting to decentralize authority, impersonalize control, and actively develop lower levels of management within a national context that lacks cultural models for such forms.

We have considered three alternative explanations to the system of authority which predominates in Mexican enterprise: (1) as a universal, early period of industrialization; (2) as a period in the development of all organizations, regardless of time and place; and (3) as a result of a specific historical and cultural background. None of these explanations is false, but each is only a partial truth. Taken together, however, the different perspectives and the comparative data have shown that the problems discussed are major ones and, despite local variations, seem to be universal.

For present purposes, the three views can be synthesized. Mexico has a long cultural tradition of rule by patrones, which often is still expected by both the leaders and the led. Moreover, its industrialization is of recent vintage and most Mexican-owned enterprises are still run by the founding fathers. The tendencies toward patronal rule are therefore still strong and yield slowly and reluctantly.

At the same time, however, other factors are increasing the pressures to change. Among the more important ones are: the growing problem of managerial succession; changing market conditions and increased competition, both internal and worldwide; and the growing influence of North American business practices, particularly a readiness to adopt and adapt new technologies. As the pressures to change steadily increase, the need to develop managerial resources in Mexico becomes all the more imperative. In the concluding section, therefore, we will examine the relation of management in Mexico to the social environment, its future needs and problems, and some implications for business management education.

CONCLUSIONS

Change in the Future

Private enterprise in Mexico is still intimately related to family enterprise. In many instances, particularly in the small and the more traditional firms, the business is seen as an extension of the family. The overlay of family-and-firm values stress stability and perpetuity, and these social functions frequently take precedence over the amount of economic profit. Control of the family firm is usually complete; investment rights, and financial and managerial control coincide,[87] and there is no separation between ownership and management. Although the general trend of development witnesses a growing separation of these functions, the distinction may be more theoretical than real, and the basic family foundation may remain unimpaired.[88]

The compatibility of family and business institutions, and of village life with factory life, requires social values which are in harmony with business in general. To survive for any great length of time, this overlap of family-and-firm values must permeate through all levels of the social fabric. In order for the artisan shop to survive rapid industrial growth, the large corporation must continue to maintain strong family values. In other words, both the artisan shop and the large corporation must play by these same family-firm rules, or else the shop must ultimately succumb to the competitive power of the larger corporation.

The family firm, then, may be seen as a positive impetus to entrepreneurial activity in early periods of modernization, and one

185

which harmonizes with communal traditional patterns. It has also survived where goals and organization of large businesses take on the
characteristics of the modest family firm writ large, and where social
function takes a precedence over amount of economic profit. When a
national ideology favors rapid economic development, however, this
"sanction pattern" is not likely to survive. Traditional family-firm
values of enterprise stability and perpetuity clash with new economic
goals of sustained investment and expansion. The more competition in-
vades the marketplace, the more vulnerable become the traditional structures and the values which are associated with them.[89]

Under such conditions, the family firm must adapt to the requirements of modern industrial enterprise or ultimately face extinction.
The issue is not whether the family firm can survive, but rather that
it cannot survive continuous and rapid industrial growth in its present
traditional form. Or, by corollary, to the extent that this form does
perpetuate itself, industrial development will be impeded. The situation becomes more or less problematical depending on two principal
factors: market pressures from without, and adaptation or resistance
to change from within.

Speaking to the first, despite variations by industry, product, and
region, the sustained rate of growth which Mexico has experienced has
steadily increased the outside pressures. While many traditional family
firms are enjoying large profits at present, the period of time during
which they will be able to continue doing so decreases rapidly.[90] The
Mexican family firm therefore faces the pressures of rapid modernization
and industrialization which do not permit the luxury of gradual change.

Regarding internal change, industrial trends in developed countries
have shown a reduction of both family ownership and family management
through time. Moreover, the firms which have remained within family
bounds and flourished have been those which were able to adapt to the
changing industrial requirements. Mexico has experienced sustained
economic growth since the late 1930's and early 1940's, and the family
heads of most businesses, from small shop to large factory, are now
anywhere between 50 and 75 years old. A necessary adaptation, therefore, is the provision of adequate managerial resources to replace the
entrepreneurs who are passing from the scene. In some instances this
has resulted in employment on the basis of competence rather than family
connection, willingness to hire and delegate authority to non-related
personnel at managerial levels, job specification, readiness to adapt
to technological innovations, and the notion that business exists to
maximize profits.

So long as market expansion outstrips productive capacity, conflict and managerial problems focus more on pressures internal to the
firm, such as those developing due to an increase in size. Increased
competition, however, creates external pressures to which traditional
structures and the values associated with them are even more vulnerable
because they are less controllable. The ability of a family firm to
absorb these stresses during the development and differentiation of
its organization and its goals depends in large part upon the nature
of the social relationships within the enterprise which we have exam-

examined. Stated somewhat differently, economic activity ultimately derives its evaluation and form from the social context and, by corollary,
some aspects of Mexican culture, social structure and personality have
adapted to the functional requirements of business, while others have not.

In analyzing the character of this adaptation and in charting its
future course, it is useful to divide the social features of enterprise
into two classes: first, those which are already in the process of
change or are likely to begin changing in the near future; and second,
those which are not likely to change for a long time to come.

Regarding these two classes of change in the Mexican family firm,
evidence of the passing of one-man rule may already be seen. With the
fathers of Mexico's industrial revolution reaching the age of retire-
ment, a new generation of industrial management is gradually taking over.
Not only are there signs that the managerial function is being dispersed
to various members of the ruling family, but one also notices a wither-
ing of the family monopoly over management positions.

Vacuums created by departing family members are more and more
being filled with non-family members, even by individuals not previously and personally known to the owners. Several middle level managers,
and even some at the top, for example, report that they get their jobs
by answering newspaper advertisements. Foreign firms and companies
whose products require technical skills and university training have
been among the ones more inclined to use this manner of locating new
management personnel, and more universalistic criteria have long been
common for industrial managers in the public sector. An emphasis on
education, and on the _título_ (degree), are reinforcing more universalistic prerequisites for obtaining managerial positions.

There is, however, a lag between the growing prevalence of these
new features in the private sector and the demise of more traditional
practices. The hiring of a non-related employee on the basis of competence, for example, is more likely to occur because an extra job has
opened up than because an incompetent relative is to be fired; nepotism
diminishes slowly, and the coupon-clipping relative may live to a
hearty old age. The emphasis placed on the value of family solidarity
is also likely to persist.

Perhaps most important is the fact that while the separation between ownership and management is beginning to grow, there is little
evidence to suggest that this is matched by a growing diffusion of
shareholdings. Under conditions of rapid expansion and the need for
financial credit, one occasionally sees a minimal dispersion of stock
ownership, but it is never in sufficient quantity to insure the independence of managerial control from the authority of the investors.

C. Wright Mills writes that "negatively, the transformation of the
middle class is a shift from property to non-property; positively, it
is a shift from property to a new axis of stratification: occupation."[91]
In Mexico this transformation is in midstream. Unlike several other
Latin American areas, the hegemony of the rural landed elite has been
broken and has been replaced, in the main, by a new industrial elite.

"Only in Mexico does there seem to have been a thorough reorganization of the upper classes in terms of power and wealth."[92] While the shift in emphasis from owner of land to owner of industry has already taken place, however, the separation between ownership, on the one hand, and power and prestige, on the other, is only beginning. The character of family firms in general is therefore likely to change considerably in the near future. Yet, we may expect that this change will represent an increased acceptance of executive-management more rapidly than in increase in its effective control over policy. In other words, cultural traditions in Mexico are yielding to industrial requirements more than they are assimilating them.

Beyond conveying power and prestige, ownership of enterprise in Mexico is also the surest route up the third ladder in the stratification triumvirate, the attainment of wealth. There is one simple fact that cannot be ignored in an assessment of management in Mexico: a man can earn a great deal more money in the rapidly expanding Mexican market by being an entrepreneur who risks his own money, than by being an executive who manages someone else's investment, whether it be the state's or another private individual's. Industrial ownership not only conveys power and prestige, it also brings wealth, which in turn adds to power and prestige. This is perhaps truer in Mexico than in other Latin American countries, where these indices, derived more from North American studies, have less applicability. The drive for economic advantage and positions of power in Mexico still derive their ultimate evaluation from the individual's ability to translate these into social position. Economic activity is still subordinate to social ends, but it is now a more readily accepted means to achieve those ends. This, of course, is truer in urban, than in rural, areas.

The increased social mobility which these changes are witness to seem to have more applicability for entrance into the upper class than into the middle class. In 1953, Beals reported that among all the Latin American countries, "barriers to upward mobility are great...but probably less so in Mexico than elsewhere. In particular, there are fewer obstacles to rising from middle to upper classes in Mexico than in most other countries."[93] The gap in educational and cultural background between white collar empleados and blue collar obreros, however, still minimizes the opportunities for upward mobility into the middle class, and there is little evidence to suggest that this will change greatly in the near future. The weakening of the traditional definition of empleados de confianza has diminished the caste-like differences between the two groups, but there are still few institutionalized ways to cross the basic dividing line. The stratification barrier in the factory is a reflection of the same barrier in society at large.

The foreman is the classical example of the man caught beneath this barrier. It is unlikely that any substantial upgrading of his role will occur in the near future to help bridge this gap. In 1958, Kahl concluded from a number of interviews with Mexican industrial workers that:

> Mexico does not yet appear to have institutionalized
> an accepted career for the middle ranks of industrial

workers. These men are neither successful members of
the working class nor accepted members of a stabilized
lower middle class. ...As the middle class grows in
size and complexity, Mexican society will probably
create a more comfortable niche for men of their type.[94]

Ten years later, the niche has not grown much more comfortable.

One consequence of the emphasis on ownership, the opportunities
for industrial profits, and the blocked mobility of skilled workers and
middle management, should be explored further. I call this phenomenon
"entrepreneurial moonlighting." Considerable emphasis on the sources
of entrepreneurship has been given to economic and psychological elements, and concern with social factors has largely focused on minority
and immigrant groups. Insufficient attention has been paid to the
interrelation between cultural values, economic opportunities, and the
industrial social structure.

Individuals at middle levels (supervisors and middle management),
whose upward progress within a firm has been blocked, often begin to
open their own small businesses on the side. These are generally in
fields related to their full-time jobs, and often utilize the knowledge,
contacts, time, and even materials gained from the company for which
they work. If these businesses fail, the financial loss is not too
great and the individual still has his other job; if the business becomes very successful, then he will terminate his employee status. Not
all employees who are blocked from rising within the employee hierarchy
engage in entrepreneurial moonlighting, however, and besides ambition,
an important factor in determining those who will and those who won't
seems to be the extent of their personal identification with the firm,
and hence, with its top man. In addition to telling us about social
change in complex organizations, the practice of entrepreneurial moonlighting may also tell us something important about the social dynamics
of economic growth and merits more attention in the future.

In line with our conclusion that an increased separation between
ownership and management does not suggest a growing diffusion of shareholdings, or a growing freedom of managerial control from the authority
of investors, the concentration of that authority and control may also
be expected to continue in the foreseeable future. Moreover, we have
seen how the delegation of authority from upper to middle levels often
results in a system of departmental autocracy. It is possible that the
growing legitimation and acceptance of executive management, its increased prestige in large industrial firms, and greater opportunities
for mobility at middle levels, will reduce this centralization, but
such a development still seems a long way off.

In consequence, the related problems of unwillingness to take
responsibility and by-passing are also apt to continue. The growing
respectability, profitability, and authority of executive-management,
however, may begin to have a positive effect on the willingness of
middle-level personnel to accept responsibility. Matters of by-passing,
and lack of horizontal communication and cooperation, seem to have a
more deleterious effect on managerial efficiency from the perspective

of organizational theory than from the viewpoint of those involved. Indeed, one may surmise that the system of authority in Mexican enterprise is really quite workable within its own cultural context or else it would not continue to flourish as strongly as it has. Its negative effects are probably greater on the internal operation of a firm than on the operation and expansion of industry.

Implications for Business Management Education

This study of management in Mexico and its relation to social change in the country has been basically qualitative. This is not by accident. Discussion, research, and writing on the subject of managerial resource development more often than not focuses on the critical needs for such development rather than on an understanding of the actual ways in which management is practiced in its daily routine and in its overall conception.[95] Resource development studies therefore tend to emphasis quantitative needs more frequently than the need for qualitative changes. The results, then, generally call for more education, more training classes and classrooms, more manpower development, and more business schools.

While poorer studies simply call for more, better ones are quick to point out that this must not be more of the same: there must be better education, better training classes, better classrooms, better manpower development, better business schools, etc. To be sure, no one is going to argue with such well-intentioned manifestos; that is, no one will argue until someone attempts to define "better" and to implement programs on the basis of this definition. Attempts at definition thereupon enter into the non-economic context of economic behavior.

Managerial incentives are culturally defined, and economic relations ultimately derive their evaluation from an individual's interpretation of social values. Economic relations may appear to operate more overtly within a social framework in peasant and feudal systems than in industrial societies, but the bond in the latter is nonetheless there. It is less easily recognizable when economic action is directed toward the achievement of pecuniary profit, but underlying the economic goal is the system of social values which gives meaning to that monetary gain.

Where economic actions do not seem to meet the end of material gains, this does not mean that rational conceptions have been abandoned. The absence of a money economy in a peasant community, for example, means imprecision, "but it does not imply either the lack of rational calculation or an unregulated system of handling expenditure of resources."[96] What it means is that rationality involves a social as well as an economic framework, and certain social frameworks limit choice and precision in economic activity more than others.

Management development and organization reflect these basic changes in the social framework, and the qualitative change beginning to be evidenced in business management education in Mexico reflects these same changes. The qualitative difference which the analysis suggests is the idea that management is not a _person_, but a _concept_, a _position_, a _function_, and a _profession_. This qualitative change does not mean an emphasis on education which is better, and thus a matter of normative definition, but rather an emphasis on education which is different, and thus a matter of cognitive definition.

The concept of management refers to an idea, representing the universal meaning and essential attributes involved in controlling and directing human activity. It is an abstraction derived from the perception of innumerable concrete instances. Similarly, the concept of manager represents the portrayal of these attributes by an individual, as distinguished from the individual himself. The role of the manager exists independently of the individual who occupies it at any given moment, and the notion of management exists independently of the concrete actions taken by a manager. This conceptualization is an essential ingredient of management education.

The idea that management is a position, not a person, strengthens the conceptualization of the managerial role. In the social organization of enterprise, those at the top of the hierarchy direct the activities of those below them. It is this position which makes them managers; it is their personal effectiveness which makes them good managers. When management is defined in positional terms, the necessary requirements may be defined according to universalistic criteria of competence. When the requirements are defined by particularistic criteria, such as family birth and connection, then management _is_ specific persons. Judged by universal criteria, an individual's education may be necessary but not sufficient qualification to occupy a particular post in management. Judged by particularistic criteria, his education may be sufficient but not necessary. Managers who think in universalistic terms are less likely to personalize their position in order to make themselves indispensable and hence secure. Given this mental perspective, they are more likely to base their security on their performance and to implant this attitude in their subordinates. Such a notion is perhaps best exemplified in the words of one Mexican executive who said:

> I am trying to instill the idea that the division
> managers have not fulfilled their job and their
> obligation to the company unless they have trained
> men who can replace them at any time. I am trying
> to show them how to spot men with responsibility,
> for better jobs. And I am also trying to prepare
> my division managers so that they can step up to
> my job at any time.

A third implication for business management education is that management is a function. The function of management is to shape and direct the utilization of natural resources, capital, and technology by human agents, through institutions and organizations. Topics such as finance, production, control, and marketing traditionally have been considered as functional areas, subject to systematic instruction. The same cannot be said of the managerial function. Unlike the other functional areas, which deal with passive agents such as materials, money, and machines, treating management as a function requires systematic instruction about the nature of human activity. This is all the more

191

difficult because of the normative quality of different values, but all
the more necessary because the teaching of management as a function is
as appropriate to a production engineer as to an accountant or a director of sales.

A fourth distinction which is of importance to the development and
performance of managerial resources is implantation of the idea of
management as a profession. In their typology of managerial elites,
Harbison and Myers distinguish between patrimonial, political, and professional managers.[97] They define patrimonial management as "business
management in which ownership, major policy-making positions, and a
significant proportion of other jobs in the hierarchy are held by members of an extended family." Political management, according to the
authors, "exists where ownership, major policy-making positions, and
key administrative posts are held by persons on the basis of political
affiliations and loyalties. Access is thus dominated by political considerations, and the orientation and interests of management are colored
throughout by political goals." The basic similarity between these two
forms of management, they continue, is that with greater industrial
growth "it becomes increasingly evident that they must rely on competence rather than connections as the standard for access to managerial
positions." This is the realm of professional management, they conclude,
toward which all forms of industrial countries are moving: "enterprise
management in which major policy-making positions and nearly all other
positions in the hierarchy are held by persons on the basis of alleged
or demonstrated technical competence rather than on relationships to a
family or to a political regime." Policy-making and administration is
not strictly speaking a profession, but business leaders who conceptual-
ize their position and function in terms of universal standards of
knowledge may appropriately be spoken of as professional management.

In sum, these are the qualitative changes, suggested by the analysis, for the development of managerial resources: to advance the notions
of management as a concept, a position, a function, and a profession.
Most important, perhaps, is that this sort of emphasis does not call for
more and better on-the-job or in-the-academy educational programs,
schools, teachers, and graduates however much they are, in fact,
needed. What it calls for is a new and different quality of mind. This
change already has begun in Mexico, and it will play a significant part
in the country's future growth.

NOTES AND REFERENCES

1. There is considerable literature on the history and development of
Mexico. Among the better sources, some of the most useful are listed below. For the colonial period: William H. Prescott, History of
the Conquest of Mexico, various editions; and Eric R. Wolf, Sons of
the Shaking Earth (Chicago: University of Chicago Press, 1959).
For the period 1810-1910: the series entitled Historia moderna de
México, directed by Daniel Cosío Villegas (México, D.F.: Editorial
Hermes, 1955-1966) six volumes; Andrés Molina Enríques, Los grandes
problemas nacionales, republished in Problemas agrícoles e industri-
ales de México, supplement to vol. V (January-March 1953) no. 1;
and Lesley B. Simpson, Many Mexicos (Berkeley: University of
California Press, 1952). From 1910 to the present: Víctor Alba,
Las ideas sociales contemporáneas en México (México, D.F.: Fondo
de Cultura Económica, 1960); Frank Brandenburg, The Making of Modern
Mexico (Englewood Cliffs, New Jersey: Prentice-Hall, 1964); Howard
F. Cline, Mexico: Revolution to Evolution, 1940-1960 (London:
Oxford University Press, 1962); Daniel Cosío Villegas, "The Mexican
Revolution, Then and Now," in Change in Latin America: The Mexican
and Cuban Revolutions (Lincoln, Nebraska: University of Nebraska
Press, 1961); Edmundo Flores, Tratado de economía agrícola (México,
D.F.: Fondo de Cultura Económica, 1961); Moises González Navarro,
"La ideología de la revolución mexicana," Historia mexicana, vol. XL
(April-June 1961) pp. 628ff; Ifigenia M. Navarrete, La distribución
del ingreso y el desarrollo económico de México (México, D.F.:
Universidad Nacional, 1960); Oscar Lewis, "Mexico Since Cardenas,"
Social Change in Latin America Today, R. Adams, ed. (New York:
Harper, 1960); Sanford Mosk, Industrial Revolution in Mexico
(Berkeley: University of California Press, 1950); Robert E. Scott,
Mexican Government in Transition (Urbana, University of Illinois
Press, 1959); Frank Tannenbaum, Mexico: The Struggle for Peace and
Bread, (N.Y.: Knopf, 1950); William P. Tucker, The Mexican Govern-
ment Today (Minneapolis: University of Minnesota Press, 1957);
Raymond Vernon, The Dilemma of Mexico's Development (Cambridge:
Harvard University Press, 1963); and also the four-volume work,
México: 50 años de revolución (México, D.F.: Fondo de Cultura
Económica, 1960-62).

2. This rule varies with the sphere of activity and with many other
conditions. Moreover, the state did not fully begin to enforce the
rule until 1959, and in many instances it has still not enforced it.

3. See Navarrete, La distribución del ingreso, op. cit., and Vernon,
The Dilemma of Mexico's Development, op. cit., pp. 94 and 208 for
opposite sides of this controversy.

4. Brandenburg reports that in 1963 over one-third of all Mexican
families--the average size of the Mexican family is 5.6 persons--
had monthly incomes of $24 or less, that over 80 percent of Mexico's
families had monthly incomes of $80 or less, and that less than 9
percent of Mexico's families had a monthly income above $175.
The Making of Modern Mexico, op. cit., p. 207.

5. See Vernon, op. cit., particularly ch. V.

6. As we shall see, for example, individual inter-generational (that is, father-son) mobility is both possible and common. While social mobility is not totally absent in caste systems, a caste, not an individual, is generally the unit which moves up or down in the stratification hierarchy. For a study of how this mobility of castes occurs, see M. N. Srinivas, "A Note on Sanskritization and Western-ization," The Far Eastern Quarterly, vol. XV (November 1955-August 1966), pp. 492-496, reprinted in Reinhard Bendix and Seymour Martin Lipset eds., Class, Status, and Power, 2nd edition (New York: The Free Press, 1966) pp. 552-560.

7. For a discussion of labor commitment and protest, see Clark Kerr, et. al., Industrialism and Industrial Man (Cambridge: Harvard University Press, 1960) ch. viii, and Clark Kerr, "Changing Social Structures," in W. Moore and A. Feldman, Labor Commitment and Social Change in Developing Areas (New York: Social Science Research Council, 1960) pp. 348-359.

8. In fairness, it should be mentioned that this particular manager regretted this manner of distinction, but feels that he has been unable to change it.

9. In contrast, Fillol describes the shortage of competent foremen in Argentina as "not so much the consequences of a lack of technically skilled or adequately trained personnel as, at least since the 1940's, a matter of a lack of incentives. Pay differences between foremen and workers have been systematically reduced (by legislation or con-tractual arrangements) in most industries." Argentina differs from the Mexican case, however, in that "foremen were usually recruited from middle-income families and were thus used to higher living standards than most workers." Apparently, the bulk of foremen came from already skilled immigrant groups. Tomas R. Fillol, Social Factors in Economic Development (Cambridge: M.I.T. Press, 1961) p. 61.

10. One insightful and witty example, from Britain, may be found in Stephen Potter's One-upmanship (New York: Holt, 1952) p. 44. "The Guv'nor addresses:
    Co-director Michael Yates as MIKE
    Assistant Director Michael Yates as MICHAEL
    Sectional Manager Michael Yates as MR. YATES
    Sectional Assistant Michael Yates as YATES
    Apprentice Michael Yates as MICHAEL
    Night-watchman Michael Yates as MIKE."

11. For a fuller discussion of the term "expressive," see ch. V, pp. 127-28, below.

12. This sub-section relies heavily on the work of John Bennett, par-ticularly Bennett & Iwao Ishino, Paternalism in the Japanese Econo-my, op. cit.; and Bennett, "Paternalism," an unpublished paper pre-pared for the International Encyclopedia of the Social Sciences.

13. Bennett & Ishino, op. cit., p. 225.

14. Eric R. Wolf, Sons of the Shaking Earth, op. cit., pp. 204, 207-9.

15. Richard N. Adams, "On the Relation Between Plantation and 'Creole Cultures'," Plantation Systems of the New World, (Pan American Union, 1959), p. 78.

16. Masataka Sugi, "The Concept of Ninjo," in Bennett & Ishino, op. cit., p. 268.

17. Michael Kenny, "Patterns of Patronage in Spain," Anthropological Quarterly, vol. 33, pp. 14-23, and J. K. Campbell, Honour, Family and Patronage: A Study of Institutions and Moral Values in a Greek Mountain Community (Oxford: Clarendon Press, 1964) use the terms "patron-client" to discuss paternalism within a communal, rather than enterprise, setting.

18. For several different points of view, setting the problem in a wider political context, see Frank Brandenburg, The Making of Modern Mexico, op. cit.; Robert E. Scott, Mexican Government in Transition, op. cit.; William P. Tucker, The Mexican Government Today, op. cit.; and Howard F. Cline, The United States and Mexico, (Cambridge, 1953).

19. Bennett and Ishino, op. cit., p. 235.

20. William F. Whyte and Allan R. Holmberg, "Human Problems of United States Enterprise in Latin America," Cornell Conference Report, October 1957, p. 3, reprinted in Human Organization, Fall, 1956.

21. Wolf, Sons of the Shaking Earth, op. cit., p. 207; underscoring mine.

22. Eric Wolf, "Specific Aspects of Plantation Systems in the New World: Community Sub-Cultures and Social Classes," in Plantation Systems in the New World, op. cit., p. 138.

23. Talcott Parsons, The Social System (New York: Free Press, 1951), pp. 79-88.

24. J. K. Campbell, Honour, Family and Patronage, op. cit.

25. For a discussion of the concept of reciprocity, in this regard, see Alvin W. Gouldner, "The Norm of Reciprocity: A Preliminary Statement," American Sociological Review, vol. XXV (April 1960) pp. 161-78.

26. See, for example, Francisco Rojas Gonzáles, "La Institución del compadrazgo entre los indígenas de México," Revista mexicana de sociología, vol. V (1943), pp. 201-14; and Benjamin D. Paul, Ritual Kinship, With Special Reference to Godparenthood in Middle America, unpublished Ph.D. dissertation. University of Chicago, 1942.

27. See Wilbert E. Moore & Arnold S. Feldman, _Labor Commitment and Social Change in Developing Areas_ (New York: Social Science Research Council, 1960) ch. ii, for a further discussion of this point.

28. Stanley J. Stein, "The Brazilian Cotton Textile Industry, 1850-1950," _Economic Growth: Brazil, India, Japan_, J. Kuznets, W. Moore, & J. Spengler eds. (Durham, N. C.: Duke University Press, 1955) p. 437.

29. Robert J. Alexander, "Brazil, Argentina, and Chile," _Labor in Developing Economies_, Walter Galeson ed. (Berkeley: University of California Press, 1962) p. 178. See also, Alexander, _Labor Relations in Argentina, Brazil, and Chile_ (New York: McGraw-Hill, 1962).

30. Peter Gregory, "The Labor Market in Puerto Rico," in Moore & Feldman, _op. cit._

31. Alexander, "Brazil, Argentina, and Chile," _op. cit._, p. 177.

32. For a fuller discussion of this process, see Stanley M. Davis, "Management's Effect on Worker Organizations in a Developing Country," _Human Organizations_, vol. 27, no. 1, Spring, 1968.

33. The same tendencies may result from the recently instituted profit-sharing law, although it is too recent to examine clearly the effects. In some firms, for example, where the _patrón_ is trying to shed his paternal role, the _reparto de utilidades_ (share of the profits)has replaced the annual _gratificación_.

34. R. Adams, _Plantation Systems_, _op. cit._, p. 78.

35. Edward Norbeck, _Pineapple Town: Hawaii_ (Berkeley: University of California Press, 1959) p. 148.

36. Bennett & Ishino, _op. cit._, chap. 5.

37. "The state set itself up as the arbiter of economic life. Unions became creatures of the state; if the state wanted strong unions, they were strengthened, and if the state wanted weak unions, they were weakened." Brandenburg, _The Making of Modern Mexico_, _op. cit._, p. 213. For additional studies of labor unionism in Mexico see, Marjorie Clark, _Organized Labor in Mexico_ (Chapel Hill: University of North Carolina Press, 1934); and for more recent treatments, Moises Poblete Troncoso & Ben G. Burnett, _The Rise of the Latin American Labor Movement_ (New Haven: College and University Press, 1960), pp. 97-107, and Robert J. Alexander, _Organized Labor in Latin America_, (New York: Free Press, 1965), pp. 183-199.

38. Bennett & Ishino, _op. cit._, pp. 230-231.

39. Whyte & Holmberg, _op. cit._, p. 39.

40. Juarez Rubens Brandão Lopes, "Relations industrielles dans deux communautés brésiliennes," _Sociologie du Travail_, (Paris), vol. III

(October–December, 1961), also reprinted in <u>La industrialización en América Latina</u>, Joseph A. Kahl, ed. (México: Fondo de Cultura Económica, 1965).

41. Juarez Rubens Brandão Lopes, <u>op</u>. <u>cit</u>., p. 215, translated from Spanish edition, SMD.

42. See, for example, Brandenburg's treatment of the labor wing within the Revolutionary Party, <u>The Making of Modern Mexico</u>, <u>op</u>. <u>cit</u>., especially pp. 119–140, 242–247.

43. P. Gregory, in Moore & Feldman, <u>op</u>. <u>cit</u>., pp. 163–184. For similar findings in Chile see, Henry Landsberger, Manuel Barrera, and Abel Toro, "The Chilean Labor Union Leader: A Preliminary Report on his Background and Attitudes," <u>Industrial and Labor Relations Review</u>, vol. XVII (April, 1964) no. 3, pp. 405–412, 419–420.

44. i.e., "Known evils are better than unknown goods."

45. For a further discussion of this point, see Stanley M. Davis, "Entrepreneurial Succession," <u>Administrative Science Quarterly</u> (Special Issue, Summer, 1968).

46. Strassman, however, notes that, "The decline of paternalism has strengthened the state's hand more than labor's, and has led to the state's holding the balance of power in labor–management disputes. This development has been to the short-run disadvantage of workers, because government and industry in Latin America tend to agree in their emphasis on tranquility and on minimizing consumer expenditures for the sake of capital accumulation and growth." <u>Continuity and Change</u>, <u>op</u>. <u>cit</u>., p. 181.

47. It is interesting to note that de Tocqueville points to the growing lack of reciprocity, in the gap between responsibility and subordination, as one of the principal causes of the French Revolution. "When we remember that it was in France that the feudal system, while retaining the characteristics which made it so irksome to, and so much resented by, the masses, had most completely discarded all that could benefit or protect them, we may feel less surprise at the fact that France was the place of origin of the revolt destined so violently to sweep away the last vestiges of that ancient European institution." Alexis de Tocqueville, <u>The Old Regime and the French Revolution</u> (New York: Doubleday, 1955), pp. 203–204.

48. J. K. Campbell, <u>Honour, Family and Patronage</u>, <u>op</u>. <u>cit</u>., p. 233.

49. Kunio Odaka, "Traditionalism and Democracy in Japanese Industry," in <u>Transactions of the Fifth World Congress of Sociology</u>, International Sociological Association, 1964, vol. III, p. 39. Odaka also discusses the ideological implications of the two viewpoints.

50. Bennett and Ishino present a third point of view of paternalism as a response to socio-economic conditions which may appear in any

country at any historical period, namely, scarce capital disproportionately distributed, low standards of living, and lack of
alternative means for attaining a livelihood. These conditions,
however, are more commonly found in pre-industrial societies and in
those with a feudal past.

51. William F. Whyte and Graciela Flores, "Los valores y el crecimiento
    económico en el Perú," in La industrialización en América Latina,
    Joseph A. Kahl, ed., (México: Fondo de Cultura Económica, 1965),
    p. 228. For similar reports on delegation in Argentine industry,
    see Fillol, Social Factors in Economic Development, op. cit., pp.
    18-21.

52. For a complete discussion of these three patterns, see Stanley M.
    Davis, "Entrepreneurial Succession," op. cit.

53. Fernando H. Cardoso describes this same situation in Brazil and its
    negative effect on expansion and investment due to limited executive
    and administrative capabilities. El empresario industrial en América
    Latina: Brazil (Mar del Plata: Naciones Unidas Comisión Económica
    para América Latina, 1963) E/CN.12/642/Add. 2, pp. 25-26.

54. Frederick Harbison & Charles A. Myers, Management in the Industrial
    World (New York: McGraw-Hill, 1959), p. 178.

55. L. C. Bresser Pereira, "The Rise of Middle Class and Middle Manage-
    ment in Brazil," Journal of Inter-American Studies, vol. IV, no. 3,
    (July, 1962), pp. 322-23.

56. Enterprise in Latin America, op. cit., pp. 8-9.

57. Heinz Hartmann, Authority and Organization in German Management
    (Princeton: Princeton University Press, 1959).

58. Ibid., p. 59.

59. Ibid., p. 61.

60. David Granick, The European Executive, op. cit., p. 309.

61. Since "centralize" means to concentrate in one place, the term
    "hoarding" is used when authority is concentrated at different
    levels and among different individuals.

62. See Michel Crozier, The Bureaucratic Phenomenon (Chicago: Universi-
    ty of Chicago Press, 1964) for similar remarks about the French
    tendency to visualize authority as something which must be had com-
    pletely to be effective. It is not something to share, as in the
    U. S. view.

63. Editors of Fortune, The Executive Life (New York: Doubleday,
    1956) p. 139.

64. Oriol Pi-Sunyer, A Regional Coalition Economy in Mexico: An His-torical Ethnography of Zamora, Michoacan, unpublished doctoral disser-tation, Harvard University, 1962, p. 354.

65. Ibid., p. 364.

66. A corollary of this restrictive control and family-centered outlook is the "reluctance to merge with other enterprises even when the separate units are much too small for optimum efficiency," and even an unwillingness to "promote joint action on industry-wide problems." Strassmann, Continuity & Change, p. 168, and Cochran, Puerto Rican Businessman, p. 108. Frederick Harbison and Eugene Burgess report similar occurences among family-centered firms in France, Belgium, and Italy in "Modern Management in Western Europe," American Journal of Sociology, vol. LX (July 1954) no. 1, pp. 15-23.

67. Thomas C. Cochran and Ruben E. Reina, Entrepreneurship in Argentine Culture (Philadelphia: University of Pennsylvania Press, 1962) pp. 266-69.

68. The respondent, here, actually used the verb conocer, which has the implication "to know someone," rather than the verb saber, "to know how to do something." In the context, he was referring to the latter kind of knowledge, but his choice of verb also stresses the importance of the personal element involved in carrying out an order. See ch. V, below.

69. For similar findings, see John Fayerweather, The Executive Overseas (Syracuse: Syracuse University Press, 1959).

70. Albert Waterston, Development Planning: Lessons of Experience (Baltimore, Johns Hopkins Press, 1965) p. 290.

71. Op. cit., p. 229.

72. Ibid.

73. Frederick Harbison and Ibrahim Abdelkader Ibrahim, Human Resources for Egyptian Enterprise (New York: McGraw-Hill, 1958) p. 65. Increased nationalization of private enterprise in the 1960's has changed the Egyptian situation significantly, but the description is nonetheless exemplary.

74. Charles A. Myers, Labor Problems in the Industrialization of India (Cambridge: Harvard University Press, 1958).

75. For an important early study of this development, see Adolph A. Berle, Jr., and Gardiner C. Means The Modern Corporation and Private Property (New York: Macmillan, 1933).

76. Alfred D. Chandler, Jr., "Development, Diversification, and Decentralization," in Ralph E. Freeman ed., Postwar Economic Trends in the United States, (New York: Harper, 1960), pp. 278-280, See also, Chandler, Strategy and Structure (Cambridge: M.I.T. Press, 1962).

77. It should be strongly cautioned that Gosplan does not stand for total decentralization of enterprise or authority and that there are many critics who doubt that any changes have occurred at all. Speculation on convergence between Russian and North American models, however, is too important to be overlooked entirely. For an excellent comparative and historical study of capitalist and communist models, see Reinhard Bendix, Work and Authority in Industry (New York: Wiley and Sons, 1956).

78. For a classical statement of this position, see Max Weber's essay on "Bureaucracy," in From Max Weber: Essays in Sociology, Hans Gerth & C. Wright Mills eds., (New York: Oxford, 1958), pp. 196-244. Weber, of course interprets this development within a very specific historical perspective, but later theorists, building on his work, have often discarded the historical setting from their analyses.

79. Philip Selznick, TVA and the Grass Roots, (Berkeley: University of California Press, 1949), p. 220.

80. Reinhard Bendix, Work and Authority in Industry, op. cit.

81. See James C. Abegglen, The Japanese Factory (Glencoe, Illinois: Free Press, 1958) and Johannes Hirschmeier, The Origins of Entrepreneurship in Meiji, Japan, (Cambridge: Harvard University Press, 1964).

82. Franco Ferrarotti, "Management in Italy," in Management in the Industrial World, op. cit.

83. Ibid., p. 240.

84. Ibid., p. 232.

85. Op. cit., p. 65.

86. R. Vernon, The Dilemma of Mexico's Development, op. cit., p. 159.

87. Wilbert Moore uses this threefold scheme to describe threefold growth of the corporation and professional management in Industrial Relations and the Social Order (New York: Macmillan, 1951), pp. 41-64.

88. "The Latin American industrialist values an enterprise mainly insofar as it is a contribution to family interests, not as an achievement in itself. His first loyalty is to the family, for he has been brought up to expect continuity and stability only in his family." W. Paul Strassmann, "The Industrialist," Continuity and Change in Latin America, J. Johnson, ed. (Stanford: University of California Press, 1964), p. 168.

89. Marion Levy speaks on this point in "Some Sources of the Vulnerability of the Structures of Relatively Non-industrialized Societies to Those of Highly Industrialized Societies," The Progress of Underdeveloped Areas, B. Hoselitz ed. (Chicago: University of Chicago Press, 1952) pp. 113-125.

90. I would estimate that this is less than one generation in the highly competitive fields and no more than two in the less competitive ones.

91. White Collar (New York: Oxford University Press, 1953), p. 65.

92. Ralph L. Beals, "Social Stratification in Latin America," American Journal of Sociology, vol. LVIII (1953), p. 336.

93. Ibid., p. 333.

94. Joseph A. Kahl, "Tres tipos de trabajadores industriales mexicanos," Ciencias Políticas y Sociales, México, April-June, 1959, p. 200. Published in English in Economic Development and Cultural Change, vol. VIII. (January, 1960).

95. For discussion on this point, see Richard N. Farmer and Barry M. Richman, Comparative Management and Economic Progress (Homewood, Ill.: Irwin, 1965).

96. Raymond Firth, Elements of Social Organization (Boston: Beacon Press, 1961) 3rd edition, p. 133.

97. Frederick Harbison and Charles Myers, Management in the Industrial World, op. cit,, pp. 68-80.

CHAPTER VII

MANAGERIAL RESOURCE DEVELOPMENT IN PERU

ROBERT R. REHDER

With the collaboration of
Nissim Alcabes and Carlos Martijena

Peru's development of effective managerial resources is directly related to the unique social-economic system within which they function. What may be sound and efficient management practice in the United States may be completely ineffective when applied within the widely different cultural and economic environment of Peru. In fact, the North American concepts of managerial efficiency must be redefined, in relation to the Peruvian environmental system's assets and constraints within which it must operate. I will, therefore, first attempt to analyze Peru's cultural and economic environment and its evolution as a necessary prerequisite to a better understanding of her managerial performance and development needs for continued modernization.

HISTORICAL PERSPECTIVES

Peru's national boundaries have changed with time, but her social-economic characteristics are broader and much older. As the third largest republic in South America, Peru contains approximately 500,000 square miles of territory and is bounded on the west by the Pacific Ocean, on the north by Ecuador and Colombia, and the east by Brazil and Bolivia, and on the south by Chile.

The Andean mountain system is the predominant geographical characteristic. Second only to the Himalayan in altitude, it extends along the entire Western edge of the South American continent as a complex of chains that divide the continent into three distinct regions: the coast, the highlands (Sierra) and the jungle (Selva).

The coast of Peru, 1,400 miles long and from 100 miles to less than 50 miles in width, is largely barren desert due to climatological conditions created by the cold Humboldt Current flowing past its coast. This same current provides a constant moderate air temperature to the Peruvian coast, averaging 70° Fahrenheit, an unusual and advantageous factor for a country located but 0°1 from the Equator. At regular intervals, rather small non-navigable rivers and streams intersect the narrow desert strip, with approximately a dozen rivers flowing all year from the Andes to the Peruvian coast, which make possible productive, agricultural valleys.

The Peruvian Andes are comprised of three great mountain chains running longitudinally through the country from north-west to south-east.

In addition, east-west ranges transverse the north-south Cordilleras, dividing the Sierra into an endless variety of high valleys, plateaus, and mountain peaks, many of which are over 21,000 feet. These physical barriers have historically resulted in dispersed population concentrations adapted to largely barren areas of rarified, dry, cold atmosphere and sparse vegetation.[1]

The Amazon basin with its vast tropical rain forest (Selva) begins at the lower Eastern slopes of the Andes and continues to the Atlantic Ocean. The area of Selva contained within the Peruvian boundaries comprises approximately 60% of its national territory but currently less than 10% of its population.[2] The sparsity of population, dispersed aboriginal groups and several population concentrations along its vast rivers, is largely explained by the environment. The Selva's tropical climate combines heat, humidity, and rainfall which favor extensive vegetative growth. However, the exuberance of jungle growth and endemic diseases and parasites have restricted native populations and limited colonization.

The extreme physical contrasts of climate and terrain are paralleled by the cultural divergencies found in Peru.

Pre-Colonial Peru

Thousands of years of cultural evolution contributed to the development of the Inca civilization, which did not emerge until the twelfth century in the Sierra near Cuzco.[3] However, the lack of a written language and the Inca's purposeful destruction and manipulation of their conquered cultures and remembered history has left vast areas open for speculation.[4]

A great deal more is known concerning the Inca history and civilization, and its profound influence is clearly evident in the Andean Indian cultures today. Social, political, and economic analysis of the Inca civilization set forth several characteristics which remain significant in contemporary Peruvian culture.

The entire history of the Incan civilization runs from the twelfth to the fourteenth century. During the latter two centuries the Incas were able to extend their empire to include the whole of Peru, Ecuador, Bolivia, and parts of Chile, Argentina, and Colombia, and greatly unify its varied and dispersed coastal and Andean cultures under a highly centralized and authoritarian state system.

The remarkable integration of diverse cultures within the Inca empire is a classic study of systematic acculturation. The basic social units within the empire were agricultural family groups, holding a small parcel of common land. These formed the base of the empire's social hierarchy, and over all ruled the Inca emperor, his nobles, and religious leaders. The social structure was highly stratified and rigid and the power of the Inca was absolute and with divine authority. Every aspect of human life was planned and organized by the state elite, including marriage, compulsory labor and military service, travel and immigration control, as well as the monumental, ingenious system of roads, cities, and irrigation. The Inca elite clearly demonstrated a genius for social organization and construction developed by a very elaborate physical, intellectual, and moral education system.[5] The social system of the Inca elite was distinctly separate from that of the masses. The individual, gradually absorbed by the state and completely subjugated to the routines of its authoritarian way of life, was guaranteed minimum subsistence.

There is some agreement among the scholars of the Inca empire that its degradation of the masses stifled their initiative and instilled rigid cultural patterns that are yet in evidence today.[6]

The Confrontation of Two Cultures

In 1532, Francisco Pizarro, with less than 200 men, disembarked on the shores of Peru, quickly captured the reigning Inca (Atahualpa), and the highly centralized empire soon fell. The history of the brief confrontation and the causes of the empire's fall form the basis for countless volumes; however, the conflict of cultures that began that year is yet underway, albeit now compounded with the demands of modernization. Louis Baudin concisely described the confrontation of the two varied concepts of life in the following statement:

> On the one side -- a people ebullient with life, restless, bold to the point of rashness; on the other -- a great empire inflexibly organized along rigid lines. On the one side, a liberalism that would have degenerated into anarchy had it not been for the King and the Church; on the other, a socialism that would have leveled existence to a complete and suffocating uniformity had it not been for an elite. On the one side, men; on the other, a state. And the drama of South America began -- a drama that continues to our own day, the drama of two races superimposed . . .[7]

The colonial period profoundly changed major aspects of Peruvian life. The Spanish, primarily interested in the exportation of the mineral wealth of Peru to finance the Spanish wars in Europe, reoriented the center of activities in Peru from the Sierra to the coast outlets and correspondingly altered its road system from the longitudinal Inca roads to short transverse roads to the sea. Lima, founded in 1535 on the central coast, quickly developed as one of the two major and highly favored Spanish colonial centers in the Americas. The coastal political, social, and economic dominance continues to this day in Peru.

The Incan governmental system, a model authoritarian organization with great but predictable demands, sanctions, and firm controls, was replaced by an equally centralized system of unlimited demands, arbitrary rules, and justice largely reserved for the conquerors and their descendants.[8]

The Spanish introduction of a money economy, concepts of private property and social-economic values based on its ownership and control were in direct conflict to the socialistic system of the Incas.

> All land was owned by the state which granted its use
> to various institutional groups but houses and movable
> property were individually owned. Land was considered
> as belonging to a man as long as he used it. The value
> of the land was derived from what it could produce from
> personal labor, and the idea of land ownership for
> prestige or personal profit was only incipient.[9]

The Spanish feudal institutions, modified types of land grant systems, included the right to a tribute in money, goods, or services from the Indians on the land. Many Indian families were dispersed as they lost control of their lands or were recruited for labor in the mines. The social and political organization of the Indians was largely invaded by the Spanish crown officials. Contemporary Indian "invasions" of haciendas and newly legislated land reform statutes clearly demonstrate the continued conflict.

The colonial social structure in Peru was dominated by the native-born Spaniards who held the highest civil, military, and religious offices. The Creole group was dominant, however, in numbers, professional and commercial activities, and natural resource holdings. Below the latter group were the many gradations of the mestizo classes, a mixture of Spanish and Indian blood, which grew rapidly due to the relatively few Spanish women who immigrated into Peru. The lower classes were comprised of the Indian masses and Negro slaves who were brought in to work largely on the coastal haciendas.

The Transplantation of a Hispanic Social Institution

The education system exported by the Spaniards and Portuguese to Latin America was not designed for the masses but to prepare the elite for service to the Church and State, closely united as in Spain under the Patronato system. Peru, as a major colonial center, received a royal decree establishing the National University of San Marcos in 1551. This was the first University charter signed in the hemisphere and precedes the founding of Harvard, the oldest North American university, by a century. As the other early pontifical universities founded in Latin America, San Marcos was patterned after the Spanish University of Salamanca, one of the four principal medieval institutions of higher education in Europe.[10] As such, San Marcos developed as an aristocratic school of professional training, isolated from its native cultural environment,with faculties of theology, law, arts, and medicine in the tradition of the major European universities of this period. The Church dominated the administration and curriculum during the development of San Marcos, providing part-time professors and receiving negligible fees. The admission of non-white races was strictly curtailed by a detailed legal "purity of blood" process. Primary and secondary education was in a like manner dominated by the Church in colonial Peru and its general classical curriculum was designed to prepare a select group for professional university study.

Spanish colonial economic regulations developed mining, controlled commodity production, and supressed manufacturing in keeping with its own economic interests. These economic regulations and inflation, combined with political and social suppression of the Creoles by the Chapetones, formed the seeds of revolution that grew in the climate of new revolutionary thought from France and North America. It was the suppressed Creole elite desiring autonomy, and not the Indian masses, who joined the revolutionary movements of Bolívar and San Martín for their own ends. The resultant independence from Spain in the early 1820's, therefore, did little to improve the Indian subjugation and social-economic segregation.[11] A small oligarchy retained the privileges, and the hierarchical social structure with its ruling and subject class remained. In retrospect, the total Peruvian cultural system, which incorporated a majority of the prevailing Hispanic cultural characteristics discussed in Chapter II, including the patrilineal extended family, authoritarian, and highly centralized institutional characteristics, was little changed by this revolution. Similarly, the aristocratic orientation and professional institutional structure of the education system did not alter significantly. With the formal abolition of the Spanish titles of nobility, the university professional titles took on new importance to maintain the oligarchy's identification and its privileges. The degree being the primary objective, there was frequently little correlation between the title earned, the effective knowledge acquired, or the subsequent activities of its holder.

The university-titled elite, both professors and students, entered into a new role of political activity involving ideological curriculum content and direct involvement in the political activity and government of the new republic. In particular, French governmental and educational influence was quite strong during the 19th century as reflected in the French type of centralized governmental control structure adopted, curriculum content at all levels, French language and general cultural values adopted. There are many indications, which will be discussed throughout the balance of this study, that the rate of cultural change which has been increasing since the 19th century is accelerating in the contemporary industrial revolution, with mixed effects on Peru's development efforts. Again, it should be stressed that the total Hispanic cultural characteristics evidenced in Peru are merely a part of its total social-economic system. They are not, therefore, subject to arbitrary value judgment, but will be analyzed in this study in relation to their augmenting and/or constraining effects on the integrated modernization process.

The Development of European and North American Business Relationships.

The second half of the 19th century saw the development of new commercial activity, agriculture on the coast, and guano trade with Europe. During the same period a small middle class of career, public, professional, and businessmen became evident, as well as a new urban commercial oligarchy, largely represented by the Civilista Party and influenced by England and France.[12] World War I and the opening of the

206

Panama Canal gave major impetus to the development of Peru's agricultural, natural resources, and manufacturing sectors, particularly textiles, and brought North American investments, education,and naval advisors. Under the pro-North American Government of President Augusto B. Leguia, United States policies played a new and important role in Peruvian politics, trade, and financing. During the first quarter of the century, North American business interests developed dominant positions in mining, petroleum, and communications, as well as foreign financing of economic overhead projects in Peru. Although foreign investments increased Peruvian exports, there was a growing awareness that only a fraction of their value remained in the country, with the remaining going to a small domestic elite who largely reinvested abroad.

> Into this general picture we must fit the fact that about 83.4 per cent of Peru's total exports were accounted for in sugar, cotton, copper, and petroleum. Then note that most of these exports were owned by non-Peruvians, especially United States citizens.[13]

In addition, there was substantial evidence that North American private business interests were instrumental in securing North American government loans for the Leguia government in return for the granting of concessions to these companies' business operations in Peru. The above later resulted in Heran W. Johnson of California conducting a U.S. Senate investigation of private business influence on official foreign financing policies.[14] While there were desirable economic development effects from the rapid growth of European and North American business activity, there developed strong exploitation associations with foreign business interests, and these associations have continuously played a major role in student reform movements.

The University Reform Movement, which had its origin in Cordoba, Argentina, June, 1918, spread to Peru one year later where the principles of reform were proclaimed by the students of San Marcos in May, 1919.[15] The deans opposed their adoption and the resultant lengthy and bitter strike was resolved one year later with the students gaining representation on the University Governing Council and freedom to adapt their school schedule to their employment working hours. The University Reform Movement in Peru was deeply involved with social justice and recognized education as the major means to improve the social-economic means of the masses. However, following severe opposition by the Leguia administration, including the imprisonment and exile of the University Reform leaders, political activity became the central means by which to achieve their objectives. The Peruvian university student has been described as a political soldier engaged in a never-ending battle for social justice.

From study both in Peru and during their exile abroad, the University Reform leadership evolved a Peruvian political party (APRA) advocating education and the development of human resources as a primary means of achieving a modern unified Latin American democracy with its

masses integrated socially and economically.[16] The Apristas recognized
the differences between North America, Latin America, and Europe and
strongly urged the development of indigenous political and economic concepts and institutions to meet their particular needs.

Although APRA espoused a strongly foreign exploitation (particularly North American) program,it recognized Latin America's need of
foreign capital but held that it should be used for the mutual benefit
of the investor and all the people of Latin America.

The Apristas advocate the peaceful achievement of power through
free elections, and although their efforts to win power have largely
been frustrated through forty years of opposition, their ideology has
deeply influenced Peru's contemporary attitudes concerning business and
foreign interests.

World War II provided even greater impetus to the further development of North American economic and national security interests in Peru.
The U. S. Government guaranteed purchases of her natural resources and
further underwrote the development of Peru's military and natural resources necessary for the support of war. Cut off from Europe, wealthy
Peruvian youth in large numbers were diverted to North American schools
and universities and established school-family relationships which have
developed inter-American cultural and intellectual understanding and
ties.[17] During the years following World War II, United States investment in Peru continued to develop to the extent that by 1953, it held
74 per cent of the direct foreign investment in Peru, concentrated
heavily in mining, petroleum, and agriculture.[18] The post World War II
years saw several unpopular governments representing the small elite
continue their close alliances with North America. Between 1946 and
1960, Peru received over $283,000,000 in economic grants and loans, and
$94,000,000 for military assistance, ranking fifth in Latin America for
total North American aid received in this pre-Alliance for Progress
period.[19] Post war economic gains were, however, of little benefit to
the vast majority of Peruvians living in the interior, as is illustrated
by the decade of the 1950's. While the annual Gross National Product
growth rate for this period was 4.5%,and the Gross National Income 3.0%
(based on 1960 prices) rising in relation, rapid increases in birth
rates and an unequal distribution of income resulted in a 2% per capita
income decline for two thirds of the Peruvian population living in the
Sierra during this same decade.[20]

The rising popular discontent and social unrest accompanying Peru's
post-war gross economic gains were clearly demonstrated during Vice
President Nixon's violent reception at the University of San Marcos in
1958. This demonstration, not easily ignored nor simply explained by
"Communism," contributed to Washington's re-examination of its Latin
American foreign assistance policy,which was reflected in the goals of
the Punta del Este Charter of the Alliance for Progress in 1960.

James C. Carey, in his study of Peruvian and North American
relationships 1900-1962, concisely reviews United States Foreign
Assistance policy in Peru.

In attempting to trace the over-all lines of the United States assistance programs in Peru, we start by noting that Peru has expected considerable aid and has received considerable aid. To a degree, both were responsible for various projects. Technical assistance starting under the Institute of Inter-American Affairs, Point Four, Operations Missions, International Cooperation Administration (I.C.A.), and later the Alliance for Progress plan were 'all alike and yet different somehow.' They were all alike in that the purpose of each was to help the United States and the people of Peru at the same time. They differed in their means of achieving this and in the extent to which each would contribute to any significant changes within Peruvian society itself.[21]

The goals of the Alliance for Progress were more clearly directed to increase the extent of beneficial change to the Peruvian society in the broadest sense, and judging from the deep Peruvian remorse at the death of John F. Kennedy, its founding inspiration, the Peruvian people fully appreciated this intent.

THE CONTEMPORARY SETTING: MODERNIZATION, ASSETS AND CONSTRAINTS

The early Incan, Spanish, and more recent North American social - economic influences on the historical evolution of Peru continue as major factors in its contemporary development. Peru's current cultural values, traditions, and social, political, and educational systems affect the development and performance of its managerial resources, as do its available human and natural resources, world markets, and population/land ratios. The remaining sections of this study represent a modest effort to further understand these relationships as a necessary basis for the effective development and performance of Peru's management resources.

The Impressive 60's: The Assets

Peru in the first half of the 1960's has maintained an impressive 5-6% G.N.P. annual growth rate based on 1960 prices.[22] Peru's rate of growth during this period has exceeded the expectations set forth in the Punta del Este Charter, in contrast to Latin America's over-all economic growth rates, which have failed to meet these initial Alliance for Progress goals. As indicated in Table I, all sectors of the economy have shown growth and vitality in recent years.

A major contributing factor to Peru's economic development has been its rapid export growth. Peruvian exports have grown at an impressive rate of 9% in the period 1950-1964, as compared to 3.4% for all Latin America. A well-known Peruvian economist, Romulo A. Ferrero, has identified three basic, interrelated causes as the most important contributing factors to this dynamic expansion of exports and economic growth: (1) a favorable economic policy, (2) the variety of natural resources of Peru, and (3) the dynamism of private enterprise.

TABLE I

GROSS DOMESTIC PRODUCT, BY SECTORS,

1950, 1955, AND 1960-64

	1950	1955	1960	1961	1962	1963	1964[1]
	(In millions of 1960 soles[2])						
Agriculture	8,860	9,787	11,317	12,313	13,558	13,445	13,998
Fishing	167	238	785	1,011	1,207	1,140	1,266
Mining	1,831	2,792	4,908	5,202	4,942	5,286	5,448
Manufacturing	5,348	7,777	10,467	11,513	12,508	13,209	13,952
Construction	1,179	1,955	1,768	2,086	2,472	2,645	2,921
Transport and Communications	1,586	2,393	3,009	3,193	3,422	3,596	3,816
Commerce	5,512	7,452	9,280	10,449	11,433	11,850	12,528
Finance	1,050	1,635	2,062	2,215	2,388	2,515	2,639
Housing	3,200	3,661	4,470	4,627	4,796	5,011	5,261
Government	3,489	3,767	4,291	4,643	4,913	5,205	5,527
Other Services	2,187	2,704	3,293	3,510	3,621	3,748	3,916
Total[3]	34,309	44,161	55,650	60,782	65,260	67,650	71,272
	(In percent of total)						
Agriculture	25.7	22.2	20.4	20.3	20.8	19.9	19.6
Fishing	0.5	0.5	1.4	1.7	1.8	1.7	1.8
Mining	5.3	6.3	8.8	8.6	7.6	7.8	7.6
Manufacturing	15.6	17.6	18.8	18.9	19.2	19.5	19.6
Construction	3.4	4.4	3.2	3.4	3.8	3.9	4.1
Transport and Communications	4.6	5.4	5.4	5.4	5.2	5.3	5.4
Commerce	16.0	16.9	16.7	17.2	17.5	17.5	17.6
Finance	3.1	3.7	3.7	3.6	3.7	3.7	3.7
Housing	9.3	8.3	8.0	7.6	7.3	7.4	7.4
Government	10.1	8.5	7.7	7.6	7.5	7.7	7.8
Other Services	6.4	6.2	5.9	5.8	5.6	5.6	5.4
Total	100.0	100.0	100.0	100.0	100.0	100.0	100.0

[1]Estimate.

[2]One sol equal to US$0.037 in 1960.

[3]Totals may not add because of rounding.

Source: National Planning Institute, Estimaciones del Producto, ingreso real y el gasto final, Statistical annex to the Diagnóstico de La Economía Peruana, Lima, 1964.

Reference: Banco Comercial del Perú "Peru 1965 in Retrospect" January, 1966, Lima.

Contemporary Economic Policy. Peru's economic policy has in recent
years contributed decisively to its export expansion and economic growth.
Traditionally, Peru has followed a relatively free and open economic
policy regarding foreign trade, exchange, and international payments
controls. In Latin America, Peru has been exemplary with relative internal and external monetary stability. By year-end 1965, gold and
foreign exchange reserves in the central bank were U. S. $153,000,000.
Since 1961, the average rate of exchange (which applies to all trans-
actions) has remained at 26.82 soles to the U. S. $1.00. However,
steadily increasing budgetary deficits (2,500 million soles in 1965) and
cost of living indexes (18% increase in 1965) could lessen the optimism
in these pictures. A series of new tax measures enacted since 1964 to
meet these increasing budgetary deficits could also decrease foreign
private investment incentives,although foreign enterprise has not been
taxed more heavily than domestic. In addition, the Peruvian government
has provided a series of investment incentives through its mining code,
electricity law, industrial and area promotion laws. These benefits,
ranging from tax exemptions and reductions, import-export duty exemptions and tariff protection,combined with increased credit activities of
the governmental banks (industrial development, agricultural, mining),
have been significant contributing factors to Peru's expanding economy.

Peruvian Natural Wealth. As Table IIa illustrates, Peru's considerable
natural resources are fortunately more diversified than most of its
neighbors,with major agricultural, mineral, and marine products contributing significantly to its total supply of foreign exchange earnings.
Again, the dominant position of the United States in Peru's foreign
trade, as shown in Table IIb, remains noteworthy.

Although Peru's cultivated land area per capita is one of the
lowest in the world (.2 hectare per capita), its fertile coastal lands
are concentrated in large haciendas whose production efficiency of
cotton and sugar cane is among the world's highest. In 1950, these two
products accounted for 50% of Peru's exports. However, today, as seen
in Table IIa, they comprise less than half that amount,due to the rapid
growth of the mineral and marine extractive industries.

Mineral exports have grown from 24% in 1950 to 37% of total exports
in 1963. Large Andean deposits of copper, zinc, iron, and lead are
reinforced by significant quantities of petroleum, bismuth, silver, and
vanadium. Again, as in the case of the large coastal agricultural
haciendas, the mining industry is highly concentrated into a few large
firms with major foreign interests, advanced technology, and requirements for high level professional scientific and managerial talent.

Since 1962, the largest Peruvian export has been marine products.
This youngest and most vigorous growth area provides an excellent illus-
tration of Mr. Ferrero's three interdependent causes of the export
expansion. The same off-shore Humbolt Current which affects the coastal
climate also makes possible one of the world's largest offshore marine
deposits of plankton, anchovy, and large fish. Although Peru's fishing
industry has steadily developed over the past twenty years, its major

TABLE IIa

PERU'S EXPORTS OF PRINCIPAL COMMODITIES, 1963-64

(In thousands of dollars)

Commodity	1963	1964
Fish meal	104,530	143,400
Copper	87,289	103,000
Cotton, raw	91,065	90,900
Sugar	63,164	63,500
Zinc[1]	15,829	39,100
Iron ore[1]	36,456	38,900
Coffee	25,573	37,000
Lead[1]	16,407	33,000
Fish oil	8,106	14,100
Fish, frozen, canned, smoked, salted, etc.	7,793	8,400
Petroleum, crude	6,491	7,000
Alpaca hair	7,085	6,600
Wool	4,126	4,400
Bismuth[1]	2,193	3,300
Silver[1]	35,802	45,300
Other commodities	29,332	29,090
Total exports	541,241	666,990

[1]Values are based on the fine content of metals.

Source: Superintendencia General de Aduanas, Departamento de Estadística, Estadística del Comercio Exterior, 1963, Lima; and American Embassy, Lima, 1965.

Reference: "Overseas Business Report", U. S. Department of Commerce, 1966.

TABLE IIb

TOTAL TRADE AND TRADE WITH THE UNITED STATES, 1950-64

(Value in thousands of dollars)

	Imports (c.i.f.)			Exports (f.o.b.)		
Year	Total	From United States	Percent	Total	To United States	Percent
1950	186,241	98,415	52.8	193,585	50,770	26.2
1951	279,681	156,681	56.0	252,516	58,964	23.4
1952	287,548	161,479	56.2	238,738	66,802	28.0
1953	292,880	160,735	54.9	221,970	84,698	38.2
1954	249,694	129,562	51.9	247,623	88,039	35.6
1955	300,291	150,216	50.0	270,860	97,513	36.0
1956	361,042[1]	178,923	49.6	311,435	114,789	36.9
1957	400,137[1]	191,058	47.7	330,006	115,369	35.0
1958	335,296[1]	156,798	46.8	291,429	111,106	38.1
1959	293,323[1]	131,693	44.9	314,203	98,529	31.3
1960	374,780	164,224	43.8	433,076	154,132	35.6
1961	469,422	207,039	44.1	496,376	178,271	35.9
1962	536,879	212,402	39.6	539,986	188,139	34.8
1963	557,062	207,642	37.3	541,241	190,861	35.3
1964	579,600	236,000	40.7	666,990	[2]206,631	[2]31.0

[1]Unadjusted figures; totals adjusted to include imports of the Southern Peru Copper Corporation are: 1956, $383,736,000; 1957, $449,605,000; 1958, $380,874,000; and 1959, $317,226,000.

[2]Preliminary official statistics.

Source: Superintendencia General de Aduanas, Departamento de Estadística, Estadística del Comercio Exterior, 1950-63, Lima; and American Embassy, Lima, 1965.

Reference: "Overseas Business Report" U.S. Dept. of Commerce, 1966.

growth began in 1957 with the development of fishmeal production using the readily available anchovy as its basic material. In 1964, Peru's production of fishmeal reached 1,550,000 tons (143 million dollars), ranking Peru number one in world fishmeal production and total live weight.[24]

The Dynamic Private Sector. The fishing industry's growth is an excellent example of the increasing importance of Peru's private sector. Private investment has contributed most to Peru's economic growth during the last ten years, although public investment is increasing due to intra-structure needs. Between 1960 and 1964, it grew from 2% to 6% of G.N.P. Unlike mining and the major agricultural export sectors, the fishing industry has been primarily developed by a large number of Peruvian and foreign entrepreneurs in small plants along the northern coast of Peru. The development of fishing has seen the growth of significant related support industry ranging from shipbuilding to the engineering and construction of entire fishmeal plants, which are now themselves being exported.

Although the private sector's primary activity has traditionally been industrial operations tied to world market activities, Peru's manufacturing has shown rapid growth recently and is currently entering the stage of intermediate industries, including such chemical products as fertilizers, caustic soda, plastics, and numerous basic metal and metallurgical products. The 4881 registered manufacturing establishments, their industry, capital, and reserves, personnel employed, and total income by sectors in 1960 is shown in Table III, while Table IV illustrates the rapid rate of new firms entering these sectors in the subsequent three years.

The dynamic growth of highly diversified private enterprise largely concentrated in Peru's northern coastal area has generated wide speculation as to its causes. As previously noted, large business enterprise in Peru has historically been dominated by foreign interests and a relatively small Peruvian elite, largely belonging to the several hundred established families, and with their extensions possessing great financial and political power. The commodity industrial sectors, in particular, traditionally involved large amounts of foreign capital, technological and managerial resources.

Significant factors in the mix contributing to Peru's recent dynamic industrial growth have been imported from abroad. William Whyte described the prominence of foreigners in Peruvian industrial activities in 1963.[25] Professor Whyte's findings were not quantified as in the United Nations Economic Commission for Latin American Studies of the industrial entrepreneur in Argentina, Colombia, and Chile. These studies found approximately 30% and 50% foreigners in respective Argentine and Chilean surveys. However, his observations were supported by the Stanford Research Institute teams engaged in industrial field research in Peru during 1963-65. Although Peruvian immigration statistics are incomplete before 1936 when its free-flow policy was restricted by legislation, large foreign populations have taken up residence in Peru

TABLE III

PRODUCTION OF MANUFACTURED GOODS, 1960

Industry	Registered Establish-ments (number[1])	Capital and Reserves (thousands of soles[2])	White-Collar Employees and Laborers (number)	Total Income (thousands of soles[2])
Food Products	1,024	1,778,723	24,188	5,684,772
Beverages[3]	192	1,020,065	7,896	1,432,541
Textiles	265	1,970,772	24,439	3,379,268
Clothing and footwear	751	309,331	11,535	932,669
Wood and cork	152	148,927	3,218	337,208
Furniture of wood and metal	351	61,164	3,651	209,363
Paper products	33	91,677	1,473	158,398
Printing	290	144,763	4,210	375,105
Leather, except shoes	94	183,387	2,788	480,479
Rubber, mostly tires and tubes	18	235,382	1,518	593,262
Chemical products, including plastic items	223	854,293	7,995	1,378,266
Metal and mineral products, except petroleum and coal	246	1,341,299	9,153	925,047
Basic metal industries	378	258,065	5,922	554,941
Manufacturers of metal products, except machinery	164	253,056	4,499	606,981
Electrical machinery, apparatus, instruments, accessories	36	37,804	838	115,147
Miscellaneous industries	664	1,354,272	17,082	2,021,941
Total	4,881	10,042,980	130,405	19,185,388

[1]Peruvian law requires the registration of all commercial entities.

[2]Average rate of exchange in 1960, 1 sol equals US$0.0366.

[3]Mostly beer.

Sources: Banco Central de Reserva del Perú, Renta Nacional del Perú, 1942-1960, 1962, Lima, Perú, pages 100 and 101; Boletín del Banco Central de Reserva del Perú, December 1964, p. 50.

Reference: "Overseas Business Report" U. S. Department of Commerce, 1966.

TABLE IV

NEW INDUSTRIAL FIRMS REGISTERED IN PERU

BY INDUSTRY, 1961-1963

	1961		1962		1963	
	Number of Firms	Employ-ment	Number of Firms	Employ-ment	Number of Firms	Employ-ment
Food	70	2,026	121	2,221	78	1,695
Beverages	10	44	20	46	5	42
Textiles	43	1,363	25	121	37	488
Shoes & Clothing	68	601	100	941	66	857
Woodworking	11	100	19	229	14	144
Furniture	25	150	18	205	19	173
Paper & Paper Products	7	111	5	44	1	5
Printing	28	401	30	340	27	678
Leather Products	13	202	3	30	4	52
Rubber Products	1	70	2	34	1	1
Chemical Products	33	656	45	888	35	929
Oil Products	--	--	1	10	--	--
Non-metallic Mineral Products	16	572	28	498	14	737
Basic Metals	4	45	1	4	--	--
Metal Fabricating	31	575	50	615	23	285
Machinery	17	509	15	432	12	96
Electrical Equipment	18	168	15	102	23	304
Transportation Equipment	34	857	62	645	39	1,872
Miscellaneous	44	425	40	278	41	493
Totals	473	8,875	600	7,683	439	8,851

Source: Dirección de Industrial y Electricidad, 1964, and published in English by the Industrial Dev. Mfg. Record, 1966.

since that date without becoming nationalized citizens.[27] In 1960, the
records of the Immigration Department showed the foreign population to
be over 67,500 including 12,000 Japanese, 8,800 Chinese, 7,500 Italians,
7,150 North Americans, 5,750 Spaniards, 3,000 Germans, 2,850 British,
1,500 Swiss, 1,500 French, 7,000 people from other Latin American countries, and 10,000 others representing most major countries in the
world.[28] These figures are considered quite conservative as they do
not reflect the large migrations prior to 1936. Since 1960, foreign
and the many private and public sector development programs have resulted in the business expansion and importation of large numbers of
high-talent manpower. In addition, sizeable numbers of Peruvian students (600 in 1966) traveling abroad for their higher education have
greatly contributed to Peru's rapid development of advanced technology
and managerial capabilities.[29] Private primary and secondary schools in
Peru representing most major nationalities are well established, inter-
racially mixed, and provide a large source of international exchange
for the elite and growing middle classes.

An easily overlooked and perhaps one of Peru's strongest assets is
her penetrating desire for progress. Peru's search for new concepts,
technology, and know-how from more advanced international sources
appears to be matched by an ability to adapt and utilize these ideas in
her own national development. A small Vicos community development project and a broad economic study by Arthur D. Little, Inc., provided a
nucleus of ideas around which Peru has built, and is carrying out with
the people, a comprehensive interior development program. The national
goals for achievement are clearly reflected and supported by large segments of Peru's population, who, in their desire for a better life, are
migrating to the coastal cities and filling the new schools with their
children. The above and other indicators of Peru's strong desire for
progress and the major problems involved, to be considered next, reflect
the significant social-economic changes taking place in Peru today.

Continuing Progress: Economic and Social Constraints.

While Peru's economic growth in the last five years has been
exemplary within the Alliance for Progress republics, so are its continuing problems. Peru's real Gross National Income advanced at an
annual rate of 6.9 percent between 1960 and 1964. However, her population's estimated annual growth rate of 2.9 percent during this period
(among the most rapid in the world) and the continued disparity of income distribution has resulted in little discernible improvement for
the majority of Peruvians living in the highlands and jungle.[30] Next
to the population expansion rate, which is sufficient to double Peru's
11 million in 25 years, stands the problem of the geographical, social,
and economic segregation of the large interior Indian populations. The
geographic distribution of the total population was estimated in 1960
to be 33% coast, 53% Sierra, and 14% in the jungle. The disparity of
national income distribution between the coastal population and the
interior population continues to increase.[31] Although the statistics
vary widely, the most conservative estimates place the per capita income
of the coastal population at three times that of the Sierra inhabitant
and over five times that of the jungle inhabitant.[32] This relationship

is yet more significant as the absolute income per capita in 1960 for
the jungle inhabitant was less than $46 (1,238 soles) per annum, for
the Sierra inhabitant approximately $88 (2,385 soles) per annum, as
contrasted with the coastal inhabitant whose per annum income was $254
(6,932 soles). The income per capita of the Limenian was estimated to
be $306 (8,312 soles) during the same year.[33]

The previously described mountain ranges physically dividing Peru
into three distinct social economic regions remain a formidable barrier
to social-economic integration.

The Sierra, containing 53% of Peru's population, also produces the
major share of Peruvian food, but very few export commodities, as crops
are primarily grown on small plots for family consumption or local markets. Productivity is understandably very low, given the scarcity of
cultivatable land, its unequal distribution owing to the before-cited
Spanish-imposed structure of large land ownership, and the lack of
knowledge and acceptance of modern farming technology. The pre-Incan
and Incan collectivist ownership of arable land and pastures, with periodic distribution of work and fruits of work, has evolved today toward
greater family possession of land with collective pasture. The semi-
feudal, middle, and large landholdings claimed by the Spanish, where
the worker received a nominal fee for working the hacienda land and a
small plot of land for his use, is still present but continues to be of
very low productivity. Non-agricultural development in the Sierra is
predominantly limited to mineral extraction which provides relatively
few employment opportunities.

Dietetic studies concur that the majority of Peruvians living in
the Sierra rural setting are seriously undernourished, with frequent
mental and physical retardation consequences in the development of
children, in addition to lowered resistance to diseases.[34]

Cultural factors again prove to be as significant as economic when
causes of the malnutrition are analyzed. Indians who work in a hacienda
several days a week for a few pennies are unable to buy the food needed
to adequately supplement their own food production. Even if foods containing badly needed proteins and calcium were economically available,
Indian beliefs concerning foods would to a large extend inhibit their
eating them. The acceptance and proper use of fertilizers, insecticides,
and animal inoculations, again when offered without cost and with expert
advice, is very slow as centuries of tradition and beliefs are not easily
or quickly changed. The essential interrelationship between social and
technical change is now gaining some recognition in Peru and social,
political, and economic pressures have placed very high expectations on
Peruvian Agrarian Reform and Rural Development Programs just now getting
under way.

The jungle east of the Sierra contains approximately 63% of the
Peruvian territory; however, it is sparsely inhabited with less than 14%
of the total population. This vast tropical rain forest is unquestionably the least understood or integrated region in Peru. The primitive

forest Indians, many of whom are only now gaining first contact with
the outside world through missionary work and exploration, present a
difficult and lengthy integration problem. The Selva's economic
development is just beginning and it currently produces less than 5% of
the national income. On the Eastern slopes of the Andes, the higher
tropical lands developing coffee, fruits, and other agricultural products have recently received considerable attention as a regional
development area of the first priority.[35]

The agricultural potential, lumber, and mineral resources of the
jungle are known to be very great; however, the climatological, geographical, and disease problems are equally great and have, to date,
limited their exploitation. Roads and communications are now opening
the way for increased colonization, but penetration is costly and difficult.

In recent years, improvements in communications and transportation
facilities primarily between the coast and the Sierra have increased the
flow of information and travelers. The transistor radio, new roads, and
air routes are opening the interior to the modern world. In Peru, as in
other parts of the world, the "have-nots'" growing awareness of the world
of plenty has excited wants. Rising expectations constrained by rapid
population growth, limited cultivatable land disproportionately distributed, and small non-agricultural employment opportunities had predictably resulted in mounting human dissatisfaction and unrest. The
above factors in addition have provided fertile ground for the growth
of radical agitation, mass invasions of large Sierra haciendas, and
large urban migrations. Rural community development is seen as a
necessary and difficult remedial action.

Vicos: The Problems of Developing Rural Communities. Planned social-
economic development of Peru's rural communities has received increasing
attention since 1951 with the advent of the Cornell-Peru project in
Vicos. Located in the Sierra of northeastern Peru the 30,000-acre
hacienda Vicos is inhabited by approximately 2,000 Quechua-speaking
Indians. For 400 years the Vicosinos had lived in poverty, isolated
from the world beyond the high Andes surrounding them in the traditional
semi-feudalistic system laid down in the colonial period. As rent for
small rocky plots of land which might provide subsistence for one family,
days of labor and other free services were paid to the hacienda administration whose authority was unquestioned. Educational and health facilities were almost completely lacking.

In fifteen years a great deal has been accomplished in Vicos.[36]
The Hacienda has been purchased by the Vicosinos and community affairs
are now directed by their elected delegates. New leadership has developed and apathy reduced as schools, agricultural productivity, and
other benefits have been accomplished through their own efforts. A
great deal more has been achieved, however, outside of Vicos by the
valuable experience it provided and interest it generated toward the
integration of Peru's and Latin America's indigenous millions. Vicos
clearly demonstrated the importance of education at all levels in

socio-economic growth and the key role of indigenous leadership development in affecting this change. The following statement by Allan R.
Holmberg, the founder and primary North American advisor for the project,
needs little amplification.[37]

> However, in the whole process of changing practices
> and perspectives at Vicos, it has been education that
> has played the key and fundamental role. It was the
> assumption of the project from the very beginning that
> without a carefully designed program of education, both
> informal and formal, it would be impossible either to
> establish or perpetuate whatever changes were proposed --
> economic, social, or ideological. For this reason, it
> has been the practice to focus on a variety of community
> hopes, and attempt, through the formation and develop-
> ment of local groups, to broaden these goals so that the
> achievement of them will also involve the attainment of
> knowledge, skills, and attitudes which will foster the
> independent growth of the community.

At the same time the Cornell-Peru project gives new insight into
the complexity and time, measured in decades, necessary to affect
significant cultural change. Although education received primary emphasis in the Cornell-Peru project, it is only recently that its value
has been recognized by the Vicosinos themselves. In 1963, twelve years
after the founding of the project, only eighteen percent of the Vicos
population aged seven or above had ever attended school.[38]

The human inputs of talent and effort over time necessary to affect
community development in Vicos have gained some recognition by national
development planners.

Traditional development programs expecting large financial inputs
to affect broad social-economic change in short periods of time are
losing favor in Latin America. The Alliance for Progress program in
Peru and the broad-range programs instigated by the Belaunde government
toward the development and integration of the rural Sierra communities
clearly attest to the impact of the Vicos project.[39]

Urban Concentration of Industry and Population. The pull of coastal
social-economic advantages, combined with the push of the Sierra's constraints, has resulted in a major population shift toward the coastal
urban areas. While there was little relative change in the proportion
of the Amazon population to Peru's expanding total population between
1950 and 1960, the Sierra is estimated to have decreased from 60% to 53%
while the coast increased from 27% to 33% during the same period.[40] With
33% of the national population in 1960, the coast received over 60% of
the national income. Industry and finance are estimated to be 90% concentrated on the Coast as well as over 66% of the commerce.[41] Agriculture
in the coastal valleys in contrast to the highlands is quite productive
with the major crops, sugar and cotton, grown on large land units for
export. The fishing industry and its related support industries,

previously described as one of Peru's most dynamic economic growth
sectors, is totally coastal. The increasing centralization of the population in the capitol Lima-Callao area is also significant. Over two
million people now live in this dominant social, political, and economic
center of Peru and over sixty percent of them were born in the provinces.[42] The nation's educational resources, largely centered in Lima,
draw thousands of talented students from the provinces -- many of whom
never return. The ambitious and talented Peruvians gravitate to Lima
because of the professional, economic, and social benefits only it can
provide,resulting in a dearth of professional and leadership resources
in the provinces. In 1957, Lima had one doctor to every 464 persons,
while five departments or states had less than one doctor per 20,000
inhabitants.[43] The concentration of professional and other high talent
human resources is now gaining recognition as a major contributor to
Peru's development integration problem. While high level manpower
gravitates to Lima from the rural areas, so do the masses of illiterate
and destitute in search of something better.

The social-economic problems arising from this tide of poor immigrants into the capitol metropolitan area are visually evidenced by the
ugly slums rising up the hills surrounding the city. The vast majority
of rural immigrants are lacking in skills to compete in the urban labor
market which, although expanding, is inadequate to meet the needs of
the labor force.

The social problems resulting from the change from rural to urban
living are in themselves of an extreme nature without the vast unemployment. The security of the family and communal relationship, life-giving
land and animals, traditional language and customs are lost in an urban
sea of disorganization.[44]

There does exist, however, in both the cities and on the large
commercial haciendas of the coast, opportunity for social mobility. The
strength of motivation behind the Sierra Indians' desire for upward
social movement to the higher status coastal Criollo is readily apparent
in Peru. From the poorest reed mat hut in the shanty towns on the
periphery of Lima emerge children and adults whose coastal dress evidences an unusual amount of attention and concern. As is typical of a
mobile group, they tend to deny their Indian cultural identity, dress,
language, etc., and affiliate with the cultural characteristics of the
coastal Criollo. Furthermore, once the Sierra Indian has adopted coastal dress and customs and mastered the Spanish language, he is difficult
to distinguish from the predominant mixed race Criollos born on the
coast.

Education, therefore, is a particularly important means to social-
economic advancement in Peru and its importance is fully recognized and
valued by those aspiring to a higher position within the Peruvian social
hierarchy. The urban poor will frequently make extraordinary sacrifices to allow their children to go to school. Once the sacrifices have
been made, and especially if the young man has completed secondary
schooling, he belongs to an elite which would little consider skilled

occupations involving manual labor, but would aspire to university admission and professional status.[45] If this poor, but ambitious, secondary level graduate gains admission to one of the now free universities, the probabilities are greater in Peru that he would choose a career in the prestigious, but overcrowded, areas of law or letters rather than fields such as medicine and education, where there are critical needs for graduates.[46]

We might project a bit further the hypothetical career development of this young Peruvian, as he characterizes in many ways the conflict of social-economic change taking place and its complex effects on him and Peru's modernization efforts. Perhaps because his father does not belong to a professional group the young man would venture into the rapidly growing, but less recognized, career in the commercial sciences. His formal education would probably consist of a five-year course of study extended several years by full-time employment and part-time study. The curriculum would be highly specialized, consisting of a large number of courses, primarily functional, in preparation for his first job, and taught by part-time professors. His placement efforts upon graduation would rely heavily on his family and especially their relationships, however tenuous, with the upper classes, as University placement and company recruiting are little used in Peru. He will, therefore, have less opportunity than his classmates from middle or upper class families in his search for an attractive position. On the other hand, his search may be broader than his fellow graduates, who are expected to wait their patrilineal turn for their chance to direct the family enterprise. He might, through a benevolent family friend, have both an opportunity as assistant to a lower-ranking public official and a junior accounting position in a large retail store. With either choice, his career advancement would be impaired by his highly specialized formal education and the limited development expectations or opportunities available within the predominant closely supervised, highly structured Peruvian organization. Peru's many new adult education programs, including management development courses, now offer opportunities for continuing education and professional associations which may enlarge the expectations and capacities of our employee as well as his employer.

The following sections will attempt to further develop the effect of these changing social and economic interrelationships on Peru's modernization manpower needs and its efforts to meet them.

Manpower Requirements

Peru's economically active population in 1965 was estimated to be 3½ million, predominantly dependents and campesinos living on a subsistence basis off the land.[47] As can be seen from Table V (Present and Projected Economically Active Population by Sector), Peru is yet a predominantly agricultural country, although the distribution of its active population is shifting steadily to non-agricultural sectors. In 1940, 62% of the active population was employed in agriculture, whereas today less than 52% are employed in this traditional sector, reflecting as well the rural-urban migration patterns.[48]

TABLE V

PERUVIAN ECONOMICALLY ACTIVE POPULATION

(Present and Projected by Sector)

| Sector | 1940 | 1950 | 1961 | 1970 | Increase 1961 – 1970 | | |
					Total	Average Annual No.	Rate
Agriculture	n.a.	n.a.	1,605	1,867	262	29	1.7%
Fisheries	n.a.	n.a.	16	35	19	2	8.9%
Mining	n.a.	n.a.	69	89	20	2	28.8%
Manufacturing	n.a.	n.a.	428	615	187	21	4.1%
Construction	n.a.	n.a.	109	274	165	18	10.8%
Services[1]	n.a.	n.a.	897	1,163	266	30	2.9%
Total	1,958	2,343	3,125	4,043	918	102	2.9%
Total enumerated population[2]	6,208	7,430	9,907	12,818	2,911		2.9%

[1]Includes transportation, utilities, commerce, government, and other services.

[2]According to the "VI Censo Nacional de Población de 1961," the total population was 10,420,357. Economically active population figures are based on the enumerated population.

NOTE: Sector figures may not total due to rounding.

Adapted from La Población, Los Recursos Humanos y el Empleo en el Perú. Servicio del Empleo y Recursos Humanos, Lima, Perú, April 1964.

The National Institute of Planning estimates a total of 400,000 workers underemployed or unemployed in Peru in 1964, and that the Peruvian economy must create 100,000 additional jobs per year in order to compensate for the population growth in the economically active age group.[49] The same publication estimates that 125,000 new jobs will be created per year based on 7% GNP annual growth rate. The implicit assumption is that the new jobs created by the projected economic growth rate should be able to keep pace with the job requirements produced by the population expansion and perhaps even reduce to some extent the continuing high rate of unemployment. The following questions concerning the assumptions underlying these statistics and the conclusions which might be inferred from them are of particular relevance to this study: Has the projected annual growth rate of 7% per annum been determined with due consideration given to the skilled and high level manpower resources necessary to achieve this high level of development? The manufacturing sector will provide an example. The National Institute of Planning's projected manufacturing sector GNP annual growth from 1961 through 1970 is 7.6%, which is somewhat higher than the 6.8% rate experienced during the 1955-61 period.[50] As seen in Table V, the economically active population in this sector is expected to increase by 187,000 persons during this period. Although these projections imply an annual growth of 3.4% per year in labor output, such increase in productivity can be achieved only with improved labor skills and the high level management resources required to effectively employ the human and capital inputs. Harbison and Myers in their book, Education, Manpower and Economic Growth, emphasize this problem.

> Many of the measures for human resource development in the short and medium planning periods have very little to do with numbers. They relate to the methods and the quality of education and training, the allocation of responsibility for upgrading manpower and the development of high-level resources.[51]

Historical studies by the Peruvian Employment Service indicate that despite an increasing demand for trained workers (total job requests increased six times between 1955 and 1963) less than one out of three of those people seeking work had the skills required to be placed. While several studies have indicated aggregate positive correlations between education level and personal income level,[52] it is also recognized that an individual's formal education will not necessarily increase his income unless his training and skills are in demand and are effectively employed.[53]

If we accept the assumption that the manufacturing sector will maintain an annual GNP growth rate from 1961 through 1970 of 7.6%, might it paradoxically be accompanied by an increase in both aggregative unemployment and unequal distribution of real income? Historical data from the period 1950 through 1961 shows the capital stock increasing about 8% per year faster than the labor force over the period. Peruvian public policy instruments, such as the 1959 Industrial Promotion Law, subsidize the importation of new capital equipment relative to old or obsolete equipment, further increasing capital-using and labor-saving change in manufacturing technology. Increasing labor benefits legislation, with little improved industrial relations climate and inadequate training and skills, further favors the substitution of capital for labor.

While increasing modern labor-saving technology could continue to increase productivity and per capita income of labor in the manufacturing sector, it may also increase aggregative unemployment; i.e., if the economy does not have sufficient capital to increase capital stock at a rate sufficient to absorb the rapidly increasing population into the active labor force. Thus, Peru's industrialization course may continue to increase mean per capita level of real income while the distribution of real income becomes more unequal (median per capita real income decreases).[54]

The above questions raised, but not answered, are representative of many concerning the consequences of Peru's alternative routes to modernization and their demands and effects on its eleven million people. If Peru is to answer her modernization problems, a much higher development and employment level of her human resources will be necessary. There are many interrelated elements and alternative strategies which a country must consider to invest efficiently in the development and employment of its human resources. Formal education is only one of these elements, which include informal educational programs, on the job training, and self development as well as an incentive system to encourage training and employment in critically needed occupational sectors. In the following sections we will consider Peru's strategic balance of these factors in her human resource development investments and policy, with special attention given to the role of higher education in the development of managerial manpower.

Peruvian Education: A Constructive Revolution

According to Harbison and Myer's comparative ranking of countries by composite index of human resource development, Peru is about in the middle, both within the 76 national sample and the 12 Latin American republics included in the ranking.[55] Peru in many ways typifies the education problems and goals of the countries at the "partially developed" level of human resources, beginning with high illiteracy levels and universal primary education goals.

Primary and Secondary Education. The 1961 Peruvian Census estimated 40% of the population above seventeen years of age is illiterate with the extremes ranging from 7% in the greater Lima area to 59% in the southern Sierra and jungle region. Again these quantitative estimates. illustrate the extent of segregation of the interior population; however, they do not adequately illustrate the dimensions of the educational problems involved, even if we consider only the present school age educational problem. The provision of a network of primary schools in adequate numbers, with teaching supplies and qualified teachers located within reach of every school age Peruvian child, is by itself a massive task. For example, it was estimated Peru needed approximately 27,000

225

additional classrooms and teachers in 1957 to enroll the illiterate children with the seven to sixteen-years age group alone -- over twice the number of primary school teachers employed in Peru that year.[56] The highly dispersed Sierra and jungle communities and the Indian languages add further dimension to the problem. If a new school is built in a remote Sierra valley and a qualified teacher is found to live there, the parents may be hesitant to send their children, and those that do come might be expected to speak little or no Spanish. These barriers, well documented in the previously cited Vicos project, further contribute to the serious retention problem as the school's learning process is not reinforced, but neutralized, by the child's home environment. In 1963, the retention of pupils from the first to the last year of the five-year primary cycle was 31%.[57] As might be expected, by far the highest attrition is between the first and second year of school, as the adaptation problems of the many non-Spanish speaking Indians to a rigidly prescribed curriculum in Spanish and developed in Lima is most difficult. The social structure, in which the lower classes are occupied by the non-Spanish speaking Indian children and the higher levels by the part Spanish "mestizos," further contributes to integration and retention problems. While the problems are massive, progress in recent years has been encouraging and there is a growing awareness of the critical role of human resource planning and development in Peru's modernization.

The National Plan for Educational Development, drafted in 1964, represents Peru's first major effort to coordinate educational planning with national planning. It further contains clear indications of a progressive decline during the last decade in the proportion of school-age children (age 5-14) not attending school and a lessening attrition rate. The proportion of children (age 5-14) not attending school is estimated to have been reduced from 26% in 1950 to 13% of the net potential in 1963.[58] The net potential used in these estimates was however, 70% of the total school age group (5-14). While several departments (states) containing urban centers were estimated in 1963 to have reached this net potential, other rural departments were estimated to have but 59% of this potential enrollment in attendance. Retention of pupils from the first to the fifth year of the primary cycle was estimated to have risen from 18% in 1955 to 31% in 1963.[59] Although attrition is yet very high, particularly in the interior urban areas, it has been declining.

The plan further reflects the general consensus that universal primary education is a most desirable and attainable goal for Peru; however, there is considerable optimism reflected in its achievement timetable. The plan does not specify how 100% of the net potential enrollment (70% of total 5-14 age group) will, as projected, be in school by 1969.[60]

The limitations of a quantitative orientation to human resource development planning without educational and employment reform is gaining recognition. Within the goals of the plan there is evidence of the need for revision of curriculum and teaching methodology toward the needs of the community and nation. Rote memorization, previously noted as a characteristic educational tool, is to be replaced by active student analysis and participation in problem solving and other learning processes. While the plan is less specific about how this is to be achieved, the growing recognition of the critical qualitative needs of the nation's educational programs is a necessary prerequisite to remedial action such as teacher training and development.

There is further basis for optimism in the progress of several creative approaches to first level and adult education, particularly in the Sierra where the need is so very great. In 1945, the Nuclear School Program was designed around the special needs, capabilities, and resources of the rural Indian. Around one central headquarters school offering the complete elementary program are up to twenty sectional schools teaching the first three years. The schools provide instruction in farming, vocational training, health, arithmetic, regional and Spanish language training, and extension work. In 1962 there were already operating 2,416 schools (central and sectional) with 5,424 teachers and 220,000 students enrolled.[61] Similar schools are being developed in the jungle. The native language is the primary medium of instruction, while Spanish will be taught as a second language. These programs, community development projects like Vicos, and the pioneering work done by universities such as San Cristóbal de Huamanga, formed the basis for the before-mentioned government's National Integration Plan for the aboriginal peoples. Recent educational legislation further evidences the desire for broader educational opportunities. In 1963, the Peruvian school system was reorganized and partially decentralized to six regional centers; in 1964, a new law was enacted granting government financed education from elementary school through the university.

The impact of government financial support for secondary and higher education has been most dramatic and necessary. Until this time secondary education presented a great obstacle to the further development of both first level (by limiting teacher training) and higher education. In 1946, legislation was enacted providing free secondary education; however, it wasn't until the 50's that the secondary education bottleneck began to break. During the period 1950-1963 secondary enrollments rose from 73,000 to 254,000 students, or from 10% to 22% of the estimated potential.[62] Rural states ran as low as 4% of their potential enrollments and over half of Peru's academic secondary schools were urban, private institutions.[63]

As the quantitative dimensions of secondary level education have improved with the postwar years, so has qualitative reform, with a comprehensive study of all aspects of the secondary system started in 1948. A major objective of the study and resultant reorganization was to coordinate academic and vocational education at the secondary level and initiate remedial action toward a variety of serious problems.

Peru shares with other developing Latin American countries a cultural tradition of academic secondary education oriented toward university admissions in large urban centers. As indicated in Table VI, the dominant position of private schools, with their limited selective

TABLE VI

NUMBER OF SCHOOLS AND STUDENTS, BY EDUCATIONAL LEVEL AND TYPE OF SCHOOL IN PERU: 1957-60

	Number of schools				Number of students			
	1957	1958	1959	1960	1957	1958	1959	1960
Total	13,560	14,315	14,864	15,403	1,372,602	1,467,176	1,603,064	1,681,299
Elementary:								
Subtotal	12,944	13,624	14,102	14,590	1,233,937	1,308,305	1,391,952	1,479,100
Public	11,422	11,799	12,231	12,700	1,065,990	1,110,742	1,184,107	1,260,400
Private	901	1,169	1,215	1,287	107,788	134,439	140,308	148,700
State supervised	621	656	656	603	60,159	63,124	67,537	70,000
Academic secondary:								
Subtotal	425	441	486	524	111,191	122,221	141,062	158,900
Public	152	176	198	222	65,922	75,895	90,553	103,778
Private	273	265	288	302	45,269	46,326	50,509	55,122
Vocational secondary:								
Subtotal	166	221	243	251	25,460	34,410	37,249	39,359
Public	129	147	169	177	22,302	27,819	31,609	33,878
Private	37	74	74	74	3,158	6,591	5,640	5,481
Teacher education:								
Subtotal	25	29	33	38	2,014	2,240	3,281	3,940
Public	19	24	28	32	1,575	1,787	2,777	3,338
Private	6	5	5	6	439	453	504	602

Education in Peru, U. S. Department of Health, Education and Welfare Bulletin No. 33, 1964, p. 43-44.

Source of data: Ministerio de Educación Pública. La Educación Actual Peruana. Documents submitted by the Government of Peru to the Conference on Education and Economic and Social Development in Latin America, held in Santiago, Chile, March 5-19, 1962. Lima: The Ministry, 1962.

enrollments is lessening with the rapidly expanding public, secondary school systems both academic and vocational. The National Plan of Educational Development proposes to further raise the attendance level from 22% in 1963 to 40% for both regular and technical secondary education in 1970.[64]

The quantitative needs of providing secondary education opportunities for the expanding numbers of primary level graduates are very great. They are, however, recognized and more easily satisfied than the chronic qualitative problems which are accentuated by the rapid growth. Vocational education has developed rapidly in recent years in recognition of the need for large numbers of technicians and skilled workers in agriculture, industry, and government.[65] In 1962, the Ministry of Public Education indicated that again major qualitative problems were undermining the vocational programs intent. The report cited that the vocational schools were not providing adequate training and skills necessary for many jobs nor fulfilling the students' expectations.[66] Furthermore, the school's specialized training orientation frequently did not provide the necessary general education for those students with the capacity and desire for higher education. A study by Harry R. White in 1964, including surveys of existing technical and general secondary schools, as well as Peru's largest firms, further supported the constraints of quality and type of student training for employment.

Closely allied to the failure of many students to find work is the fact that nearly all the secondary technical schools of Peru teach the same unneeded skills. Hence, many students leave such schools without either a marketable skill or a good general education (thought by some employers to be more important than specialized training).[67]

Studies by William Whyte have indicated the low social status of manual work in Peru.[68] This cultural constraint, supported by the previously cited limited access and high attrition characteristics of the Peruvian educational system, contributes to the high school graduate's strong preference and expectation for professional status achievement through university study. While Peru's need for skilled and technical workers increases, these vocational school systems' limitations and the cultural blue collar barrier provide serious constraints to their satisfaction.

Peruvian university rectors have been in a favorable position to evaluate the deficiencies of the expanding numbers of vocational academic secondary school graduates. Luis Alberto Sánchez, Rector of the University of San Marcos, has found that secondary school preparation suffers from the quality of instruction, with excessive rote memorization and inadequate preparation in mathematics and scientific fundamentals, compounded by a lack of library and laboratory facilities.[69] The shortage of secondary school teachers in Peru has been partially met in Lima and the larger cities by the part-time teaching of lawyers, engineers, and physicians. The European educational influence characterized in Peru, concentrating general education at the secondary level and

professional specialization in the university, places further burden on
secondary education. After successive years of mounting unsuccessful
applicants, several major universities in Lima as well as one provincial
have initiated first-year preparatory programs in basic general studies.[70]

Since the 1950's Peru has greatly increased her investment in education and several promising new programs have been developed at the
secondary level such as the comprehensive school centers (gran unidad
escolar). In 1964, over 21% of the national budget was expended on education and this rate has been steadily rising about one percent per year
since 1955.[71] From 1960, over thirty of these centers have been established
and offer both vocational and pre-university academic education. Such
multipurpose schools can develop a fundamental and flexible educational
base on which the student may further build and adapt vocational skills
to changing technology or continue on to professional education.

However, the critical resource in this program's successful development will again be highly qualified teachers. The Peruvian Ministry of
Education in cooperation with Columbia University's School of Education
under the Alliance for Progress have undertaken several programs designed
to satisfy this need for educational leadership. Expanded scholarship
programs for study abroad and educational television with especially designed curriculum and teaching materials are two parts of this program
designed to increase the level of education and greatly multiply its
impact.

University Education. Peru's system of higher education has undergone
far greater change since 1950 than in its previous 400 years of existence, but its greatest challenges lie ahead before it can achieve its
full potential role in the modernization process.

In 1950 there were four national and one private university in Peru
providing, primarily, education in the traditional professions.[72] Peru,
as a major Spanish colonial center with the first university on the
hemisphere combined with its active role in the university reform movement of 1918, previously described, contained at that date the major
characteristics and problems of the "Latin American University" discussed in Chapter II. Part-time students, faculty, and administrators,
combined with the active political involvement and inadequate research
facilities, were not producing the quantity nor quality of high-talent
human resources needed for Peru's modernization. However, with the mid-
century came significant progress toward these goals.

The provision of free secondary education (enrollments at this
level rose from 73,000 in 1950 to 254,000 in 1963) and the social-
economic forces previously described resulted in mounting demands for
higher education. University enrollments between 1950 and 1963 rose
from 17 to 55 thousand, and, with the additional incentive of free
tuition starting in 1964, are projected to reach 110,000 by 1970.[73]
These growing pressures soon overtaxed the facilities of the existing
universities and paved the way for the establishment of new universities
throughout the country.

The five Peruvian universities operating in 1950 were joined officially by the National Engineering University in 1955 and the National Agrarian University in 1960, both located in Lima. The latter institutions had been founded in 1866 and 1902, respectively, as schools but did not gain university status until the above dates. In 1959, the National University of Huamanga was reopened as the second university in the Sierra.

Since the enactment of the University Law of 1960, eighteen new universities have been founded (including six additional in the Sierra and jungle regions) and four more are in the process of organization. Under this law, which recognizes the private university, half of the eighteen new universities have been privately founded.

The University Law of 1960 in many ways reflects the growing, but often conflicting, forces for change in Peruvian higher education. While explicitly prohibiting political activities in the university, it legally establishes student representation (co-gobierno) in their governing bodies, believed by many Latin-American scholars to be the basis for student political involvement and power. While the students' involvement in national politics and frequent university strikes has most adverse educational effects, their reform movements, beginning with the before-mentioned 1919 Cordoba Proclamation at San Marcos, has also accelerated many desirable changes in the highly structured Peruvian universities. The law further grants the central government the legal basis for founding and financing new universities, but again does not provide for the coordination of their development once established. With the rising public and political pressures for higher education, the explosion of new universities in Peru is understandable, if not predictable from comparative development studies.[74] One might, however, question the adequacy of the manpower and academic planning considerations preceding the rapid commitment of future public funds when the university's autonomy, once founded, is guaranteed by law. Unfortunately, the majority of the newly authorized universities, particularly those in the interior, do not have adequate resources, monetary or human, to develop the breadth or level of skills and talents needed. Nevertheless, in sparsely equipped autonomous universities, part-time teachers and students will meet in accelerating numbers, interrupted only by their frequent conflict protests and strikes.

What career specialities and educational standards are currently being institutionalized within these new Peruvian universities for generations to come? Will they further accelerate the historical (1950-1959) oversupply of graduates in the traditional fields of law and letters but contribute little or less to the relative decline, during the same period, in critically needed scientific and medical manpower areas? University enrollments in the specialized areas of law and letters between 1950-1959 increased respectively 2% and 6% of the total percent. University enrollments in the areas of medicine and basic sciences between the same period decreased respectively 10% and .5% of the total percent.[75] The answers to these and other central problems will be determined by Peru's national leadership. Public recognition has

recently been given to strategic manpower planning and the vital quantitative and qualitative needs and prerequisites for Peruvian high-talent
human resource set forth in the 1964 Plan of Educational Development.
The government's awareness of these problems represents a necessary and
most encouraging step toward the missing coordinated development of
Peru's institutions of higher education.

Peru is fortunately not without the educational leadership necessary
to translate these objectives and plans into programs of action, as exemplified by the substantial progress of several of its institutions of
higher education.

The early Peruvian leader in university proletarianism beginning
in the 1940's was the National University of San Marcos. The oldest
university founded in the hemisphere, San Marcos remains Peru's largest,
with approximately 60% of its 15,000 enrollees drawn from the lower
social-economic classes in 1964. In recent years less than 40% of the
student body was born in Lima. The rapid university student population
expansion has not helped efforts to overcome its almost classic Latin
American university problem syndrome; however, increasing Peruvian and
international assistance holds promise for increasing progress.

The National Agriculture University established high educational
goals and is building a solid foundation for their achievement. Since
its founding as a university in 1960 (previously the School of Agriculture established in 1902), renewed emphasis has been placed on the
continuing development of a well-qualified faculty. Of the national
universities in 1964, it achieved the highest proportion (75% of 289
faculty members) and total number (216) of full-time professors. The
faculty includes 64 members with advanced degrees at the masters or
doctoral levels, while 38 additional faculty in 1964 were preparing for
advanced degrees from North American or other universities abroad. New
faculties (schools) have been developed, including schools in the basic
and social sciences. A general one-year educational core curriculum
common to all schools has recently been initiated which includes basic
courses in the humanities, physical and social sciences. In addition,
their continued recognition of advanced elective and required courses
taken outside a faculty reduces duplication of offerings and facilitates
the more flexible and economic use of limited educational resources. In
1963-64, the University's Graduate School (founded in 1959) initiated an
eighteen-month post graduate program leading to a masters level degree
in several fields related to agriculture. To a large measure, the integration and coordination of curriculum, faculty, and institutional
development was made possible by the full-time efforts of its administrative leadership and staff.

The National Engineering University has been a major contributing
factor to Peru's essential human resources in the engineering sciences,
many of whom have advanced to positions of high public and private
managerial responsibility. While, as noted previously, there was a
relative decline in Peru's total university enrollment in the medical
and basic sciences between 1950-1959, the Engineering enrollment, during

the same period, more than tripled to include approximately 13% of the total enrollment.[76] Over 62% of this substantial growth was accounted for by the Engineering University. Although established in 1876 as the National School of Engineering, its major development has taken place following its achievement of university status in 1955.[77] Its faculty development program has received continuing emphasis, with approximately 100 of its 670 professors employed on a full-time basis in 1964. Like the National Agricultural University, it has both expanded and integrated its curriculum, including the addition of a common core curriculum for entering students, a new School of Economics, and a post graduate program in civil engineering. Having attracted substantial North American and international monetary and manpower assistance, the Engineering University's ambitious development plans show excellent promise.

The University de San Cristóbal de Huamanga, located in the Sierra city of Ayacucho, has recently re-opened after being closed for over seven decades. Its organization and curriculum today represent a thoughtfully planned departure from the traditional university pattern toward a program to meet the specific social-economic needs of the provincial region it serves. Emphasis has been placed on providing an intensive educational program through the employment of a full-time faculty and administration while prohibiting partisan politics. As the student body is predominantly Indian, the Quechua language is incorporated into the curriculum and a preparatory one-year general course of study is required for all entering students. It is designed to both fulfill the individual's basic educational needs as well as provide pre-professional orientation. It is worthy to note that following this preparatory program a majority of the students have substantially re-oriented their entering career choices. Purposeful efforts have been made to integrate the curriculum internally as well as environmentally through required field research and community study.

Higher Education for Management: Concepts, Commitments and Strategies. Management education as a specialized area of formal study in Peru has a brief but intensive history characterized by merging North American and Peruvian concepts and practices in a variety of changing educational institutions. The resultant educational programs are predictably diverse, and a review of their development reveals several significant innovations and many remaining problems in the development of management education to meet the particular needs of Peru.

Peru's enrollments in its faculties of economic and commercial sciences, an important source of its managerial manpower, more than doubled during the 1950's to just under 4,000 students as Peru's industrialization gained momentum and the universities were opened to greater numbers. The large influx of businessmen, government personnel, and returning Peruvian university students from North America following World War II provided a growing awareness of the potential role of high-talent managerial resources in economic development. Other major Latin American universities in Mexico, Brazil, and Chile had already established schools of public and private administration. It is, therefore,

quite understandable why, in 1959, the first Peruvian school of administration was founded at the northern coastal University of Trujillo. As
indicated by its title, The Professional School of Business Administration was patterned after the highly specialized programs of the
traditional Latin American professional schools. Major concentrations
in economics, accounting, and law were offered by the founding faculties
of economics and commercial sciences with classes totaling at least 24
hours per week. Enrollments have since grown to over a hundred predominantly part-time students who, upon completion of a five-year program,
including a thesis, are awarded the degree of Executive in Business
Administration.

Since the founding of the first school at Trujillo in 1958, an
average of one major new program in administration has been established
each year, predominantly in Lima.

In 1959, the business community founded the Peruvian Business
Administration Institute (IPAE) in Lima. It is patterned after the
American Management Association, conducting evening and weekend seminars
for Peruvian businessmen in the traditional functional business areas.
The growth and orientation of this institution since 1959 is reflected
in its 1963-64 program. During this year 36 seminars in such fields as
marketing, finance, and personnel administration were attended by over
1100 businessmen.

San Marcos University established its School of Administration
within the School of Economic Sciences in 1961. As in the case of the
University of Trujillo, the founding economics and commercial science
faculties gave strong initial direction to the program in administration,
and their combined enrollment at San Marcos has quickly grown to over
3,000 students.

Under the provisions of the University Law of 1960, three new private institutions of higher education with administration orientation
were established during 1962-63 in Lima. The University of the Pacific
was founded early in 1962 with strong support from the business community and academic leadership provided by the Society of Jesus coordinated
with the University of Loyola in Chicago. The program is therefore more
closely aligned to a North American undergraduate curriculum in business
administration and offers a bachelor's degree after four years of study.
The school is growing rapidly with approximately 200 students currently
enrolled in its four-year program and over 300 businessmen annually
attending its three-month business extension courses.

The University of Lima was established in 1963, again with considerable private sector support and North American academic counsel.
Its faculty of arts and sciences offers a rather broad four-year bache-
lors degree program providing mathematics, humanities, and social
science studies, and including some basic courses in business administration. An additional year of more specialized business administration
study qualifies the student for the title of Master in Social and Economic Sciences. The university which has had an enrollment of 575

students in 1965 also offers doctoral as well as continuing education programs.

The third private institution established during the 1962-63 period was the Graduate School of Business Administration (ESAN). Founded and supported initially under the Alliance for Progress Program, the school was organized and staffed by the Stanford University Graduate School of Business. The nine initial North American and European faculty members and more recent Peruvian replacements are all engaged on a full-time basis in the school's teaching and research programs. ESAN's eleven-month post graduate program was essentially adapted from the core curriculum of the two-year Master of Business Administration Program at Stanford University and requires the full-time study efforts of the current enrollees. In addition to the latter Masters Degree program, ESAN offers several continuing management development programs each year. The school's research includes the development of Peruvian case material and draws upon its 10,000 volume management and social science library.

In addition, the Agrarian University, in 1963, undertook a department of administration in its faculty of social sciences. Oriented toward the development of managerial resources for agriculture as well as business administration, the five-year program is quite broad, including required courses in the physical and biological sciences. Although the program is yet small (fifteen students in 1965), the Agrarian University, with assistance from North Carolina State University, first concentrated on the development of its faculty and curriculum and has made exemplary progress.

In 1964, the National Office of Rationalization and Training of Public Administration (ONRAP) was established as the first Peruvian educational institution for the development of public sector administration and leadership. As in the case of the Graduate School of Business Administration (ESAN) previously described, ONRAP was founded under the Alliance for Progress with joint Peruvian and North American support. With advisory and staff assistance from the New York Institute of Public Administration, ONRAP's functions include a series of courses and seminars for various levels of public officials of from one to eight months duration. Again paralleling ESAN's program, considerable effort is being extended toward the development of a permanent Peruvian faculty in both national and foreign universities to carry on the institute's varied teaching and research programs, including case development.

In addition to the above major programs, several universities now include courses in administration as part of their professional curriculum. The National University of Engineering, for example, includes Administration and Economics courses in the Schools of Mechanical and Electrical Engineering and Industrial Engineering. The Catholic University of Peru also includes courses in business administration within its Faculty of Economics and Commercial Sciences as does the National University of San Agustín of Arequipa.

At the time of this writing several entirely new undergraduate programs in business administration are in various early stages of development, including one at the private university of Santa María in Arequipa and an entirely new private school of business administration with North American sponsorship to be located in Lima. In Peru, as in many other Latin American countries, higher education for business administration is growing so rapidly that the government is considering licensing its graduates and requiring certain administrative positions to be restricted to those so certified.

The proliferation of new Peruvian schools and programs of administration with wide variations in curriculum level and orientation, but sharing financial and faculty resources, readily invites internal conflict and expert advice from abroad. Regardless of how knowledgeable a foreign consultant may be in their specific field of expertise applied in the host country, the burden of carrying out the recommendations typically remains behind when the advisor departs. Peru has already been the gracious recipient of countless foreign advisors' "problems and remedial action reports," but, as in other modernizing countries, these are frequently not carried out as intended, if at all.

The reasons typically cited in defense of the performance short-comings or failures seldom fail to include the advisors' lack or under-standing of the country and its complex problems and the recipient's inability to carry through the most carefully constructed plans.

In March, 1962, Stanford University was invited to study Peru's management education needs. The university responded by sending a faculty team which, following discussions with Peruvian leaders in the public, private, and academic sectors, submitted a report recommending the creation of a graduate school of administration. In September, 1962, the governments of Peru and the United States then requested that Stanford University establish, as a part of the Alliance for Progress Program, Latin America's first school of administration to operate exclusively at the post-graduate level. Recognizing this unusual and challenging opportunity, the Stanford Graduate School of Business Administration undertook the achievement of its own recommendations. The plans and strategies undertaken, the unexpected problems and complications overcome, as well as the compromises, adaptations, and innovations required, challenged many basic concepts and attitudes of the North Americans and Peruvians involved. An analysis of this specific undertaking may provide a truer understanding of Peru's managerial resource development problems and some insights from this inter-American experience toward their solution.

ESAN: A Bold Approach to Managerial Resource Development. The new graduate institution of administration was named in Spanish, the Escuela de Administración de Negocios para Graduados, and abbreviated ESAN. ESAN was chartered as a private Peruvian educational institution with complete financial and faculty autonomy planned for within from five to ten years. The school was not founded within an existing Peruvian educational institution because its intended goals and development efforts

236

required the complete autonomy and freedom for innovation that an independent organization could best provide. On the other hand, ESAN fully recognized its dependence upon the established universities for continuous counsel and support and established, therefore, an advisory council with senior representation from major universities.

The institution's basic objective from its inception was to assist in the development of the high-level managerial resources needed for Peru's continued modernization.

The school's original orientation was to the private sector, not unlike its founding North American institution. However, exclusive leadership development efforts within one sector, the predominating pattern in North America, did not, in time, appear possible or desirable. The prominent businessman is most often quite influential in Peruvian public affairs, while the government, as is common in Latin America, owns and administers several major enterprises in addition to its many regulatory functions. An understanding of the interdependent relationship between the public and private sectors in Peru's development process is therefore essential. In addition, the need for high-level managerial talent and technology in Latin America's educational and public institutions is no less great, and perhaps more important at present, than in the private sector.

Intensive post graduate and executive level programs were chosen as ESAN's major educational undertaking for several reasons. Peru's increasing development efforts and involvement in a changing world of competitive markets and advancing technology have created new levels of intellectual and leadership demands. The complex and substantial social-economic problems just reviewed certainly demand no less intellectual capacity, educational development, and social responsibility than those of the highly advanced industrial countries.

By concentrating its limited resources on post-graduate and executive level continuing education programs, it was possible for ESAN to draw upon the proven intellectual and leadership talent from a broad range of academic and professional fields including the military and the Church. Rather than joining in direct career competition with the established prestigious professions in Peru for the most talented university applicants, ESAN could select from and contribute to the further development of their honor graduates and successful alumni.

It was believed, and later substantiated, that talented graduates of Peru's several overcrowded professional fields would find new career opportunities by combining, for example, their legal or letters degree with post-graduate management education. The substantial advantages and entrepreneurial potential of basic engineering or military sciences, broadened with professional management education experienced in North America, were also anticipated in Peru. The post-graduate and executive orientation of ESAN was seen, moreover, as a major asset in its goal to assist in the establishment of high academic standards of teaching, research and faculty development.

A primary task of ESAN was, therefore, to develop simultaneously a highly qualified Peruvian faculty and an institutional framework, including research facilities, which would support full-time faculty teaching, research, and professional achievement. A preliminary search for faculty candidates was instigated by the Stanford faculty team members during their first months in Peru, but the problems were more complex and extensive than anticipated. While a dearth of Peruvians with post-graduate degrees in administration was expected, the most serious shortage of potential faculty with adequate social science foundations was not. While there were many qualified lawyers, engineers, and accountants with senior faculty appointments teaching part-time in the universities, their background was highly specialized in their respective fields, necessitating several years of post-graduate work to develop new professional concepts, tools, and capacities. Furthermore, when these talented professionals were interviewed, they were less than enthusiastic with the idea of undertaking two to six post-graduate years of study abroad, even with full living and study scholarships provided. Their general disinterest was not unjustified, however, considering their already promising careers and opportunities to hold senior university faculty rank by part-time teaching within their professional field. A doctorate in a Peruvian university might be earned, further enhancing their credentials, by an additional year of work in their professional area without serious career interruption, financial loss, or the complete social economic adaptation required to live abroad as a student. While early efforts to locate well qualified potential faculty willing to study abroad were largely unsuccessful, once ESAN was established, its Master's program proved to be the major source of such candidates and will be further discussed later in this chapter.

During its early development ESAN also sought to make its basic objectives better known to the business, government, and academic communities, while at the same time seeking advice and counsel regarding how these might best be accomplished in Peru. The university advisory board previously mentioned and several short-duration executive development programs held with business, government, military, clerical, and academic representation were most helpful in this regard.

Research: A Basis for Adaptation and Growth. Research and the library were among the very first departments at ESAN to undertake their related and important functions. The leading contemporary institutions of higher education throughout the world are deeply committed to the creation, as well as transmission, of knowledge. Their questions concern what might be, in addition to what is or has been. ESAN recognized, too, that it must first attempt to identify the contemporary problems and practices of Peruvian management within their complex environmental settings as a basis for meaningful future research. The initial method of inquiry was the case study involving the examination of the many interrelated factors affecting the unit under study, be it a person, work group, organization, or larger system. The case study proved a most effective system of information exchange through which the faculty could rapidly become familiar with a broad range of Peruvian management problems and behavior, as well as introduce and seek applications for new concepts and tools. It established, therefore, a basis for continuing communication and exchange of ideas between the professional school and the broad management profession which it serves. In addition, the case study proved to be one of the school's most important tools of instruction for the graduate and executive development programs and will be discussed in the next session. Based on an analysis of one unit, the case study seldom proves anything by itself; however, it can be an excellent source of insights and raw material for more fundamental research.

In time, ESAN became a center for a wide variety of research carried on both by its own faculty and visiting scholars from North and South America. Increasing applications of analytical tools from mathematics, economics, and the behavioral sciences were evidenced as well. ESAN's library was of great assistance, with its professional staff rapidly developing one of Latin America's most complete contemporary collections of Spanish and English publications in the social sciences. A special effort was made to open the library's resources to active use by the academic and management community through the development and distribution of annotated bibliographys, open book shelves, and liberal circulation policies. Serious problems were encountered, however, in the location of current publications in Spanish. The general scarcity of empirical research in Latin American universities has already been noted; however, this need is most apparent in the social sciences. In Peru, the need for trained social scientists to carry out all manner of inquiry concerning its modernization process, and management capable of directing and evaluating this research, is critical and clearly an important challenge to ESAN.

The Master of Administration Program. Ten months after the first Stanford faculty team members arrived in Peru, ESAN admitted its first Master of Administration class. This program was to be the school's primary academic undertaking involving the nine faculty members and fifty post-graduate students' full-time efforts for its eleven-month duration. While there were some reservations expressed by many Latin Americans regarding the school's ability to attract university graduates to such an intensive program, necessitating their delaying or leaving their career occupation, this problem did not materialize. The total number of applicants was four times larger than the fifty-member class planned for. This gratifying response was in no small measure due to the advance efforts mentioned above, as well as an extensive university visitation and meetings program.

While the total number of applicants was adequate, their qualifications were often difficult to evaluate.

Admissions and Financial Assistance. The faculty's admissions criteria were several. The candidate was to have a bachelor's degree, or its equivalent, from an accredited university. While no specific undergraduate major or series of courses was prerequisite, the program was designed primarily for individuals who had completed their university studies in the liberal arts, law, physical and social sciences, rather

than business administration.[78] It was recommended, however, that
students considering future application to ESAN include in their university programs, when possible, several courses in the basic analytical
areas including mathematics and statistics, the social sciences, emphasizing economics and the behavioral sciences, and communications skills,
especially Spanish grammar and written composition. These broad subject
areas, providing the basic concepts and cognitive tools with which a
graduate program in administration must build, were also, unfortunately,
most often deficient in the applicant's professional curricula and
required early adaptation and compensation in ESAN's program. Considerable admissions effort was, therefore, given to the identification of
valid and reliable indicators of the applicant's verbal and analytical
abilities. In addition to the individual's past academic record, which
was often difficult to appraise because of significant variations in
institutional standards, two scholastic aptitude examinations were
selected for evaluation. These tests were developed especially for university level Spanish-speaking Latin Americans by two internationally
recognized psychological testing institutions.

Scholastic aptitude testing is a quite new idea in Peru, as in most
of Latin America. While extensive evaluation of tests and scores
remain, their potential value in the selection of promising students for
the Latin American University, suffering from swelling application and
attrition rates, is very great. The ESAN admissions faculty committee
was also well aware of the limitations of such tests and the need to
seek other indicators of the applicant's special talents, especially
evidence of high achievement and entrepreneurial leadership potential.
Personal interviews and complete employment and educational histories
with letters of recommendation were required of each applicant. Additional consideration was given to the applicant's place of residence
recalling the great interior problems, and intended career, recognizing
Peru's special needs for professors of administration and administrative
talent in religious and military institutions as well as in government
and private organizations.

Financial considerations involving the institution's continuing
monetary needs and the student's ability and willingness to invest in
his personal development presented several unexpected problems. Tuition
levels in Peru are very low, with the public universities virtually without
fees and the private universities averaging but several hundred dollars
per year. Although the latter tuition is nominal by North American
standards, the student from the lower socio-economic classes of Peru
would find this difficult to pay without full-time employment. After
considerable discussion among the faculty and consultation with its
advisory board, it was, nevertheless, decided that ESAN would set its
tuition among the highest being charged by private Peruvian universities.
In 1963 these tuition charges ranged between three and four hundred
dollars per academic year.

There were several important considerations in setting this relatively high level of tuition. Although ESAN was being underwritten by
the Peruvian and North American governments during its early development

years, it did want to help establish a better understanding of the potential values and real costs of education upon which would rest more than the future of ESAN. While the advanced industrial nations' dependence on and investment in educational programs of all kinds continues its accelerating growth, the part-time minor role of higher education in Peru's modernization process is inadequate. The concept of personal or national investment in education has little meaning unless it results in intellectual growth marked by increasing capacity and talents needed and valued in the society. It was ESAN's contention that its well qualified faculty, student body, and administration devoting their full efforts to study and research could give new meaning to the value of educational investment.

While ESAN believed its tuition level was appropriate, it did not want to exclude any student who could otherwise qualify for admission. It instigated, therefore, a loan program for needy students to defer their educational costs until following graduation when they are able to undertake repayment of the loan. This program, although quite unusual in Peru, is well received and greatly facilitates ESAN's ability to enroll talented graduates from varied geographical and socio-economic sectors of Peru.

Curriculum Development and Methods of Instruction. ESAN's eleven-month masters degree curriculum was initially adapted from the core requirements of Stanford University's eighteen-month Master of Business Administration Program. The total program planned for nineteen courses, including six elective seminars in the major subject areas, was distributed across four quarters. The major subject areas were Organizational Behavior and Industrial Relations, Mathematics and Statistics, Macro and Micro Economics, Accounting and Control, Finance, Marketing, Production and Management Policy. The student work load was designed to be between 16-18 hours of classes per week with each class requiring approximately two hours of additional preparation. Soon after the program was underway, however, internal changes in course direction and content were indicated as well as several new areas of study.

One of the earliest problem areas to appear, as might be anticipated, involved communications. As the North American faculty's Spanish language problems were anticipated, a simultaneous translation and written translation staff were employed on a full-time basis. The translators were highly trained, and with the aid of multichannel translation equipment, similar to that used in the United Nations, the ESAN faculty not fluent in Spanish were able to carry on their classes with little difficulty. While simultaneous translation was possible in the classroom, those faculty not fluent in Spanish were severely handicapped in their constant associations with students and management during the vast majority of their working day. While these faculty were all taking Spanish language programs in Peru, it was unanimously agreed that if they had undertaken an intensive language program before leaving for Peru, their adaptation and effectiveness would have been really enhanced.

While the North American faculty's Spanish language communication problems were anticipated, the Peruvian students' were not. These centered primarily in written communications and resulted in the addition of a new course in Spanish composition and written analysis of cases. The students' English language knowledge was not an admissions requirement, however, the students were later encouraged to study English and assistance was provided. The importance of a second internationally used language to Latin American management so intensely involved with other countries needs little justification here. English was preferred not only because of its very wide commercial usage, but also because the majority of basic and applied publications in the broad fields concerning administration are published in English. With first-quality Spanish translations of current publications in administration and its related fields in extremely short supply, the critical continuing self-education of Latin American management and their total career effectiveness can be facilitated by the development of English language capacities.

Far greater curriculum changes took place, however, within the existing major course offerings than through the addition of new courses during ESAN's early years. The perennial academic debate between the universalists of management theory postulating that management is a science based on truly universal principles and yielding "one best way" and those that maintain that its principles are culture bound was not at all popular among the ESAN faculty. Perhaps it was because they were fully occupied attempting to evaluate and relate their field's concepts and technology to the Peruvian social system and organizational behavior. It was apparent that while some concepts and technology were more readily applicable to Peruvian problems, others were not at all. This sorting and relating process was initially made even more difficult by the North American faculty's personal aculturation to their new environmental system. For many months, the perceptual clues and communications inputs relied upon for learning had to be relearned before they could be effectively utilized to contribute to the understanding of the host country.

While the faculty found significant variations among their fields of study as to the extent their concepts, developed primarily from North American or European experience, were of direct relevance in Peru, their analytical, economic and behavioral tools of inquiry proved equally applicable to Peruvian managerial problems. The field of industrial relations, for example, involves workers, managers, government administrators, and their organizations interacting within a social-economic, political-legal environment. John Dunlop first analyzed these elements on a systems basis in 1958.[79] While developing the consistency and unity of an industrial relations system, he emphasized that changes in one facet of the system will disrupt its equilibrium and create new relationships (attitudes, rules, behavior) between its members and their organizations. He further pointed out that efforts to affect the direction of change in the system is greatly facilitated by analyzing its historical development and the consequences of past changes within the system through time.

The industrial relations professors at ESAN found that recent systems concepts, in combination with other basic quantitative and social science tools of analysis, made possible highly promising new approaches to research and teaching in their field in Peru. At the outset, normative values concerning the "one best way" to achieve harmonious industrial relations was replaced by comparative analysis of representative international industrial relations systems with special attention given to Peru and Latin America. Such studies yielded valuable insights concerning the integrated functions of each country's industrial relations sub-system within its unique society. The many reasons why the Spanish, British, and Yugoslav industrial relations systems each developed over time certain distinct characteristics and their relative effectiveness within that nation provided an excellent comparative base for the study of the Peruvian systems evolution. The traditional historical, legal and other descriptive approaches to the study of Peruvian industrial relations were no longer ends in themselves, but now formed the foundation for further inquiry concerning its internal and external interrelationships and the effects of changes in these factors. For example, Peru has had in the 1960's a particularly high level of union-management industrial disputes. Studies such as those conducted by William Foote Whyte concerning labor, government, and management's cultural attitudes and related behavior in Peruvian industrial relations produced needed insights concerning the causes of its industrial conflict.[80] These studies, incorporating attitude measurement combined with recent empirical and field research contributions from the behavioral and quantitative sciences interrelating, bargaining behavior, conflict, technology, task and structure, provided invaluable new concepts and tools with which to approach the challenging industrial relations problems of Peru.[81,82] Studies of union-management relations at the plant level are as yet quite rare in Latin America and proved to be a particularly promising area for continuing study by the ESAN and visiting scholars. Intensive studies of industrial conflict and subsequent resolution with management change within one plant, for example, yielded a series of interesting and meaningful research hypotheses concerning interrelationships between leadership style, organizational structure, and behavior.

The above problems were also incorporated into a series of cases for student analysis in organizational behavior, industrial relations and policy courses.[83] This series along with others focusing on problems in finance, marketing, and other areas provided an invaluable basis for management-professor-student exchange and learning. As previously noted, the case development process provided the faculty with current Peruvian problems within their actual setting, as well as the opportunity to exchange ideas with management. Within the classroom these cases were representative of the actual problem and provided both students and faculty the opportunity to test concepts and the application of tools in complex open-ended systems.

While the case method is certainly a well recognized method of instruction in North America, it has proven to be particularly valuable in Latin American management education. If used properly, the case

method immediately emphasizes the Latin American students' problem
solving responsibility in direct contrast to his traditional passive
role of note taking and memorization of material from authoritative
sources. The student faced with the multiple and interrelated systems
of the problem situation will seek information, potentially useful tools,
and advice from a variety of sources, but he is the final authority in
his choice of remedial action. He gains insight and experience from
planning for change rather than passively anticipating future uncertainties. Through case and research assignments which bring the student
into the field, the students learn by analyzing problems, attempting
their solution, and comparing actual or potential results with their
goals. As this process simulates the actual managerial decision process and is consistent with the findings of dynamic learning theory, it
represents a most promising,although entirely new,approach to management
education in Peru.

The case method, combined with other active problem solving forms
of instruction are, therefore, of primary importance in the achievement
of ESAN's goal to further strengthen the students cognitive processes
in order to increase his own effectiveness in dealing with future managerial problems in Peru.

The use of small study groups to help in the preparation of cases
and team research projects was further observed to provide social support
and enrichment of the learning process which extended beyond the classroom.[84] The ESAN library stacks were completely open and the entire
building purposely designed to be a pleasant place to browse and study,
rather than a forbidding,maximum security depository of national trea-
sure. Its separate rooms were also a favorite place for group case
preparations and the analysis of materials gained from field research.

It is of additional interest to note that the Peruvian students at
ESAN proved themselves highly motivated, mature, and capable scholars.
At no time has there been student reform movements or threat of strike
so very common in Peru and Latin America. While the students and alumni
do not participate directly in the administration of ESAN, their con-
structive suggestions and advice, actively sought and freely given, continue to play a significant role in its development.

Placement: Feedback and Change. As ESAN's Masters of Administration
candidates were fully occupied with their eleven-month academic program,
all but a few on leave from their organizations, including the military,
sought career opportunities. University placement functions are not
common in Latin America. ESAN's faculty and staff began by introducing
this procedure and their graduates to the Peruvian management.

The strong demand for ESAN's first graduates and the excellent,
career opportunities they received has been particularly gratifying,
considering the newness of the school and its professional program.
While several graduates started new firms, the majority have been employed throughout the private and public sectors. Of particular interest
has been the significant number who are engaged in a full or part-time
academic career.

Twelve of ESAN's first class of fifty Master of Administration program graduates alone were teaching part or full-time in schools of administration soon after their graduation. The universities included several in the provinces, including the University of Cuzco. This high level of academic career choices was seen to create a multiplier teaching effect from ESAN's master's graduates. With it, however, came greater recognition of the multiple roles its graduates must be prepared for and the implications for the curriculum.

Basic concepts and analytical tools applicable to the constantly changing systems of Latin American administrative problems appeared of even greater importance to ESAN's graduates with highly diversified career expectations involving the teaching and practice of management in public, private, and institutional organizations.

At the same time, the positions of leadership and responsibility many of these graduates would soon occupy in their country's public and private institutions raised concern regarding the curriculum's adequate consideration of public policy and its interrelationship with the private sector and national development. The major issues of public policy now confronting Peru were previously seen in this chapter to inextricably involve the private sector. Peru's most difficult problems concerning alternative routes and priorities in national development involve every aspect of present and future, public and private sector relationships and operations. These problems demand the objective analysis, research, and informed public discussion in which ESAN's graduates must be prepared to play a major role.

The interrelationship of technology and growth with people and task-oriented structures applies equally to an industrial, agricultural, or government organization, as both revisionist changes in Soviet block countries and greater North American central regulation and welfare control illustrate. Questions must be openly raised and objectively analyzed concerning the assets and constraints of various capitalistic socialistic, communistic, and other social-economic systems for satisfying Peruvian national priorities. ESAN cannot fail to adapt its curriculum and research to include such critical Peruvian problems as agriculture administration, land reform, and interior integration, including those most sensitive areas concerning military expenditures and foreign mineral rights. The integration of political science with the other social sciences now involved in ESAN's curriculum and research would appear essential, although it would add further pressures to lengthen the programs.

Furthermore, separate institutions of higher education for the study of public and private administration is a North American dichotomy which is increasingly less justified there on academic bases alone. Nevertheless, in Peru, as in other Latin American countries, where the separation of the sectors is far less distinct and resources, particularly qualified teachers, are most scarce, separate public and private institutions of administration (ESAN and ONRAP) have been established through North American assistance. Consideration should be given to the exploration of ways these two organizations could work more closely and mutually benefit from each other's resources if not undertake a complete merger.

Henry D. Aiken sums up what might be ESAN's curriculum policy in the following statement:[85]

> In a world in which all moorings have been washed
> away, what the student needs nowadays is not an
> anchor, for which he no longer has any use, but a
> pair of compasses, a strong keel, and a first-rate
> set of pumps.

The Development of ESAN's Future Faculty. ESAN has found its master's degree candidates to be an excellent source of potential faculty for its future staff needs as well. Several graduates each year have been selected on the basis of their achievement and interest to continue their studies in major North American Universities. Stanford University remains a natural preference; however, every effort has been made to avoid the domination of one university in the development of ESAN's future faculty. Several faculty candidates have already enrolled at Columbia and the University of California at Berkeley, and future candidates should include European universities in their application considerations.

While a diversity of education experience for ESAN's future faculty is not overly difficult to insure, questions concerning their level of academic achievement prove less easily resolved. As an educational institution offering only post-graduate degrees, the academic qualifications of its faculty is of special significance. In the well established Latin American school of administration offering primarily undergraduate programs, the Master of Business Administration degree from a major North American university, or its equivalent, is most highly regarded, but no longer uncommon among its faculty. As these schools increase their post-graduate and research programs, North American or European education at the doctoral level is receiving increased emphasis. Many universities in Latin America already have faculty with North American or European doctoral level degrees in the social sciences, including a small number in administration. Although there are as yet relatively few teaching in schools of administration, their numbers are slowly increasing each year, as indicated in the preceeding chapters.

The ESAN faculty, while recognizing the desirability of doctoral level study for its future Peruvian faculty, soon gained an appreciation of why North American doctoral level degrees have increased so slowly and the related problems involved. We might consider briefly a master's degree candidate at ESAN who has proven to be an outstanding student and would like to continue his education in North America preparatory to an academic career. As his English language skills are marginal, he will have to work very hard in Peru before he will be able to embark on his studies abroad. If an all expense scholarship is awarded, he will be able to live comfortably alone, but dependents will provide a further set of adjustments and financial problems. As he anticipates the uncertainties of cultural adaptation and academic challenges involved, he will also weigh the cost of possible failure abroad against the many career opportunities, including the academic, that will be his upon graduation. He also recognizes that among the limited number of full-time academic positions in Peru, very few offer salaries competitive with the private sector. If he decides to apply to North American universities and successfully passes the competitive entrance examinations in English, he will most likely be placed in a masters or non-degree category until he can demonstrate his capabilities at that university. While this is a common North American university admissions practice, the student may discover he will have another year of study before he can complete his second masters degree prior to being considered for admissions to the doctoral program. At any step in this long process the student may well decide to accept an attractive offer in industry, rather than continue on with uncertainty and subsistance living. This is particularly true if there is inadequate encouragement, financial support, and future job security offered by the sponsoring institution. If he gains acceptance to the university's doctoral program and receives the necessary support, he may embark on several additional years of study. Assuming he passes the examinations, he will next be required to develop a doctoral dissertation proposal, have it approved, and then complete the work to the satisfaction of his supervisory committee. After several years abroad, our candidate will probably be anxious to return to his own country and undertake the completion of his dissertation there. Financial considerations alone may make his return without the degree mandatory. While this has been a common practice among the Latin American Ph.D. candidates from North American universities, the problems of completing the dissertation at a great distance from the degree-granting university are very great. The Ph.D. candidate upon returning home would most likely undertake a full-time academic position at his sponsoring institution if one was available. Large blocks of free time would be limited as the demands for his newly acquired knowledge and skills and his long-delayed financial needs will both be substantial. Communications with his dissertation advisors would also be most difficult and their guidance and motivation may be seriously impaired. As faculty dissertation committees undergo change over time, so do their expectations. In addition, many North American universities have recently placed limits on the number of years allowed the candidate to complete his doctoral degree.

The cultural, academic, and financial barriers for our ESAN candidate, with others from Latin America, are clearly very great. However, their advance recognition can facilitate remedial planning if the sponsors and candidates first believe the added costs are justifiable. This problem, of course, can only be answered in light of the individual institution's objectives and resources. In the case of ESAN, there would appear to be several major reasons why its expectations and plans should emphasize their future faculty's achievement of North American or European doctoral degrees at carefully selected universities. If ESAN seeks to become a distinguished Latin American institution of post-graduate education in administration, it must develop a faculty fully able to evaluate, apply, and contribute to its diverse and expanding body of knowledge. Perhaps the greatest distinction between the North American master of business administration and the better doctoral programs in administration is the relative time and emphasis placed on investigation and experimentation toward the extension and application of knowledge. The doctoral program seeks the development of skills, tools, and conceptual frameworks which, applied through systematic investigation, contribute to interpretation and prediction. In conjunction with the latter, they seek the development of a scientific outlook, openminded-ness as to possibilities, but reluctance to accept a fact until defi-nite evidence is demonstrated.

If ESAN's future faculty cannot evaluate the expanding research of its field's international contributors, it must then continuously rely on, and often wait for, its translated interpretations and applications by scholars from other countries. As new research and information are growing at unprecedented rates, the leaders in each field are also in the process of dynamic change. Many of the leading names and concepts in the field of management in the World War II period are no longer receiving this recognition today in North America and Europe. Many of their textbooks, however, largely normative and based on North American and European experience, are currently the most popular in Latin America. Unfortunately, this situation is often reinforced and perpetuated by well-meaning North American advisors. All too often concepts, textbooks, courses, and entire curricula no longer in use by leading North American and European scholars are exported, presumably because it is assumed that Latin American management problems are also at an earlier stage of development. Old textbooks never die, they are sent to developing nations and there institutionalized.

North American faculty at ESAN soon discovered that Peruvian management problems, such as those previously discussed in industrial relations, were most often different, but no less complex to diagnose nor difficult to change than their counterparts in the advanced indus-trialized countries. It was most often the recent concepts and tools, as those from systems analysis, bargaining behavior, and conflict theory, which proved to be of greatest value in dealing with unexplored problems and social-economic systems. In other areas of management vital to Peru, such as agriculture, education, and development administration, classi-cal management theory concerned primarily with industry and government is again of limited value.

If the limitations inherent in the majority of classical management concepts are to be recognized in Latin America and replaced by the ana-lytical tools and scientific findings which can be of significant value in the solution of its difficult and unique problems, it will require the application of skills and capacities currently developed primarily at the doctoral level in mathematics and social sciences at select North American universities.

ESAN, as an independent graduate institution with favorable re-sources and support both in Peru and North America, is furthermore in a

unique position to develop, in time, an internationally recognized
doctoral program, providing it can first achieve a nuclear Peruvian
faculty trained abroad at the Ph.D. level in outstanding universities.
Such a program would not only make possible the accelerated development
of highly trained doctorates in Peru and throughout Latin America, but
also, through their research and teaching, geometrically increase high
level managerial manpower as well. Such a doctoral program in the basic
sciences has already been achieved, for example, by the Chilean University Federico Santa María. While the varied costs of training a core
ESAN faculty abroad at the doctoral level is indeed very great, their
projected value added would appear to be significantly greater.

Non-degree Management Education. The international growth since World
War II of continuing management education has been no less significant
than the development of university degree programs in administration.
In many Latin American countries, as previously seen, it has been the
independent institutes for executive education which have paved the way
for new schools of administration. The Peruvian Business Administration
Institute (IPAE) has, for example, played a key role with several other
such institutions in gaining recognition and acceptance for management
education throughout Peru.

ESAN's first educational program in Peru was a management development program jointly sponsored with IPAE on the southern coast of Peru
in August, 1963. It was a residential seminar involving the full-time
efforts of twenty-seven Peruvian executives during its continuous four
weeks duration. The program included fifty-six class sessions of one
and one half hours duration distributed over the following areas:
production, managerial accounting, marketing, finance, policy, organizational behavior, and industrial relations. In addition, four guest
speakers were chosen to introduce broader public policy issues. The
format and content at this time strongly resembled Stanford University's
executive programs, and, unlike specialized courses limited to one
functional or more fields, it was of much greater breadth and stressed
general management problems involving the total organization and its
environment. While this program was the first of its kind ever held in
Peru, it was enthusiastically received and provided an invaluable base
of information, experience, and support for the establishment of ESAN's
future degree and continuing education programs.

Seven faculty members from four major Peruvian universities were
among the twenty-seven managers participating in this first seminar.
These faculty representatives subsequently organized themselves into an
informal inter-university group in order to exchange information and
further the development of management education at their respective universities. The executive alumni in a similar manner formed a vital base
of enthusiastic support without which ESAN's future would have been
indeed bleak. It was furthermore ESAN's first educational undertaking,
and like the case development program, it provided invaluable insights
concerning Peruvian management values, practices, and problems. This
information, in turn, initiated a continuous process of evaluation and
adaptation in an effort to better fit ESAN's limited educational resources

to Peruvian management needs. For example, it was discovered at this
first management program that many Peruvian executives, including those
from the largest firms, did not feel they had adequate management support to permit a comfortable several weeks absence from the office. As
a result, an additional executive program was undertaken with a new
format, including several in-residence weekends near Lima and bi-weekly
evening sessions distributed over three months in Lima. This program,
offering approximately 25% more program hours with far less time away
from their firms, was so heavily over-subscribed that two sections with
fifty members each were finally accepted.

Of greater significance, however, to the ESAN faculty were the
questions raised concerning the extent, causes, and effectiveness of
centralized organizational structures in Peru. What, therefore, are
the curriculum implications involved? How might centralized and/or
family dominated organizations affect the development aspirations and
opportunities of future ESAN and other professional degree graduates in
Peru?

While searching for the answers to these, a steady stream of new
questions arose from a growing array of additional non-degree programs
undertaken. These ranged from resident management programs of several
weeks duration in major northern and southern cities to public sector
programs for the Peruvian Ministry of Labor and Development Corporation.
Each program generating program requests and compelling opportunities
forced a re-appraisal of strategic questions concerning ESAN's basic
goals, resources, directions, and development.

ESAN's Future: Strategic Reappraisal. As is so often the case with
the press of growth and limited relief from operational problems, long-
range planning, although recognized to be of critical importance, proved
difficult. Furthermore, the strategic problems involved did not lend
themselves to the certain identification of one way which ESAN could
best assist in the development of the high-level managerial resources
needed for Peru's continued modernization.

The faculty was generally divided in support of two divergent
strategies to achieve the latter primary institutional goal. One group
held that ESAN's greatest potential contribution remained in the development of administrative talent in all sectors and at all management levels
in Peru and secondarily, other selected Latin American countries. Its
members, therefore, advocated that ESAN's current degree and non-degree
management programs be lengthened and enrollments expanded. In addition,
new programs were proposed for small businessmen and entrepreneurs,
union leaders, government administrators, and teachers in all areas of
Peru and in other Latin American countries when possible. The thrust of
this strategy was then a direct assault on a broad range of Peruvian and
other Latin American private, public, and institutional management needs
through the expansion and development of ESAN's management programs.
This proposal called for a sharp acceleration of a pattern of growth
which had emerged during ESAN's first year of operation. The monetary
resources which would be required for this expansive growth were

generally seen to be self-financed by the programs with help anticipated from North American foundations, USAID, and the Peruvian private sector. The faculty resources were to be supplied by an expanded ESAN staff and past program graduates.

A second faculty group supported a less direct, two-step strategy emphasizing ESAN's unique graduate orientation and qualifications for the advanced education of outstanding leadership talent in management education as well as business and public administration. These men would then shape and develop generations of Peruvian management resources. Only one new post-graduate program for Peruvian and select Latin American faculty, whose theoretical and research interests involve business, public, or educational administration, would be added to ESAN's current professional master's degree and non-degree management program. The management programs, while resisting further expansion, would increase their emphasis on improved instruction and the specific adaptation, innovation, and development of management education for Peruvian and Latin American high-talent resources. The faculty and the management programs were seen, in addition, to provide valuable mutual benefits. ESAN's institutional framework and management programs would provide the faculty program participants teaching and research experience in private, public, and educational administration areas, as well as academic and administrative standards and procedures which may be of value when they return to their own universities. The faculty program would, in return, afford talent and research resources for the continuing study and development of Peruvian and Latin American management problems and educational requirements. The financial resources for the new faculty program were to be derived from its tuition and the current operating income from the Peruvian and North American governments. The tuition plus living expenses were expected to be largely underwritten by the faculty members' sponsoring institutions. The existing ESAN faculty and staff was believed adequate to man this additional program if the management programs were not expanded.

A formal decision regarding these two alternative courses of action was not made by the original ESAN faculty before most of its members completed their planned time abroad and had to return to their home institutions.

A new and increasingly Peruvian faculty is now replacing ESAN's founders. They inherit both the significant foundations established and many high aspirations yet to be achieved.

ESAN is an infant compared to Peru's older educational institutions, and its contribution as a Peruvian institution remains to be established. However, Peruvians and North Americans from many sectors and professions, meeting and working together through ESAN, have already learned a great deal from each other concerning the similarities and dissimilarities of problems, strategies, and potential of management education in their countries.

Management Education: Directions and Implications for Peru. The preceeding would indicate that Peruvian management problems are often quite different but seldom less difficult than North American management problems. The human and technological resources and the organizational structures which Peruvian management coordinates, as well as the environmental system within which it must operate, are distinctive. Furthermore, the Peruvian manager's value system and cognitive processes, themselves a function of his cultural and educational system, were seen to add a further dimension of variance from their North American counterparts.[86] The wholesale importation of North American management courses and curriculum is, therefore, not adequate to meet Peru's management education needs. This is most particularly the case when the educational materials imported are from the classical period of management theory, based largely on normative North American and Northern European experience. If such material is rigidly adopted and taught within a highly structured Peruvian institution of education, the inadequacies are compounded. The latter situation, unfortunately, is not only prevalent in Peru, but in the majority of Latin American countries where hundreds of new management education programs and institutions are now in the development process. Once established, these educational programs will be at least as difficult to change as their counterparts in North America have proven. Hundreds of thousands of young men and women, generations of potential leadership talent, will not receive the education so necessary to their individual and national development.

It is, therefore, the qualitative dimension of management education in Peru and Latin America which is of the highest priority. Without a foundation of highly trained and talented Peruvian faculty to provide academic leadership, the development of management education necessary to meet this country's specific needs will be severely constrained and continuously dependent on external "experts." The seed of academic leadership talent is far more significant than traditional lower life form propagation analogies might infer, for this human seed is capable of shaping the environment to suit its needs as well as adapting to it.

The foregoing discussion supported the position that post-graduate study, preferably in a doctoral program at select universities abroad, was essential to develop this academic leadership talent. However, those familiar with North America's graduate programs in administration alone will appreciate the great variety of curriculum content, teaching, and research emphasis offered today. More specifically then, what type of graduate study abroad will provide Peru's future leadership in administration with the knowledge, skills, and tools necessary to build the academic institutions and programs which will subsequently further develop the nation's management resources?

Graduate programs in administration retaining an apprenticeship character, with course materials based largely on descriptive studies of North American business firms and their functions, although declining, remain well represented. Peruvian and other Latin Americans who receive their training abroad at these institutions can be expected to further this already all too prevalent orientation in their own countries.

During the last decade, in particular, the descriptive-normative approach to management is increasingly being displaced by a second generation of theoretical concepts and tools from the mathematical and social sciences, supporting disciplined analysis, and empirical research, both in the laboratory and the field. Such fundamental disciplines are now providing a common basis for the study of administration in business, public, and educational organizations as well as on a comparative international basis. While the integration of these basic disciplines within the study of administration is far from complete, they have already caused major changes in the business-oriented curriculum of leading North American graduate schools of administration. Several newer institutions, such as the Graduate School of Administration at the University of California-Irvine and the Administrative Science Department at Purdue University, have completely redesigned their graduate programs around these disciplines underlying the study of administration. While such programs are yet in the early development stage, they should be of very great interest to Latin America's academic leadership in administration. As can be seen from the Purdue administrative sciences doctoral program (Exhibit I at end of chapter), heavy emphasis is placed on quantitative and behavioral research tools and their problem-solving applications in both the laboratory and the field. The development of these skills and capacities should represent a major criterion in the selection of programs of graduate study abroad for those Peruvians and Latin Americans desiring intellectual development applicable to a broad range of contemporary and future management problems. The significance of the mathematical and social sciences to the Peruvian and other Latin American graduate students of administration is their value in the development of systematic description, interpretation, and prediction, as well as normative models within their own countries. Their graduate study program must provide more than theory and techniques, as these men of responsibility and future influence will be confronted with values and goals, alternative strategies of organization and national development far more varied than the western industrial pattern, which itself is proving much more complex than the historical stereotype. Technological and economic capacity has proven to merely intensify questions of values and social welfare and there is, as yet, little concensus among nations as to the means or ends of their development. One thoughtful North American's recognition of the non-material elements involved with the development of more effective methods for controlling the future is reflected in the following statement by Max Ways:[87]

> By 1977, the U. S. should understand more clearly that
> its highest satisfactions are derived from the way we
> go about forming our choices and organizing our action,
> a way that stresses persuasion over force and arbitrary
> authority, a way that extends to more and more men
> shares of responsibility for the future. By 1977, it
> may be clearer that we are not just pursuing a material
> "more", that what matters to us is how we formulate our
> goals and how well we pursue them; that in worldly pro-
> gress, as in another, the destination is inseparably
> bound up with the way.

In this regard, the total resources of the university must be considered, as the scientific, value-free orientation of most North

American schools of administration will prove inadequate. Select North American universities with broad international interests and involvement, such as Chicago, Columbia, Cornell, Harvard, and Stanford Universities, have a particularly rich diversity of offerings. In addition to a full compliment of courses in the humanities and social sciences, such universities support interdisciplinary institutes and centers specifically concerned with the complex interrelationships of population, health, education, and social-economic development. The diversity of foreign experience and nationalities represented by students and faculty at such universities, in addition, contribute to the Latin American scholar's scope of experience and viewpoints essential to his development of new and creative approaches to his national problems.

It is interesting to further anticipate the educational directions Peruvian scholars receiving such extensive training abroad would advocate for the development of their country's management resources; that is, if their return to a position of academic leadership is adequately provided for. As the five-year, professional university program in business administration is most common in Peru and Latin America, it may not be unrealistic to assume that several returning professors would soon be involved in the academic planning of such a program. If an ideal situation were to be constructed for these academic architects, the following might be assumed: a leading Peruvian university with a nucleus of well-qualified, full-time faculty in balanced fields received a substantial grant to develop a five-year program in administration. As this university did not previously have such a program, the returning professors were advised that their primary objective was the development of a program specifically designed to meet the needs of Peru's future management. In order to gain some insights as to possible results of such future planning, the author presented a similar hypothetical situation to fifteen schools of administration faculty from eight different Latin American republics during a seminar at Stanford University's International Center for the Advancement of Management Education in 1966. The faculty from each country was to develop such an educational program and review it with the seminar members. The programs were quite varied and the curriculum discussions often provocative.

The curriculum for Peru, as outlined on the following page, was developed by the author with the collaboration of Carlos Martijena and Nissim Alcabes, both Peruvian ESAN graduates then doing post-graduate work at Columbia and Stanford Universities, respectively. This curriculum represents an attempt to consolidate their combined inter-American management experience and inquiry within a university program specifically designed to develop Peru's future management leadership. The curriculum is included to stimulate debate concerning the needs, objectives, and new directions of management education. While the relationship between the program's design and course content and the preceeding discussion of future Peruvian management needs is, hopefully, evident, several points require amplification.

It was, at the outset, a challenge to provide for both the breadth and depth of study indicated earlier in this chapter within the

PERUVIAN SCHOOL OF ADMINISTRATION

Five-Year Curriculum Proposal

Course Title	Hours/Week

Year I

First Semester

Philosophy I: Comparative-value Systems	3
Behavioral Sciences I: Physiological Psychology (including laboratory experimental methods)	4
Modern Mathematical Analysis I: Basic & Advanced Sections	3
Communications I:	
Spanish Written Composition I	3
English I (including language laboratory)	4
	17

Second Semester

Economics I: Macro Economic Theory and Analysis	3
Behavioral Sciences II: Psychology (including laboratory experimental methods)	4
Modern Mathematical Analysis II: Basic and Advanced Sections	3
Communications II:	
Spanish Written Composition II	3
English II (including language laboratory)	4
	17

Year II

First Semester

Economics II: Micro Economic Theory and Analysis	3
Behavioral Sciences III: Social Psychology (including laboratory experimental methods)	4
Modern Mathematical Analysis III: Calculus - Basic and Advanced Sections	3
Communications III:	
Hispanic-American Literature and Arts	3
English III (including language laboratory)	4
	17

Second Semester

Political Science I: Basic Concepts and Theory	3
Modern Mathematical Analysis IV: Calculus - Basic Advanced Sections	3
Basic Science: Physics or Chemistry I, (including laboratory)	4
Economics III: International Development Economics	3
Communications IV:	
English IV (including language laboratory)	4
	17

PERUVIAN SCHOOL OF ADMINISTRATION CURRICULUM PROPOSAL, (Continued)

Year III	Hours/Week
First Semester	
Western Civilization I: Area Studies: History Culture, Art	3
Applied Mathematics: Statistics I	3
Basic Science: Physics or Chemistry II (including laboratory)	4
Philosophy II: Social Responsibility of Administrators in the Modern World	3
Communications V:	
English V (including language laboratory)	4
	17
Second Semester	
Western Civilization II: Progress & Problems	3
Applied Mathematics: Statistics II	3
Management Operations and Systems Analysis I: Mathematical Programming and Decision Theory (including laboratory)	4
Political Science II: Latin American Public Policy Issues	3
Communications VI:	
English VI (including language laboratory)	4
	17

Year IV	
First Semester	
Organizational Behavior I: Basic Concepts and Theory (including laboratory)	4
Inter-American Historical and Contemporary Social-Economic Relationships	3
Financial Management I	3
Managerial Accounting and Controls I	3
Management Operations and Systems Analysis II: Mathematical Programming and Decision Theory (including laboratory)	4
	17
Second Semester	
Organizational Behavior II: Research Methods and Applications (including laboratory)	4
Legal Environmental Factors in Peru and Latin America	3
Financial Management II	3
Managerial Accounting and Controls II	3
Management Operations and Systems Analysis III: Management Information Systems (including laboratory)	4
	17

PERUVIAN SCHOOL OF ADMINISTRATION CURRICULUM PROPOSAL, (continued)

Year V	Hours/Week
First Semester	
Management Logistics	3
Industrial Relations, Peruvian Issues and Comparative Systems	3
Latin American Development: Problems and Strategy	3
Student Field Research Project and Seminar	8
	17
Second Semester	
Elective*	3
Elective*	3
Elective*	3
Student Field Research Project and Seminar	8
	17

*Electives can be drawn from specialized courses in public, private, or institutional administration, including: small business management, production operations, international business, and the multinational corporation, public finance, agricultural administration, university administration, hospital administration, public health policy, manpower planning and development.

traditional five-year duration of Peruvian university professional programs. The curriculum, as presented, is quite demanding and best suited for select students of high intelligence and sound secondary level preparation. This, of course, raises problems for the many talented but underprivileged students in Peru. The addition of a sixth year would allow for a broader and more flexible pre-professional program with the inclusion of highly desirable remedial and elective courses.

The program's first three years are devoted to general education, emphasizing both the fundamental concepts and methods of inquiry in the sciences and the integration of the humanities and social sciences in interdisciplinary area studies. The pre-professional years further contain integrated course sequences in mathematics and the social sciences, which are essential prerequisites to the fourth and fifth years of study. The final two professional years are focused on the development, integration, and application of core disciplines and tools upon which management is founded.[88] The entire program's research emphasis provides for an interdisciplinary focus of concepts and methods on problems of significance to Peruvian and Latin American management in a wide variety of public and private organizations. The electives in the fifth year of study provide the student with an opportunity to focus more sharply on his particular administrative career interests.

Approximately one half of the student's final year of study is devoted to his field research project. The latter is the culmination of the program's dynamic learning emphasis, which includes the student's active solution of problems in the classroom with case discussions and analytical tool development as well as in laboratory and field research. This orientation is specifically designed to develop an analytical framework for realistic problem solving, the application of ideas and tools from the basic disciplines to the current international, national, and institutional problems of Peru. This analytical approach develops additional theory application controls through its demand for validity tests of proposed solutions. The ultimate objective of the students and faculty involved in this program is, then, the continuous development and application of basic theories, tools, and conceptual frameworks which will contribute to the solution of problems confronting Peruvian management. The achievement of this goal necessitates, therefore, that this educational development relationship be continued after the five-year professional degree program is completed.

One last point concerning the above curriculum deserves clarification and it brings us full circle to the study's primary emphasis, the critical need for academic leadership talent in Peru and Latin America. The ideas and directions represented by this program are sterile academic dreams unless some parts are considered worthy of trial and brought to life within an institutional environment suitable to support and further their development. This will demand a high level of academic leadership talent -- a diversity of administrative and academic capacity and skills as yet in critically short supply in Peru and all of Latin America. Unlike the advanced industrialized nations, Latin America has little demonstrated that it sees its future progress tied to present educational investment in human talent. Nevertheless, the quality of Peru's and Latin America's future society will be sharply constrained without the high-level leadership talent necessary for its accelerated advancement.

Those who set the educational standards today and implement the decades of future actions required for the systematic development of this leadership talent will, even if by default, also determine the development level of Latin America's future society.

EXHIBIT I

PURDUE UNIVERSITY KRANNERT GRADUATE SCHOOL OF INDUSTRIAL ADMINISTRATION

Department of Administrative Sciences

Typical Plan of Study for a Ph.D. Candidate in the Administrative Sciences - 1967*

Stem:	Decision-Making Structures	Individual & Social Foundations of Decision-Making Behavior	Research Methods
Semester 1**	Administrative Sciences 661 Utility and Decision Theory	Psychology 646- Group Structure and Process; Psychology 649- Cognitive Organization	Econ. 670- QUANTITATIVE ECONOMICS I
Semester 2	Administrative Sciences 662 Small Group Competition and Conflict	Psychology 647- Social Interaction and Influence	Econ. 671- QUANTITATIVE ECONOMICS II. Adminis. Sciences 605- Laboratory Experimental Methods
Summer	Administrative Sciences 606 – Laboratory Research Project, and Competence Examination in a Foreign Language.		
Semester 3	Administrative Sciences 663 Cooperative Groups and Organizational Structures	Administrative Sciences 656 – Seminar in Organizational Theory and Management. Sociology 607- Seminar in Current Issues and Sociological Theory.	Adminis. Sciences 610- Simulation Models of Decision-Making.
Semester 4	Administrative Sciences 664 Societal Choice and Individual Values.	Sociology 609 – Seminar Elective	Adminis. Sciences 615- Field Study and Survey Methods.
Summer	Administrative Sciences 616 – Field Research Project, and Competence Examination in Mathematics.		

Typical Plan of Study for a Ph.D. Candidate in the Administrative Sciences – 1967* (Continued)

Stem:	Decision-Making Structures	Individual & Social Foundations of Decision-Making Behavior	Research Methods
Preliminary Exams	Examinations on the Structure Stem	Examination on the Foundations Stem	Examination on the Methods Stem
Dissertation	Dissertation research and examination on the dissertation subject.		

*While this program appears to be fixed, in practice flexible programs are devised to meet particular interests and particular competencies.

**Students are required to become actively engaged in research during their first semester in the program. This usually takes the form of an affiliation with faculty research in which the student takes considerable responsibility.

Reproduced with permission of the Purdue University Department of Administrative Sciences.

NOTES AND REFERENCES

1. For a comprehensive description of the diverse geological characteristics of Peru see Robinson, David A., _Peru in Four Dimensions_,
   American Studies Press S.A., Apartado 4217, Lima, 1964.

2. Owens, R. J., _Peru_, Oxford University Press, London, New York,
   1963, p. 5.

3. von Hagen, Victor, _The Ancient Sun Kingdoms of the Americas_, The
   World Publishing Company, Cleveland, New York, 1961, pp. 419-422.

4. Osborne, Harold, _Indians of the Andes: Aymaras and Quechuas_,
   London, Cambridge, Mass., 1952.

5. Prescott, William H., _History of the Conquest of Peru_, Random
   House, Inc., New York, p. 774.

6. Baudin, Louis, _A Socialist Empire: The Incas of Peru_, D. Van
   Nostrand Company, Inc., Princeton, New Jersey, New York, London,
   1961, pp. 198-208.

7. Baudin, _op.cit._, p. xvii.

8. Owens, _op.cit._, pp. 30-31.

9. Robinson, op.cit., p. 7.

10. Benjamin, Harold, _Higher Education in the American Republics_,
    McGraw-Hill Book Company, New York, p. 12.

11. Bassdre, Jorge, _Meditaciones sobre el Destino Histórico del Perú_,
    Lima: Ediciones Huascaran, 1947, p. 115.

12. Chaplin, David, _The Recruitment of the Peruvian Industrial Labor
    Force_, Dissertation, Princeton University, University Microfilms,
    Inc., Ann Arbor, Michigan, p. 32.

13. Carey, James C., _Peru and the United States - 1900-1962_, University
    of Notre Dame Press, 1964, Indiana, p. 60.

14. Carey, _op.cit._, pp. 62-63.

15. See Chapter II for a discussion of the major conditions of University
    reform in Latin America cited at the World Congress of Students,
    1921, in Mexico.

16. Kantor, Harry, "Aprismo: Peru's Indigenous Political Theory," _The
    Dynamics of Change in Latin American Politics,_ John D. Martz, ed.,
    Prentice-Hall, Inc., Englewood Cliffs, New Jersey, 1965, p. 88.

17. Bernstein, Harry, Making an Inter-American Mind, University of Florida Press, Gainesville, 1961. See Chapter V for a summary of the lineage of intellectual inter-American tradition.

18. Investment in Peru: Basic Information for United States Businessmen, Department of Commerce, Washington, 1957, p. 5.

19. Operations Report, International Cooperation Administration F.Y., Office of Statistics and Reports, Issue 1960, No. 4, Washington, November 23, 1960.

20. Plan Nacional de Desarrollo Económico y Social del Perú 1962-1971, Banco Central de Reserva del Perú 1962, Lima, Perú.

21. Carey, op.cit., p. 130.

22. Overseas Business Reports, U.S. Department of Commerce, Washington, D. C., July, 1965.

23. Ferrero, Rómulo A., "El Desarrollo Económico del Perú en el Período 1950-62," Cámara de Comercio de Lima, Perú, April, 1965, p. 18.

24. Overseas Business Reports, op.cit., p. 5.

25. Whyte, William F., "Culture, Industrial Relations and Economic Development: The Case of Peru," Industrial & Labor Relations Review, Vol. 16, No. 4, July, 1963.

26. "The Industrial Entrepreneur in Latin America," U.N. Economic Commission for Latin America, E/CN. 12/644/Add. 4, March 18, 1963.

27. Owens, R. J., op.cit., pp. 12-13. Since 1936 only about 2,000 persons have become nationalized Peruvians.

28. Owens, R. J., op.cit., p. 13.

29. During the academic year 1962-63, there were 335 Peruvian students plus 28 faculty enrolled in North American universities alone, and in 1966 this number has been estimated to be over 600 scholars.

30. La Población, Los Recursos Humanos y el Empleo en el Perú, República del Perú, Servicio del Empleo y Recursos Humanos, Lima, Perú, April, 1964, p. 3.

31. Chaplin, David, "The Peruvian Elite and Industrialization: A Study of Variations in the Distribution of Wealth in an Industrializing Society," August, 1963. A paper read at the American Sociological Association Convention in Los Angeles, California.

32. Ferrero, Rómulo A., op.cit., p. 18.

33. Ministerio de Hacienda y Comercio, Boletín No. 6, 1958-1962, p. 48.

34. Collazoa, Carlos C., et al., La Alimentación y el Estado de Nutrición en el Perú, Ministerio de Salud Pública y Asistencia Social, Servicio Cooperativo Interamericano de Salud Pública, Instituto de Nutrición, Lima, 1960, p. 277.

35. A Program for the Industrial and Regional Development of Peru, Arthur Little, Inc., 1960, Part II, Plan Peru-Via.

36. Dobyns, Henry F., Tenth Report of the Cornell-Peru Project, Lima, Peru, December 1, 1961.

37. Holmberg, Allan R. and William F. Whyte, Human Organization, Special issue dealing with human problems of U.S. enterprise in Latin America, Vol. 15, No. 3, Fall, 1956, p. 17.

38. Dobyns, Henry F., "The Strategic Importance of Enlightenment and Skill for Power: The Vicos Case," The American Behavioral Scientist, VIII, No. 7, March, 1965, p. 25.

39. In March, 1966, a pioneering $20 million loan was made from the United States-financed Social Progress Trust Fund, administered by the Inter-American Development Bank for the expansion of a broad-ranged rural community development program in Peru now engaged in activities including agrarian reform cooperatives, education, and the development of local community leaders.

40. Dobyns, Henry and Mario Vásquez, editors, Migración e Integración en el Perú, Monografías Andinas #2, Editorial Estudios Andinos, 1963, Lima, Perú, p. 38.

41. Ferrero, Rómulo A., op.cit.

42. Dobyns, Henry, op.cit., p. 38.

43. Roemer, Milton, Medical Care in Latin America, Pan American Union, Organization of American States, Washington, D. C., 1963.

44. Patch, Richard W., "Life in a Callejon," American Universities Field Staff, West Coast South American Series, Vol. VII, No. 6, June, 1961. See this article for an excellent study in depth of urban disorganization in Peru.

45. Whyte, William F., op.cit., p. 586-7. Professor Whyte's survey of Peruvian high school students indicated the low status of manual work by this group throughout the country. It should be noted, however, that the very high attrition rates through the primary and secondary levels in Peru (approximately 5% of those children entering the primary schools complete the secondary level) does make his sample group an elite in Peru with expectations of reaching professional status in the tuition free public universities.

46. University Enrollment Statistics in Peru by Areas of Specialization, 1950-1959, Banco Central de la Reserva, Programación del Desarrollo, Lima, November, 1963, Vol. 3.

47. La Población, Los Recursos Humanos y el Empleo en el Perú, op.cit., p. 23.

48. Analysis and Projections of Economic Development: VI The Industrial Development of Peru, United Nations Economic Commission for Latin America, 1959, p. xxiii.

49. Instituto Nacional de Planificación, Programa de Inversiones Públicas, 1964-65, Projections of economically active population are based on a 2.9% rate of total population growth.

50. Instituto Nacional de Planificación, loc. cit.

51. Harbison, Frederick, and Charles A. Myer, Education, Manpower, and Economic Growth, McGraw-Hill Book Company, New York, 1964.

52. Miller, Herman P., "Annual and Lifetime Income in Relation to Education," American Economic Review, December, 1960.

53. Thomas, Lawrence G., The Occupational Structure and Education, Prentice-Hall, Englewood Cliffs, New Jersey, 1956, p 6-8.

54. For an interesting analysis of the effects of Peru's industrialization upon aggregate income and employment from which the following concluding quotation is taken, see Chaplin, David, op.cit.

55. Harbison, Frederick, and Charles A. Myers, op.cit., p. 33.

56. Robinson, David, op.cit., p. 773.

57. Plan de Desarrollo Educativo, 1965-1969, Ministerio de Educación Pública, Lima, 1964.

58. Loc.Cit.

59. Loc.Cit.

60. Loc.Cit.

61. Bulletin #33, U.S. Department of Health, Education and Welfare, Education in Peru, 1964, p. 11.

62. Plan de Desarrollo Educativo, 1964, op.cit., p. 100.

63. Education in Peru, op.cit., p. 42.

64. Loc.Cit.

65. See Table VI.

66. Informe sobre el Desarrollo de la Educación en el Perú durante el Año, 1962, Ministerio de Educación Pública, p. 66.

67. Possible Effects of Selected Educational Policies and Programs on Income Size and Distribution in the Industrial Sector of Peru, Unpublished Dissertation by Harry R. White, Stanford University, Comparative Education Center, 1965, p. 87.

68. Whyte, William F., op.cit., p. 586.

69. Sánchez, Alberto Luiz, La Universidad no es una Isla, University of San Marcos, Lima, Peru, 1961.

70. Education in Peru, op.cit., p. 45.

71. Informe sobre el Desarrollo de la Educación en el Perú, op.cit., p. 93-94.

72. National University of San Marcos, founded in Lima in 1551.
National University of San Antonio Abad, founded in Cuzco, 1598.
National University of Trujillo, founded in Trujillo in 1824.
National University of Arequipa, founded in Arequipa in 1825.
Pontifical Catholic University of Peru, founded in Lima in 1917.

73. Plan Nacional de Desarrollo Educativo, 1965-69, op.cit.

74. "In general political and social pressures make for emphasis on quantity, whereas the achievement of rapid economic growth makes it imperative to emphasize the quality of high-level manpower required for development." F. Harbison and C. Myers, op.cit., p. 174.

75. University Enrollment Statistics in Peru by Areas of Specialization, op.cit.

76. Loc.Cit.

77. Total enrollment is projected to grow from 3,444 students in 1964 to 8,000 in 1971.

78. The undergraduate majors of ESAN's first Master of Administration Class were:

Engineering –		Other –	
Civil	9	Public Accounting	7
Elec. and Mechanical	4	Law	3
Agriculture	5	Economics and Commerce	5
Mining	2	Military Science	2
Industrial	4	Earth Sciences	3
Petrol	3	Theology	1
	27	Administration	2
			23

79. Dunlop, John T., _Industrial Relations Systems_, Henry Holt & Company, New York, 1958.

80. Whyte, William Foote, _The Management Elite in Latin America_: _Management Strategy in Industrial Relations in Peru_.

81. Fouraker, Lawrence, Siegal, Sidney, _Bargaining Behavior_, McGraw-Hill Book Company, New York, 1963.

82. Rapaport, Anatol, _Fights, Games and Debates_, The University of Michigan Press, Ann Arbor, 1960.

83. The Balnor S. A. case series, as well as other ESAN cases, are now available in Spanish through the Harvard Inter-collegiate Case Clearing House.

84. Orth, Charles E. III, _Social Structure and Learning Climate: The First Year at the Harvard Business School_, Division of Research, Graduate School of Business Administration, Harvard University, Boston, 1963.

85. Aiken, Henry D., "The University II: What is a Liberal Education?" _The New York Review of Books_, Vol. VII, No. 7, pp. 25-26.

86. For an interesting study indicating the differences between the problems of Brazilian top managers and their North American counterparts, as well as the variance in the rules by which they operate, see: Oberg, Winston, "Cross-Cultural Perspectives on Management Principles," _Academy of Management Journal_, VI (June, 1963), pp. 129-143.

87. Ways, Max, "The Road to 1977," _Fortune_, January, 1967, p. 197.

88. The Amos Tuck School of Business Administration at Dartmouth, New Hampshire, has successfully followed a "three-two" (pre-professional-professional) program for many years.